Dyslexia and Inclusion

Assessment and Support in Higher Education

MARION FARMER PHD,
University of Northumbria,

BARBARA RIDDICK MA,
University of Sunderland
and
CHRISTOPHER STERLING PHD,
University of the South Bank

Consultant in Dyslexia
PROFESSOR MARGARET SNOWLING
University of York

D0238961

W
WHURR PUBLISHERS
LONDON AND PHILADELPHIA

First published 2002 by
Whurr Publishers Ltd
19b Compton Terrace, London N1 2UN, England
325 Chestnut Street, Philadelphia PA19106, USA

British Library Cataloguing in Publication Data

A catalogue record for this book is available from the British Library.

ISBN 1 86156 314 0

Printed and bound in the UK by Athenaeum Press Limited, Gateshead, Tyne & Wear.

Contents

Preface   vii

Chapter 1   1
Identifying students with dyslexia

Chapter 2   11
Approaches to assessment

Chapter 3   24
Investigating and assessing the writing of students with dyslexia

Chapter 4   52
Assessing and supporting numeracy

Chapter 5   60
Assessment and support relating to emotional adjustment and
mental health

Chapter 6   68
Evaluating university students' experiences of assessment
and support

Chapter 7   117
Profiling the student's course: which aspects of the course cause difficulty
with students with dyslexia

Chapter 8   148

Views of academic staff on support for students with dyslexia

Chapter 9   182

The perspectives of student support staff

Chapter 10   224

Conclusion

References   230
Index   237

Preface

There is a growing need for universities and other higher education institutions to understand and address many issues in relation to the access of students with dyslexia to the full range of higher education courses. This book has been written in response to that need, and although the data we report and discuss come from students and staff in the university sector, the material should be equally applicable to staff and students in other institutions in the higher education sector. This preface outlines the material contained in the book's various chapters and the approaches we have taken in developing our understanding of the varied aspects of the topic.

In the Report of the National Working Party, *Dyslexia in Higher Education: Policy, Provision and Practice* (Singleton 1999), dyslexia was defined as 'a complex neurological condition that occurs in approximately 4 per cent of the population, and which primarily affects the acquisition and use of written language, memory and organizational skills'. Almost by definition, therefore, individuals with dyslexia are likely to have difficulty in coping with many aspects of the formal education system as we know it, including the final and most demanding phase of higher education. In this book we attempt to present the perspectives of academic and support staff at universities who are involved in making higher education inclusive and accessible to all, together with the views of students with dyslexia who experience the effects of those attempts. The material has been developed from data collected from several qualitative and quantitative studies, from discussions with colleagues involved in work in the area and from consideration of the increasing literature relating to dyslexia in adulthood. It has not been our intention to consider theoretical issues around the deficits underlying dyslexia. However, the material collected in our studies does provide plenty of food for thought in relation to debates on 'what' dyslexia is and 'who' is dyslexic.

Our primary aim has been to contribute to the development of understanding and practice in the inclusion of dyslexic students, at a time when access to higher education has widened hugely in the UK and the continued increase of this access is urged. The excellent Report of the National Working Party on Dyslexia in Higher Education (Singleton 1999) gave an overview of the then current state of practice with regard to dyslexia in HE and made many important recommendations. Following the report's publication, Singleton informed the British Dyslexia Association's international conference (University of York, April 2001) that HESA statistics indicated that the number of students entering higher education who declared themselves to be dyslexic had increased from 0.44 per cent in 1994/95 to 0.97 per cent in 1998/99; furthermore, a recent survey conducted by Singleton and Aisbitt (2001) indicated that around 1.1 per cent of students were known to be dyslexic on entry into HE, and a further 0.8 per cent were diagnosed after entry. There has in fact been an overall increase in the number of students with dyslexia attending higher education institutions of 41 per cent in 5 years. We can therefore conclude that around 2 per cent of students entering HE in the academic year 2001/02 will be dyslexic and that this proportion is likely to rise over the coming years. Singleton and Aisbitt's survey also showed that, although around 20 per cent of institutions said that they had changed their policies on assessment and identification following the 1999 report (Singleton 1999), 70 per cent of institutions had apparently made no changes. The picture with regard to changes in the provision of support was rather better in that around 35 per cent of institutions said that they had developed their support services following the report. However, 60 per cent reported no change.

Some of the continuing problems and issues reported by Singleton and Aisbitt were as follows:

- variability in relation to responsibility for the funding of the initial assessment which gives access to the Disability Support allowance (some universities pay for this while others expect the student to pay)
- the time taken to process DSA applications
- the lack of availability of tutors trained in understanding and dealing with dyslexia
- the lack of awareness of the nature and problems of dyslexia of teaching staff in higher education
- the need for more effective identification procedures
- the need to embed support for students with dyslexia throughout HE institutions rather than leaving it to central services

- the continuing bar on admission of dyslexic students to some courses
- the attitudes of some academics to literacy skills.

The chapters that follow in this book will be seen to bear directly on these issues. They probe the attitudes, understanding and practices of teaching and support staff, explore the students' experiences of assessment, consider the general principles of assessment of students with dyslexia, look at the complexities of the assessment of reading, writing, spelling and numeracy, and reflect on issues relating to the emotional adjustment of these students.

Issues relating to assessment are considered in the earlier chapters. Thus, Chapter 1 addresses the debates around the principles of assessment that should be used when assessing students with dyslexia in higher education, returning to the debates around the 'discrepancy' definition and putting the case for a 'modular' approach. Chapter 2 takes a further look at assessment approaches, considering particularly those areas that traditionally have been considered to be impaired in dyslexia. These two chapters are based on reflections on our current state of knowledge and understanding of the development of dyslexic individuals. Chapter 3 goes on to consider the difficulties endemic in the assessment of writing skills, skills which are seen by staff and students to be the most problematic and the most important in terms of achieving academic success. Much of the material in this chapter is based on data obtained from a recent empirical investigation of the writing of students with dyslexia at one university. Chapter 4 addresses the assessment of another neglected area, numeracy. Here the label 'dyscalculia' is considered and the relationship between impairments in literacy and numeracy discussed. Chapter 5 again reports recent empirical research findings on the emotional adjustment of students with dyslexia. The links between cognition and emotion are discussed and issues concerning the assessment and support of emotional and mental health are debated. Turning from the views of the assessor to the views of the assessed, in Chapter 6 we address students' perceptions of assessment and their anxieties and concerns in relation to this experience; for many, the assessment of their dyslexia is the key which unlocks the door to new self-understanding and awareness and also access to support – financial, educational and emotional. The material in this chapter is based on data collected by means of questionnaires and interviews at two universities. The students' reflections on their experience of assessment in this chapter also lead on to their views on support.

Chapter 7 addresses the other side of the assessment equation: assessing the requirements of the courses themselves and the greatly varying skills and abilities which they demand of their students. Academic staff from a range of disciplines describe in their own words the demands of their courses and the difficulties which they may present to the student with dyslexia. This chapter and Chapter 8, which reflects on the support provided by academic staff, highlight the considerable differences between courses in their experience of students with dyslexia and the consequent widely varying practices which academic departments have adopted in relation to these students. So, for example, it is conservatively estimated that 10 per cent of students following courses in Fine Art may be dyslexic (Thomas 2000), while in subjects in the Humanities such as History, or in Modern Languages, the dyslexic individual may be a *rara avis* indeed. In both Chapter 8 and Chapter 7 we hear the voices of staff expressing their concerns, interests and creative solutions in relation to the support of students with dyslexia.

Chapter 9 is in three sections and contains material from interviews carried out with support staff in a university which is well advanced in its provision of access to a wide range of students with disabilities and students from backgrounds where higher education has not been traditional. These staff are employed centrally within the university to assist students. Once again, the voices of the staff can be heard and their vast experience and endeavour and examples of good practice in supporting students can be demonstrated. The book's final chapter provides a summary and concludes with recommendations for future development of good practice.

We hope that the variety of methods used to develop the material for this book will permit educationists, staff, students and researchers alike to develop a greater understanding of many different aspects of the issue of inclusion of students with dyslexia. Inclusion for all is not easy, and it is not cheap, as we have learned from the experiences of teachers and support workers within the primary and secondary education sectors. Dyslexia is not a simple concept, easily definable and measurable in terms of the 'deficits' displayed by those who are dyslexic. In fact, there are positive and negative sides to dyslexia and, for those with determination, academic success need not be a wild dream. We hope that for many a greater understanding will emerge from reading this book and that, in consequence, attitudes and practice will change to facilitate the implementation of the inclusive agenda.

Marion Farmer
Barbara Riddick
Christopher Sterling
June 2002

CHAPTER 1

Identifying students with dyslexia

In recent years there has been a significant increase in the number of students in higher education in the UK. In particular, most universities have changed their entry criteria to permit and encourage applications from persons from unconventional educational backgrounds. So where once most students were 18-year-olds with A Levels at minimum grades there are now substantial numbers of older students without formal qualifications, students from different ethnic backgrounds where English is a second language, students with learning disabilities, and some who have more than one of these characteristics. The problem that concerns us here is how we are to distinguish students with dyslexia from students with other types of educational disadvantage. Three populations of students are of particular concern because they often perform at levels normally associated with a learning disability: students who are not able to meet the intellectual demands of a degree course; students from ethnic minorities for whom English is not the first language; and students from deprived backgrounds who have missed the educational opportunities on offer. The problem is important, partly because financial support and special concessions are, rightly or wrongly, only available to students with diagnosed learning difficulties. Unfortunately, the solution to this problem of differential diagnosis is not immediately obvious.

Dyslexia was once defined as 'a disorder manifested by difficulty in learning to read despite conventional instruction, adequate intelligence and socio-cultural opportunity. It is dependent on fundamental cognitive abilities which are frequently of constitutional origin' (World Federation of Neurology 1968). The most salient feature of this definition is that it is one of exclusion: dyslexia can only be diagnosed once other causes of poor reading such as low intelligence, inadequate education, social and emotional problems and overt brain damage have been discounted. The problem is that people with these other problems cannot be diagnosed as dyslexic. So, for example, in principle a Bangladeshi child with English as a second language and from a socially deprived area could not be diagnosed dyslexic. Fortunately, since this definition was produced psychologists have made considerable progress in understanding dyslexia with the result that diagnosis is now based on more 'positive' characteristics, principally the existence of a phonological deficit. However, this has not solved all the diagnostic problems. In this chapter we examine some of the issues, often controversial, that surround diagnosis.

Traditionally, as the definition indicates, people with dyslexia are people who underperform relative to their intellectual ability. So, if an intelligence test indicates that a person is of normal intelligence but a reading test indicates that reading is much poorer than would be expected on the basis of the IQ score, then the person is (probably) dyslexic. The assessment of reading ability and intelligence is based on the person's performance relative to his/her peers on appropriate psychometric tests such as the Wechsler Adult Intelligence Scale and the Wide Range Achievement Test (reading). The discrepancy criterion for the diagnosis of dyslexia serves the critical function of distinguishing the dyslexic poor reader from the generally backward poor reader (GBR), someone whose poor reading ability is consistent with their low intelligence. The implication of the discrepancy criterion is that people with dyslexia and GBRs are poor readers for very different reasons: the dyslexic because of a specific impairment or difficulty and the GBR because of generally inadequate intelligence. The diagnosis has, of course, major educational and financial implications, especially for remediation. It could be argued that GBRs are not capable of being helped to any worthwhile degree because of their low intelligence but that people with dyslexia will benefit from remediation because of their adequate or high intelligence. The ethics of this are, of course, questionable, but that is the assumption implicit in much of educational policy. The question is whether or not it is justifiable to distinguish between dyslexics and GBRs.

The logic of the differential diagnosis position is that GBRs are poor readers because their low intelligence makes it more difficult to learn the alphabet, to learn the rules and regularities that link the spellings of words to their sounds, and to learn the many idiosyncrasies of English spelling. In addition, their low intelligence also impedes their ability to derive the meaning of a sentence from the component words, to combine meanings of sentences, and to draw inferences from sentences and text. Their limitations in this regard extend to spoken as well as written language. Their general intellectual impoverishment extends across the board to more general cognitive abilities such as problem-solving and concept formation and to other academic subjects. Evidence for general backwardness in GBRs comes from studies such as that by Stanovich et al. (1986), who showed that precocious 9-year-olds (1 year ahead), slightly backward 11-year-olds (1 year behind) and severely backward 13-year-olds (3 years behind) had the same general profile on a range of tasks, indicating that the backwardness was not specific. In the same study, they followed the precocious 9-year-olds and weak 11-year-olds over two years and found the latter falling behind on a range of tasks, not just a few. In contrast, the problem with dyslexic reading is attributed to a specific deficit in a general background of adequate intellectual function. Hence the term 'specific reading difficulty'. Their development is assumed to be different from that of GBRs in that although they lag behind their peers the lag is confined to literacy. Their development in other areas is assumed to be normal, although in practice this is not the case because their reading and spelling deficit impedes the development of other skills, such as vocabulary development, which depend on literacy. Evidence for a specific lag comes from longitudinal studies such as Manis et al. (1993) and Snowling et al. (1996).

Research over the last 20 years has converged on the finding that a major specific cause of dyslexic poor reading is a phonological deficit. Phonology is the area of human language that is concerned with speech sounds, the perception of speech sounds in spoken language, the production of speech sounds in spoken language, memory for the combinations of speech sounds that make up the words in our vocabulary, and so on. There is now a considerable body of evidence that phonological ability (e.g. being good at rhyme and breaking words up into their component sounds or phonemes) is causally related to reading ability. Thus, studies have shown that a child's early phonological ability is a good predictor of later reading ability (e.g. Bradley and Bryant 1983; see Wagner and Torgeson 1987 for a review). Another body of evidence indicates that people with dyslexia perform significantly poorly on a range of tasks that require phonological skill (see Rack 1994 for a review). For example, they are poorer even than younger children of the same reading ability on a phoneme deletion task (Manis et al. 1993) which involves removing a specified phoneme from a target word and reporting the result (e.g. *table* to *able*, or *blink* to *bink*). The problem is also one that persists into adulthood. Conners and Olson (1990) found dyslexic children to perform poorly on a pig latin task and Pennington et al. (1990) found adult dyslexics to be similarly impaired. These two substantial areas of investigation provide solid evidence that the specific impairment in dyslexia is a phonological one. A direct link between poor phonological skill and poor reading is found in the problems people with dyslexia have with reading nonwords (Rack et al. 1992).

Support for the discrepancy diagnostic comes from a classic study by Rutter and Yule (1975). In a large survey of all 9- and 10-year-old children on the Isle of Wight they distinguished two types of poor readers: those whose reading ability was 2.4 years poorer than would be expected from their IQ (dyslexics), and those whose poor reading was consistent with their IQ (GBRs – 2.4 yrs behind). The two groups differed in important ways. The gender ratio was different (equal in the GBRs, more boys in the dyslexics). There was a greater prevalence of neurological and motor disorders in the GBRs. Both groups had delayed language but a follow-up when the subjects were 14 years old found that the dyslexics had made less progress than the GBRs on reading and spelling but more progress on arithmetic and maths.

However, the discrepancy definition of dyslexia and the idea that GBRs and people with dyslexia are poor readers for different reasons have come under attack from a number of researchers. Siegel (1989, 1992) argues that the measurement of IQ is irrelevant to the diagnosis of dyslexia. This is because the discrepancy diagnostic uses IQ tests such as the WISC to work out a person's expected reading ability but an examination of the subtests that comprise the WISC reveals that they are either irrelevant to the kinds of abilities that we would expect to predict reading ability or they tap skills and abilities that would be degraded by having a learning disability. It is not clear, for example, why being good at block design or maze learning should predict reading ability in any reader. On the other hand, being dyslexic might discourage reading and so tend to produce poor performance on the vocabulary or information subtests. Thus, calculating expected reading ability from these components of the WISC does not make sense, for different reasons. Empirically, Siegel (1992) showed that that IQ did not correlate with reading skills in either reading disabled or normal readers. She also cites the existence of hyperlexics who are above average readers with below average IQ. More damaging evidence against a difference between GBRs and people with dyslexia comes from a number of studies who have found that the two groups do not differ on a range of tasks such as phoneme deletion, verbal short term memory and rapid naming (e.g. Fletcher et al. 1994), tasks which are clearly related to phonological impairment and not general intelligence.

Given this, are there any differences between GBRs and people with dyslexia? Stanovich (1988) has proposed a phonological-core variable-difference model which identifies both the similarities and differences. This argues that both GBRs and people with dyslexia are poor readers because of a phonological deficit. Because of this they have the same profile for all skills and abilities that are dependent on phonological ability. Hence they are poor both at single word reading and at related abilities such as verbal short-term memory. The difference between the groups, according to Stanovich, lies in skills and abilities that are relatively unconnected to the phonological core. So, people with dyslexia will not be impaired on tests of visual learning and reasoning ability because these are distant from the phonological core and depend on their general intelligence. GBRs, in contrast, will be impaired on these non-core tests to the extent that their general intelligence is low. An interesting case is reading comprehension. Gough and Tunmer (1985) have proposed that reading comprehension depends firstly on the ability to decode single written words and secondly on the ability to derive the meanings of sentences by combining the meanings of the single words in the appropriate way. Combining the two models indicates that dyslexics are impaired in single word reading (phonological core) but not comprehension (because the ability to combine meanings is related to general intelligence and not phonological ability), while GBRs are impaired on both single word reading and comprehension. Thus, dyslexics will have poor reading comprehension only to the extent that their poor single word reading disrupts comprehension processes (which in themselves are normal) whilst GBRs will have poor reading comprehension partly because of poor single word reading and partly because of low intelligence. There is a third group, hyperlexics, who are impaired on comprehension but not on single word reading. A potentially interesting diagnostic which stems from this is to use the discrepancy between reading comprehension and listening comprehension to distinguish between dyslexics and GBRs (Joshi et al. 1998). In GBRs both reading and listening comprehension will be poor, while in dyslexics only reading comprehension will be poor.

Given this argument and evidence against the differential diagnosis of GBRs and people with dyslexia, should dyslexia assessment include IQ tests and use discrepancy as a diagnostic? In spite of the strength of the arguments above we think that it should, with qualification. First, intelligence is not irrelevant to reading ability. Torgeson (1989) argues that reading ability is generally correlated with intelligence, so that intelligent people tend to be good readers while less intelligent people tend to be poorer readers. Because the correlation is not perfect (no correlation is) we expect to find people where intelligence and reading ability seem unrelated. Torgeson (1989) points out that even in Siegel's (1989) data poor readers tend to have low intelligence score while good readers tend to have higher scores. Second, the anti-IQ argument suggests very strongly that phonological deficit is the only cause of poor single word reading. The problem of why some people are poor readers is considered solved! In our view, psychology has not a sufficiently glittering history of being right to justify such confidence so early. The position completely discounts the fact that the ability to read is underpinned by a number of general cognitive abilities which are related to what most people consider intelligence such as, for example, the ability to abstract rules and regularities from a mass of complex information. This is exactly what is required when learning the complex relationships between spellings and sounds, particularly in English, which has so many ambiguities and irregularities. Siegel (1989) is right in arguing that the intelligence tests used do not relate very convincingly to this kind of cognitive ability. On the other hand, they do give some idea of a person's ability to form concepts and abstract patterns of similarities and differences (e.g. the vocabulary and similarities subtests of the WISC; the progressive matrices). They give an indication of the general cognitive ability of the individual, which includes something of the specific cognitive skills that underpin reading ability. It is significant that even those who argue against discriminating dyslexics from GBRs eliminate from their sample individuals with IQ scores less than 85–90 (Siegel 1992; Fletcher et al. 1993). Given that people with an IQ score of 85 and above are definitely within the normal range they are actually eliminating what would normally be considered generally backward participants from their comparisons! Rutter and Yule (1975) did not exclude anyone from their sample. Where there is room for improved diagnostic procedures is in the replacement of lengthy and tiring IQ tests such as the full WAIS with shorter tests that provide reasonable estimates of general cognitive ability. In the longer term we need to consider which tests best measure the kind of cognitive abilities we consider to underpin reading ability.

A second problem for differential diagnosis comes from students with poor reading and spelling skills but for whom English is not the only or first language. Consider the simplest situation, where the person is reasonably literate in the first language but is having reading and spelling difficulties in English. The question is whether their literacy problem is due to interference from the first language, to dyslexia, or to both.

The literature on bilingual or second language readers indicates that there is a good deal of strategy transfer. Thus there is evidence that literate Chinese people, who have learned to read a logographic script by developing a sight vocabulary, tend to adopt a visual, whole-word strategy when reading English. Indeed, in Singapore, a multilingual society, this is encouraged by teachers who regard this as the optimal strategy for learning an orthography as irregular as English (Rickard Liow 1999). The problem that strategy transfer poses for diagnosis is that good logographic reading may disguise dyslexia. A Chinese person who is dyslexic in English may be hard to identify because their logographic reading compensates for the underlying problem. Evidence for how good compensatory logographic reading can be comes from Campbell and Butterworths' (1985) case study of a highly intelligent university student (English monolingual) with a huge sight vocabulary, whose dyslexia was only discovered when she was asked to read nonwords and unfamiliar words. This kind of evidence suggests that diagnosis of dyslexia in good logographic readers will need something more than tests of reading ability. In this respect nonword reading seems to be a good discriminator. LJY was a 12-year-old Chinese boy who was competent in Chinese but was four years behind in English. He had a good sight vocabulary but found reading nonwords almost impossible and his attempts at these were largely real words (Rickard Liow 1999). This suggests that, like all people with dyslexia, he had poor phonological ability and presumably he would perform poorly on tests of phonemic awareness.

Although phonemic awareness is probably the best diagnostic in such cases it needs to be treated with caution because of the evidence that phonemic awareness also depends on the nature of the first language. Rickard Liow and Poon (1998) compared three kinds of (non-dyslexic) Singaporean children on their phonological awareness ability. The best skills were found in the Malay speakers, whose (other) written language is alphabetic and very regular. The next best skills were found in English speakers. The poorest skills were found in the Chinese group whose written language is logographic. This is consistent with the finding that experience with an appropriate (alphabetic) script itself enhances phonemic awareness (Morais et al. 1979). Diagnostically, it means that phonemic awareness will also depend on the client's other language.

The situation is simpler for those people whose first language uses a regular alphabetic orthography such as Turkish or Spanish. There is evidence that phonological awareness in the first and second language of bilinguals is correlated and that phonological awareness in the first language is correlated with literacy in the second language (Durgunoglu et al. 1993). This suggests that information about reading and writing ability in the first language can make a valuable contribution to diagnosis in English. The problem with such transfers is that while readers of regular orthographies such as Italian are very good at grapheme–phoneme transcription (better than their English counterparts) they don't seem to pick up on the larger spelling units that occur in English (Goswami 1999). So someone transferring from, say, Portuguese, will be very good at grapheme–phoneme transcription but will find the irregularities a major problem (Fonseca 2001). In short, their reading problem will be word-specific and their phonemic awareness adequate, so distinguishing them from dyslexic readers whose phonemic awareness is impaired should not be a problem.

The third problematic group consists of those students who have a poor educational history for social and economic reasons. They may have left school early because their families couldn't support them; they may have had extended absences from school for health reasons; they may have played truant or been in frequent trouble with the authorities; and so on. They have returned to education because they are dissatisfied with their job and their status. They feel they are under-achieving and see higher education as the way to remedy their predicament. In our experience, although these students struggle academically, they see their problem as being one of dealing with the generally 'foreign' demands of academic life, rather than a specific problem. The problem is most marked in, and may be confined to, the first year. If they do present, their profile is likely to be one of general slowness in most tasks, with little evidence of impairment on tasks such as phonological awareness. In this respect they will be distinguished from their educationally deprived peers who are also dyslexic.

Discriminating dyslexics from other populations is not the only problem posed by diagnosis. There is a growing literature proposing different causes of dyslexia. The claim generally made by this research is that phonological impairment is not a sufficient theory to explain all the reading failure that is generally referred to as dyslexia. Other causes also exist. This is a highly contentious issue and we will consider only the most powerful of these alternative views.

Initially Boder (1973) and subsequently Coltheart and colleagues (e.g. Coltheart et al. 1983; Castles and Coltheart 1993) have argued that there are two kinds of dyslexics. First, there are those whose problem is phonological in nature and who are characterized by difficulty in phoneme–

grapheme and grapheme–phoneme transcription. Their defining characteristic is great difficulty in reading nonwords. Coltheart and colleagues refer to these as phonological dyslexics and they are the same population we have referred to in our discussion of dyslexics with phonological impairments. The second type of dyslexic is the surface dyslexic, whose major problem lies in the reading of irregular words such as *yacht* and *colonel*. The dispute is about the causes of the surface dyslexic pattern. On the face of it the problem seems to be one of orthographic memory – remembering the letters and letter sequences in these words, where the sound structure is of little help. This seems to be the explanation implied by the proponents of surface dyslexia. However, there is no real evidence that these dyslexics have a problem with remembering visual patterns. The alternative explanation is that the surface dyslexic pattern is also the result of a phonological impairment, but a much milder one. Manis and colleagues (Manis et al. 1996; Manis et al. 1999) seem to be on the way to a solution. They compared both phonological and surface dyslexics with reading age controls and found that the pattern for the phonological dyslexics was one of developmental deviance, with the dyslexics being poorer even than much younger reading age controls on phonological tasks. This is the deviance pattern. In contrast, the surface dyslexics produced a profile that was very similar to the younger readers, implying that the problem was one of developmental lag. Their various subskills were commensurate with those of younger readers. Manis et al. (1999) call this subgroup delayed dyslexics.

Unfortunately, diagnosis cannot wait on a resolution of this issue. However, we can proceed pragmatically. First, it seems that most people with dyslexia show both patterns (Manis et al. 1996). They have problems with both nonwords and irregular words. Furthermore, it seems that most dyslexics also show some phonological problems, even if in some cases, this is mild and more consistent with delay than impairment. Accordingly, we don't need any special tests to identify the majority of surface dyslexics. Single case evidence suggests, however, that there will be some cases which show the pure surface dyslexic pattern (e.g. Coltheart et al. 1983): no phonological impairment but very poor performance on reading and spelling irregular words. These can be dealt with on a case by case basis.

Conclusions

This chapter has sought to identify some of the problems of dyslexia diagnosis without seeking to claim that answers to these problems currently exist. Many of these problems do not currently have a satisfactory solution. The problem that needs much attention is that of the role of intelligence in reading ability. The argument that intelligence is irrelevant to reading does not sit comfortably with our experience. The argument that (all) reading impairment is due to phonological impairment may be dominant at this point in time but its weaknesses suggest that it is somewhat premature for us to consider the problem solved. The question of second language learners, and similarly, that of the educationally-deprived poor readers, is an interesting one but one which is, in principle, solvable through the use of core tests which tap underlying cognitive abilities. The problem that is likely to prove theoretically intractable for some time but which can be dealt with pragmatically is that of subtypes.

In the next chapter we consider in greater depth the problems that some of these issues pose for assessment.

CHAPTER 2

Approaches to assessment

The purpose of this chapter is to identify areas of performance which reliably discriminate dyslexic adults from their nondyslexic peers. At first sight this seems a relatively straightforward enterprise. We go to the extensive literature on dyslexia and select a subset of tasks on which dyslexics have been found to differ. These can then be put into a battery which can be administered conveniently and quickly. However, on closer examination we find a number of problems with this seemingly straightforward strategy. In the first part of this chapter we will identify some of these problems, and consider their importance and how they can be dealt with.

We are reaching a point in the dyslexia literature where the list of reported differences between dyslexics and normal readers seems endless. In theory this should make diagnosis easy because of the choice of tests available, but in reality there is an uneasy sense that not all these differences are meaningful or large enough to be useful. Test batteries reflect this state of affairs. They tend, for example to be large, often taking several hours to compete. This is undesirable, not just in humanitarian terms but also because of the fact that many differences will arise because of fatigue, anxiety and boredom rather than because of genuine cognitive differences. Test batteries also tend to differ substantially in content, something which is seen in the batteries compiled by, for example, Hanley (1997), Nicolson and Fawcett (1997) and Hatcher et al. (in press). The reason for this is partly theoretical. Some tests in these batteries are not found in the others because the authors have different theories about the nature of dyslexia. However, given that there is now a consensus that phonological impairment is a major cause of dyslexia we would expect not just significant theoretical overlap, which there is, but also agreement on the specific tests that should be used to test for differences in these areas of agreement. While certainly there is similarity between tests, the degree of difference and diversity is unhelpfully large for someone looking for a battery, or even looking to put together their own battery of the best tests.

Clearly we need to try and reduce the number of diagnostically useful tests by identifying the most discriminating tasks. However, while there is a huge literature on childhood dyslexia there is a dearth of research on adult dyslexia, making the identification of a few critical tests difficult. Although we can extrapolate from the childhood research we need to do so with caution, especially because of evidence that dyslexic adults learn to compensate for their problems (e.g. Lefly and Pennington 1991). This means that we have had to rely heavily on the rather few adult studies. Fortunately, many of these are of a high quality, with relatively large samples of dyslexic adults and clear results.

The major factor in deciding the components of a test battery is, of course, theoretical orientation. So someone who holds that dyslexia is a phonological problem is likely to discount tests of, say, visual memory. The battery by Hatcher and et al. (in press), for example, reflects their view that dyslexia is a problem of impaired phonology. It emphasizes phonological skills and gives no attention to the possibility that visual memory may be a cause of dyslexia. In contrast, the battery by Hanley (1997) reflects the view that dyslexia can also be caused by a visual/orthographic problem and so contains a test of homophone discrimination. Similarly the screening test by Nicolson and Fawcett (1997) involves a test of postural stability which is grounded in their theory that dyslexia involves an impairment of motor control located in the cerebellum. We think it best to take a pragmatic approach and make decisions based on how established a particular finding is. Thus, that dyslexics and controls differ on tests of phonological awareness has been replicated many times. To our knowledge no one would disagree with this, it is theory-driven and so should be a critical part of any test battery. On the other hand, the finding that people with dyslexia have motor problems is empirically less well established and is theoretically less well founded. It therefore seems best to omit this from any list of critical tests. In order to maximize the reliability and validity of recommended tasks and tests we also consider it best to keep to those that show substantial differences between dyslexics and nondyslexics. Typically, research findings indicate that a statistically significant difference has been found between dyslexics and control participants. What this means is that a dyslexic group has been found to be reliably worse, as a group, on particular tasks than has a nondyslexic group. However, although reliable, the difference may not be very large, and so unhelpful in discriminating between individual dyslexics and controls. Suppose, for example, that a group of dyslexics make, on average, 8/20 errors on a spelling test while the controls make 7/20 errors. Although this difference may be statistically significant we would be reluctant to base diagnosis on such a small difference because it is likely that many controls will make 8 or more errors and many dyslexics will make 7 or fewer errors. We would be more confident, diagnostically, if the average difference was bigger – say 7/20 errors for controls and 14/20 errors for dyslexics – because the two groups' scores would be less likely to overlap. We would probably find that a criterion of, say, 10 errors would separate the majority of dyslexics from the majority of controls. A good example of a substantial difference is the spoonerisms test by Hatcher et al. (in press). We shall consider this later.

We also need to differentiate tasks on the basis of their diagnostic specificity. We need to be clear on whether a difference in performance indicates only a dyslexic impairment or whether it also reflects other causes of poor reading. Reading comprehension is an example of a diagnostically ambiguous task. A student who complains of having severe problems understanding text might be dyslexic, but we would be unwise to make a diagnosis on the basis of poor reading comprehension because there are other reasons why reading comprehension might be poor. S/he might, for example, have a problem with grammar and understanding complex grammatical structures, in spoken as well as written language. So, because of its diagnostic ambiguity, reading comprehension can contribute to, but cannot be the sole basis of, diagnosis. A number of other tasks, covered later in this book, such as proofreading fall into this category. In contrast, there are tasks where performance is much more specifically and unambiguously related to dyslexia. Tests of phonological awareness fall into this category. Poor performance on tests of phonemic awareness is strongly suggestive of dyslexia and therefore carries much weight in the diagnosis. However, even this is not proof-positive because of the evidence that phonemic awareness is itself partly dependent on learning to read. Thus Morais et al. (1979) found poor phonemic awareness in Portuguese illiterate adults compared with literate adults. These people were illiterate for social and economic reasons, not because of any disability. This evidence indicates that while poor phonemic awareness may occur because of a phonological problem it can also occur because of not having had the opportunity to learn to read. Whilst the distinction between diagnostically specific core tests and diagnostically ambiguous secondary tests is not always easy to maintain it does help us to decide the weight we want to give the results of a particular test.

There are three further issues that apply to all test batteries. The first of these is the problem of 'recovered' or compensated dyslexics. A number of research papers (Felton et al. 1990; Kinsbourne et al. 1991; Lefly and Pennington 1991) have reported that a significant proportion of childhood dyslexics appear to have 'recovered' when they reach adulthood. So, even though they satisfy the criteria for dyslexia as children their adult diagnosis is open to question. Assuming childhood misdiagnosis is not the problem, then the most plausible explanation is that these adults have learned to compensate for their various impairments. Many dyslexics are likely to have learned a variety of strategies for dealing with their problems. If they write an essay, for example, they may avoid words which they know they find difficult and develop an appropriate alternative vocabulary (Sterling et al. 1997). LA, a dyslexic of our acquaintance, is very good at tests of reading comprehension because she is extremely canny at looking in the text for key words that occur in the question. Given this ability to compensate, many such dyslexics are able to perform above their true ability on many tests of functional ability such as writing and reading. However, they are less likely to be able to compensate on core tests.

The second, relatively intractable, problem in diagnosis is the Matthew Effect (Stanovich 1986). This is simply that someone who begins with an impairment is likely to show a bigger deficit than would be expected as time progresses because of a snowball effect. For example, someone with a reading problem is likely to avoid reading because they find it difficult and not very enjoyable. The less they read the more they fall behind their peers both on reading and on other skills that are dependent on reading: their vocabulary will not have the same opportunity to grow; their knowledge of the world, so often gleaned from books, will be limited; their social contacts may deliberately exclude their intellectual peers because they feel inferior; and so on. Most importantly, they may lack the confidence to tackle tasks they can actually do and so are likely to underperform and present a distorted picture of their disability. This means that the impairment we measure is a combination of some 'true' deficit' and these secondary effects. These secondary effects are most likely in tests which depend on reading, e.g. the vocabulary, information and similarities subtests of the WAIS.

The third problem concerns the existence of norms, or base data about the performance of a nondisabled group against which potentially dyslexic performance can be assessed. If the diagnosis uses standardized tests such as the WRAT or WAIS then norms for a representative sample of the general population will have been collected. The problem arises with nonstandardized tests, such as those of phonological awareness, for which such norms do not exist. Typically, what happens here is that the researcher or diagnostician has collected performance from a matched group of nondyslexic controls and makes a judgement about impairment based on performance relative to this group. For the population being discussed here this control group is a group of students. This can cause problems, firstly because this control group may not be very large, and secondly because someone who is dyslexic relative to a group of students may not be dyslexic relative to the general population. This is, of course, the discrepancy diagnostic problem in a slightly different guise and its solution is more a matter of theoretical orientation than simply collecting more representative norms.

Given these rather numerous cautions and caveats we move now to a consideration of the kinds of tests most likely to yield reliable and useful differences between adult dyslexics and their chronological peers.

Core indicators

Phonemic awareness

It is now generally acknowledged that impaired phonological awareness is a core deficit of dyslexia. The difference between dyslexic children and both chronological age and reading age controls is now well documented and so we can be sure we are dealing with a real and substantial effect. The question is whether this impairment persists into adulthood. The evidence indicates that it does (e.g. Bruck 1990, 1992). The issue that is much less clear is which tests of phonological awareness are best placed to identify this difference. In generally, we can discount tests which require manipulation of large phonological units such as the syllable because adults show no evidence of having problems with these (e.g. Bruck 1990). The phonological problem in dyslexia lies principally with phonemes, the component sounds that make up a word (e.g. 'kuh', 'ah', 'tuh' for *cat*). The next question concerns the task that should be used. One task that has been used is phoneme counting. In this task the testee has to count the number of phonemes in a target word. So, if the target was *company* the number of phonemes would be seven. The results of studies which have used this task suggest that differences exist but that the overall level of performance in both dyslexics and controls is quite good (Bruck 1992), and only the more severe dyslexics are likely to make enough errors to distinguish them from the controls. Thus, Bruck (1992) found that adult controls made almost no errors counting 30 monosyllabic nonwords with between 2 and 4 phonemes, while the dyslexics got about 1/5 wrong. Hanley's results (1997) suggest that the difference is even smaller. Notice that the task could be made more discriminating by using longer words which would induce relatively more errors from the dyslexics.

Another task that is frequently used is phoneme deletion, requiring the person to remove a phoneme from a target word and report the result. The phoneme to be deleted can be the first, last or in the middle of the target. Task difficulty can also be increased by using words with consonant clusters. Bruck's (1992) task required deletion of the first or last phoneme of consonant-vowel-consonant nonwords (e.g. *dom*), consonant-consonant-vowel-consonant nonwords (*stom*) or consonant-vowel-consonant-consonant nonwords (*domp*). The dyslexic error rate was about 40 per cent while that of the controls was about 10 per cent . The majority of controls (those within one standard deviation of the average) made between 0 and 28 errors whilst the majority of dyslexics made between 20 and 57 errors. A phonological task that is at least one step more difficult than phoneme deletion is the pig latin task used by Pennington et al. (1990). In this task the testee is required to delete the first phoneme of a target word, e.g. *dog* to *og*, move the deleted phoneme to the end of the target, *og-d*, and add 'ay', producing *ogday*. Although it is not possible to deduce the size of the difference between dyslexics and controls from the paper, it seems that the difference was particularly marked when the target involved consonant clusters. So going from *blow* to *lowbay* was harder than from *man* to *anmay*. The dyslexic error rate was about 80 per cent compared to about 60 per cent for the controls. The same task was used by Gottardo et al. (1997) who found that dyslexics made twice as many errors as controls. Again the precise ability of the task to discriminate is not computable. Another complex phonological task, somewhat similar to pig latin, is the spoonerism task used by Hatcher et al. (in press), Hanley (1997) and Rack (1997). In this task the names of famous people are read out and the task is to exchange the first phoneme of each name. So *Bob Dylan* becomes *dob bylan*. The data from Hatcher et al. (in press) suggest that this task is very powerful in discriminating dyslexics from controls.

One reason for describing three phonological tasks – phoneme counting, phoneme deletion and pig latin – is that they can be combined to provide a composite task of graded difficulty. For example, very mild dyslexics might be able to do the counting and possibly the deletion but fail on the pig latin, while a very severe dyslexic might fall at the first hurdle of counting. Within each task the difficulty can be varied by manipulating the length of the word and the number of consonant clusters. This composite task has potential.

Nonword reading

This task is now generally acknowledged to reflect a person's phonological ability, because it requires both grapheme–phoneme (letter to sound) transcription and then a blending of the resulting sounds. The review by Rack et al. (1992) has argued that failures to find differences between dyslexics and controls reflect methodological flaws in the investigating study rather than the absence of a difference. So, to maximize discriminability one needs to be careful about the type of nonwords used and how they are generated. Bruck (1990) found that her dyslexic students made about 15/40 errors when reading one and two syllable nonwords while controls only made about 2/40 errors. Furthermore, reading time for the dyslexics was just over two seconds per word, compared with less than one second per word for controls. However, the difference could be bigger than this suggests because the nonwords were constructed by changing a few letters in a real word to produce a nonword with the same structure (e.g. *planet–plamid, fringe–pringe, rickshaw–cullshew*), allowing an analogy strategy to be used. Hanley (1997) reports that his dyslexic students were most impeded in reading nonwords when they were unable to find an analogy for a given nonword and instead had to rely on grapheme–phoneme conversion, i.e. converting letters to sounds and blending the result. Nonwords without real word analogues seem best suited to nonword reading tasks.

One variation used by a number of researchers is a jabberwocky passage, which is composed largely of normal prose but which contains nonsense words at frequent intervals (e.g. Nicolson and Fawcett 1997). A sample (from Hatcher et al., in press) is 'Once upon a time a tawndy rapsig named Gub found a tix of pertollic asquees. So chortlich was he with his discovery that a murtled . . .'. They found this to be the best discriminator in their battery. Gross-Glenn et al. (1990) argue that these passages are particularly good for discriminating compensated dyslexics from controls. A problem with using this task as a diagnostic is that it is not a pure test of nonword reading. There is the distinct possibility that a nonword reading impairment makes only a limited contribution to the overall difference, with the real causes of the difference lying elsewhere.

Indeed, Gross-Glen et al. (1990) suggest that it is the switching between words and nonwords that dyslexics find difficult. This task is in danger of becoming yet another difference which has not got a clear theoretical underpinning.

Other core indicators

There are two other tests of underlying cognitive deficits which are argued to be intimately connected with the core deficit in dyslexia but which, on closer examination, are not as attractive discriminators as they first appear.

Short-term memory

Short-term memory is usually tested using the digit span test from the Wechsler Adult Intelligence Scale. In this test one is required to recite back, in the correct order, sequences of digits (or letters or words) read out by the tester. Dyslexics have shorter digit spans than nondyslexics(the average number they can recite back correctly) and this test is one of the so-called ACID tests of dyslexia. Results from the adult literature, however, (e.g. Hanley 1997; Hatcher et al. in press) indicate that the difference in digit span between dyslexics and controls is really quite insubstantial (about one according to Hatcher et al. in press). More worrying is the finding by Pennington et al. (1990) that differences only existed for a clinical sample of dyslexics (referrals to clinics), not from a sample of familial dyslexics (third generation dyslexics in dyslexic fami-lies). This suggests that impaired digit span may be associated more with a broad syndrome of disabled reading and less with a 'pure' dyslexia. Accordingly, we suggest that while it may provide supplementary diag-nostic information it is not a core diagnostic difference. The second test is rapid naming (Denckla and Rudel 1976). In this test the testee is presented with numbers, letters, objects or colours (all highly familiar) and has to name each stimulus as quickly as possible. It is a test of access to spoken words (names) and therefore comes under the general umbrella of phonological ability. Again, the evidence from adult studies is not clear. Rapid naming as an independent core test is only useful for the naming of objects and colours because naming letters or digits is actually a variation on reading words out loud and so is not independently core. The study by Pennington et al. (1990) found no differences between dyslexics (either clinical or familial) and controls. Accordingly, we do not regard this as being a very helpful addition to a battery.

IQ

The merits of including an IQ test were discussed in the previous chapter. While it is important to have a measure of general intelligence it is not necessary to administer the full WAIS. Given that we want an estimate of intelligence one option is to use only the block design and vocabulary tests of the WAIS. These have been found to correlate well with the full WISC, the children's version of the WAIS (Sattler 1982). An alternative is the progressive matrices test and a test of vocabulary. The function of these estimates in the diagnosis is simply to ensure that the client is within the normal range of intelligence.

Indicators of a functional deficit

Single word reading

It is generally acknowledged that the main locus of the dyslexic reading deficit is in the reading of single words and so a test of single word reading should reveal clear differences between dyslexics and their peers. A number of such tests exist but the most popular in the dyslexia literature is the Wide Range Achievement Test (reading). One of the advantages of the WRAT is that it has norms for a huge age range (5–75 years), allowing an adult's reading difficulty to be compared to the reading of younger readers and to be expressed in terms of age or grade equivalent. A disadvantage for non-United States users is that it is standardized only on a United States population. A number of studies indicate that the WRAT (reading) is a good discriminator of dyslexics from matched controls. In a study by Felton et al. (1990) the impaired group had a mean standard score of 78, with the majority of scores (within one standard deviation of the mean) falling between 66 and 90. In contrast, the control group had a mean standard score of 105, with the majority falling between 96 and 114. Thus only those dyslexics and controls with standard scores between 90 and 96 were in a diagnostic no man's land. Similar results were reported by Bruck (1990) and by Kinsbourne et al. (1991). In all these studies the adult dyslexics all had childhood diagnoses of dyslexia. However, a problem highlighted by two of these studies is the existence of compensated dyslexics. Both Felton et al. (1990) and Kinsbourne et al. (1991) tested a sample of borderline cases (also with childhood diagnoses of dyslexia) and found them to produce scores which fell between the clear dyslexics and controls. These cases weaken the discriminatory power of the WRAT (or indeed any test) and suggest that in such cases other sources of evidence, such as the person's history, should be given special consideration.

One problem with the WRAT (reading) is that it is a graded difficulty test, in which the words to be read become more and more difficult and reading ability is indicated by how far into the test the person gets. So it is actually a test of reading vocabulary and dyslexics could score badly partly because they are poor readers and partly because they have a poor reading vocabulary, consequent on finding reading a stressful activity that is best avoided. One solution to this problem, suggested by Hanley (1997) is to assess vocabulary independently and only favour the dyslexia interpretation of poor reading performance if the person's vocabulary is, say, within normal limits for their age. A potential candidate for this is the vocabulary subtest of the WAIS.

An additional, informal source of information is the incidence of reading errors. We would expect dyslexics to have many more false starts, repeated attempts and dysfluencies than the control groups for words that they eventually get right. We would also expect regularization errors, pronouncing an irregular word according to rules (*pint* to rhyme with *hint*), and visual guesses (*causal* instead of *casual*). However, we are reluctant to identify a diagnostic pattern of errors because of the fact that we are dealing with adults who will use any and every strategy available to them to produce an acceptable result.

Single word spelling

Compared with dyslexic reading there is a dearth of information about dyslexic spelling. What is clear, however, is that spelling ability may be a more powerful indicator of dyslexia than reading. The most obvious reason for this is that while guessing will go quite a long way in reading, especially when there is context, guessing is much less successful in spelling because precise information about letter identity and sequencing has to be produced correctly. The most popular standardized spelling test in the dyslexia literature is again the WRAT (spelling). It too has been standardized for a huge range of ages which means that age and grade equivalents can be calculated.

The literature on adult dyslexia reveals that the WRAT (spelling) is a good discriminator of dyslexics from controls. Lefly and Pennington (1991) found standard scores for their dyslexic sample to be 89, with most cases (within one standard deviation) falling between 75 and 103. The mean for the controls was 109, with most cases falling between 101 and 117. Bruck (1990) and Kinsbourne et al. (1991) obtained similar results. We see from these results that the WRAT (spelling) is a good discriminator of dyslexic from normal spellers. However, a problem is again posed by compensated dyslexics. In the Lefly and Pennington (1991) study these adults produced error rates that were between the dyslexic and control groups but markedly closer to the controls. Thus, their standard score was 105, with most scores falling between 96 and 114, very similar to the control results. Again, historical information should be given due weight.

The same cautions apply to interpreting standardized spelling tests as to reading tests. Like the WRAT (reading), the WRAT (spelling) is a graded difficulty test so that poor results could be due to poor spelling ability or to a poor spelling vocabulary because of impoverished experience – which could in turn be due to motivational or socio-economic reasons. Dyslexics are likely to do badly both because of poor ability and because of poor spelling vocabulary. As before, we can partly compensate for this ambiguity by setting a minimum requirement for vocabulary and by placing relatively greater reliance on core tests.

Unlike in reading, where the evidence is ambiguous, relative ability to spell different kinds of words is a supplementary source of diagnostic information. The biggest differences between dyslexics and controls are found for irregular words (Bruck 1993; Hanley 1997; Sterling et al. 1997). In Bruck's (1993) paper dyslexics had a mean error rate on very irregular words (such as *yacht* and *leopard*) of 80 per cent , with most scores (within one standard deviation) falling between 67 per cent and 93 per cent . The comparable figures for the controls were a mean of 31 per cent and a one standard deviation range of 15 per cent and 37 per cent . There was very little overlap between the groups. Hanley's (1997) results were similar. Differences are also found for the spelling of regular words but the relatively low error rate for both groups and the relatively small difference between dyslexics and controls suggests that this is not a powerful discriminator. (Bruck 1993 found error rates of 23 per cent and 6 per cent for dyslexics and controls respectively.) Evidence from a free writing study by Sterling et al. (1997) suggests that what is salient about dyslexic spelling is the fact that they make errors that nondisabled readers simply do not make, on irregular but very common words such as *friends* and *their*. This difficulty cannot be ascribed to spelling vocabulary because of the highly familiar nature of these words and is therefore an important source of supplementary information.

Background indicators

Finally, in our concern with scientific and clinical rigour we should not forget the value of less quantifiable, more subjective information. Thus, if someone is a dyslexic adult it seems likely that their educational experiences will reflect this. In a book of interviews (Riddick et al. 1997) we found that dyslexics consistently reported negative experiences which resulted both from their treatment by the educational establishment and from their own anxiety and lack of self-confidence. The diagnostic value of such qualitative information should not be forgotten. Two sources of information are particularly valuable.

Educational history

In general, persons with childhood diagnoses of dyslexia are also likely to be dyslexic as adults, albeit compensated. However, less equivocal documents recording childhood achievements, including reports from educational psychologists and other professionals, are also a valuable source of information. In many cases, especially with older adults, such a documented history may not be available, in which case the client's self-report of problems at school is a good substitute. Thus, reports of having been in remedial classes or having been particularly poor at reading and spelling should be noted as markers. More subjectively, self-reports of frustration at being unable to deal specifically with print, or of discrepancy between a person's perceptions of his or her own ability and performance at school should also be noted. The value of this kind of information has been supported by Riddick et al. (1999) and by Gillis and DeFries (1989).

Genetic loading

Given the evidence that dyslexia has a significant genetic component, information about reading difficulties in a client's family is valuable (Gilger et al. 1991). Ideally, an unambiguous diagnosis of dyslexia in father, mother or sibling is sought. What is more likely is a vague report that one member of the family had or has problems reading. These reports need to be treated with caution, especially if the client is older, because the problem may have been the result of social disadvantage or lack of educational opportunity. Vogler et al. (1985) have calculated that, assuming a prevalence of reading disability in the general population of 5 per cent, 35–40 per cent of boys of with one affected parent will also be disabled. The likelihood for girls with one affected parent is slightly less (15–20 per cent).

Conclusions

In previous sections we argued that the large number of tests used by the majority of test batteries reflect a lack of diagnostic confidence. Although there is overlap, between them they present a bewildering array of tests, all of which are claimed to make a significant contribution to diagnosis. In some cases, the choice is not explained and the rationale for their inclusion is only that dyslexics do more poorly on them. We have tried to use the data available to home in on a few tests or tasks which reliably discriminate dyslexic adults from their nondyslexic peers. In doing this we have ignored many other tests and tasks which also show differences between dyslexics and their nondisabled peers, such as reading comprehension and writing, for example. The intention is not to discount the value of these. What is being argued for in this chapter is the need for test batteries to discriminate between different kinds of tasks. In some cases, the tests are of core diagnostic significance; in others, they have a supplementary role to play in diagnosis; and in still others, they have no diagnostic role to play because poor performance can occur for other reasons. In these cases, they provide information about weaknesses and about where support should be directed. There is also a need for the tests in a test battery to have more than just face validity – their inclusion should be justified on theoretical grounds with an explanation of why differences would be expected.

One consequence of discarding the 'shotgun' approach to diagnosis in favour of targeted testing is that fewer students may be diagnosed as dyslexic. People who would previously have been diagnosed as dyslexic on the basis of marginal impairments on a number of tests may now not qualify. This is no bad thing. In diagnosis we are being presented with an individual who is underperforming and we are being asked to state whether this is due to the condition know as dyslexia. A positive diagnosis brings with it financial help as well as concessions such as extra time in examinations. We are naturally loath to deprive someone who is disabled of these compensations and may therefore be inclined to set more lax criteria for a positive diagnosis. However, there are many reasons why a student in higher education might be having problems meeting the academic demands made by their course and only one of them is dyslexia. Many students underperform because of social and educational problems, as well as because they cannot meet the demands of a course. Diagnosing someone as dyslexic who is not does not benefit the person concerned in the long term because that person then has a diagnostic label which may disadvantage him/her later in life. The short-term benefits cannot compensate for this. Misdiagnosis also does harm to all those who are truly dyslexic because it diminishes the severity of the disability in the eyes of the general population and, most importantly, in the eyes of those who control budgets. In short, we need to be more rigorous in our diagnostic criteria.

CHAPTER 3

Investigating and assessing the writing of students with dyslexia

In this chapter many references are made to a study carried out by Farmer et al. (2001). As the work is as yet unpublished, in order to set the scene for the chapter, the method used in the study is first described. Some of the results were reported at the International British Dyslexia Association Conference at the University of York, 2001. Further analyses will be reported in a paper currently under preparation (Farmer et al. in preparation). In this study, a group of dyslexic students from a wide range of disciplines within one new university was compared with a group of nondyslexic controls on a wide range of measures. The dyslexics were volunteers obtained by circulation of a request to students registered and recently assessed as dyslexic by the student support services. The controls were obtained by asking the students with dyslexia to recruit a friend from their course or department. The details of the sample are given in Table 3.1. Their scores on standardized assessments are given in Table 3.2. The standardized assessments used were the Wechsler Adult Intelligence Scale (Wechsler 1981) which gives a verbal IQ (VIQ) and a performance IQ (PIQ) and the Wide Range Achievement Test Reading and Spelling tests (Wilkinson 1993). Reading standard score (Read SS) and spelling standard score (Spell SS) are reported.

As can be seen from scrutiny of these tables, the method of selection of controls did not always produce well-matched pairs, as sometimes, in fact, the friend who volunteered to act as a control was a housemate or other friend, rather than someone from the same course. Since there was, however, a systematic link between the members of the pairs, matched-pairs analyses were used when analysing the data. In this sample there were significant differences between the groups in terms of verbal IQ $(t(15) = 3.72, p = 0.002)$, but not in performance IQ $(t(15) = 1.61,$

Table 3.1. Details of the sample of students participating in the investigation carried out by Farmer et al. (2001)

Control			Dyslexic		
Age	Sex	Course	Age	Sex	Course
22	F	Human Organisations	21	F	Human Organisations
29	M	Dip. S.W.	29	F	Dip. S.W
22	M	Geography	22	F	Contemporary Photo Practice
22	F	Government and Politics	18	F	Travel and Tourism
25	F	Psychology	20	F	Psychology
21	M	Graphic Design	21	M	Graphic Design
20	M	Maths	21	M	Geography
22	F	Sociology/Social Research	18	F	Travel and Tourism
20	F	Marketing	20	F	Marketing
26	M	Economics	21	M	3D Design
31	M	Computing for Business	37	M	Computing for Business
22	F	3D Design	22	F	3D Design
27	F	Fine Art	21	F	3D Design
23	F	Law	22	F	Business Admin.
21	F	Fine Art	21	F	3D Design
20	M	Geography	23	M	Geog/Env. Management

Table 3.2. Group means for standardized assessments carried out by Farmer et al. (2001)

	Controls				Dyslexics			
	VIQ	PIQ	Read SS	Spell SS	VIQ	PIQ	Read SS	Spell SS
Mean	120.4	127.0	120.37	110.75	98.37	117.6	110.00	92.13

p = 0.128). There was also a significant difference between the groups for mean reading SS (t (15) = –4.92, p = 0.000) and spelling SS (t (15) = 5.42, p = 0.000). As part of the study, students' literacy skills were further assessed in a variety of ways, as were their perceptions of their own ability as writers, their perception of the importance of writing and also their levels of anxiety. The results of these assessments are reported and discussed in this chapter and also in Chapter 5.

Writing is the activity in academic life that has, perhaps, the most importance for students as it provides the basis for the majority of assessments they must undergo in order to achieve their qualifications. Clearly, in order to be able to produce relevant and interesting material in their writing, students must acquire information and knowledge in a variety of ways, including reading. But, ultimately, output in writing is of primary importance in staff assessment of student academic achievement in most degree courses. Further information about the importance of writing in assessment can be found in Chapter 7, which discusses the demands of different university degree courses.

Before considering the assessment of writing skills in detail it is of interest to note here that the quality of student writing in higher education generally is a cause for concern. Winch and Wells (1995), summarizing a variety of studies of higher education institutions, report that students have a general problem in relation to the secretarial skills involved in the handling of spelling, punctuation and morphosyntactic rules and some students have compositional as well as secretarial difficulties. Farmer et al. (2001), in information obtained from the staff responses to the questionnaire described in Chapter 7, found that 70 per cent of staff from a wide range of disciplines said that some students who had not been identified as being dyslexic had similar problems in writing to those identified as dyslexic. Several staff commented on the widespread nature of the difficulties in the production of text shown by students in general. It seems likely that the widening access to higher education over the last decade has allowed students to gain admission to university courses who have lower levels of educational attainment and come from a wider range of educational backgrounds. It is likely that lower levels of attainment in the development of writing will be found in this group. This is of relevance to the discussion of the writing of dyslexic students since if many students are seen to have difficulties with writing, the difficulties experienced by students with dyslexia may not be particularly apparent to teaching staff. They may simply consider that students with dyslexia are part of a group of 'bad writers' without understanding the origin of their difficulties.

An additional problem for students in the production of writing in higher educational settings may also be the types of writing expected on academic courses. Many academic disciplines ask for an impersonal style and will not accept anecdotal evidence or personal opinion. Certainly 'correctness' in adopting the academic style required is emphasized by many courses and disciplines (Crème and Lea 1997). Lea and Street (1998) suggest that, for students, their own identity as writers is of great importance. This identity 'may be challenged by the forms of writing required in different disciplines, notably prescriptions about the use of impersonal and passive forms as opposed to first person and active forms, and students may feel threatened and resistant . . .'. Pollak (2001) suggests that this challenge will be intensified for those who have been identified as dyslexic. The written word differs from the spoken word in many ways.

Students who are comfortable with the spoken word, but very uncomfortable with the heavy demands made by different levels of processing in the production of the written word, may have particular difficulty in adopting the formality of the written voice that is required.

Problems of writing faced by students with dyslexia

Singleton (1999) suggests the problems dyslexic students face when writing can include:

- an intractable spelling problem, often concealed by the use of an automatic spellchecker
- confusion of small words such as *which/with*
- omission of words, especially when the writer is under pressure
- awkward handwriting and/or slow writing speed
- an unexpected difference between oral and written expression, with oral contributions being typically of a much higher quality than written accounts of the same subject matter in terms of structure, self-expression and correct use of words.

Recent studies suggest that to this list can be added:

- difficulties in adopting the appropriate code of writing (Pollak 2001)
- slowness and difficulties in detecting errors in proofreading (Hatcher 2001; Farmer et al. 2001)
- restricted/inappropriate vocabulary (Raskind and Higgins 1995; Sterling et al. 1998; Farmer et al. 2001).

If we consider research into the writing of adult dyslexics we find that difficulties in spelling are fairly well documented (see, for example, Bruck 1993; Sterling et al. 1998) and there are many well-known tests of spelling to assess these (see discussion in Chapter 2). However a review of the literature related to other aspects of writing shows that there is a dearth of investigation into the writing of dyslexic students at any stage of education. The HEFCE report, *Dyslexia in Higher Education* (Singleton 1999), devotes some space to describing the difficulties of writing in examination conditions for university students and also the difficulties which grammatical errors in the construction of text may present to the assessor; however, no back-up research evidence is presented. The authors acknowledge that there are no standardized tests of writing ability and handwriting speed for this population so an assessment of difficulties in these areas is often omitted in the original process of identification of the dyslexic student. The issue of writing is also generally neglected in books and papers on dyslexia. McLoughlin et al. (1994) suggest that 'dyslexics will make characteristic errors such as omitting words and missing out prepositions and pronouns they intend to include' but this assertion is based on one paper on learning-disabled college students by Gregg (1983). In a recent edited book of papers, *Dyslexia: Theory and Good Practice* (Fawcett 2001), the index gives only two, very passing, references to writing. A chapter in the same book on identification and intervention in adults (Kirk et al. 2001) has a very brief section on dyslexia in post-school education and, under the heading 'Supports', mentions five key areas (organization, reading strategies, note-taking, presentations and study techniques) in which adult dyslexics may need training. Writing, however, is not mentioned. Rudel (1981) reported that students with dyslexia gave anecdotal accounts of problems with ordering information and coming to the point when writing but there is little research evidence to support this. However, studies by Aaron and colleagues (e.g. Aaron and Phillips 1986) do indicate that dyslexics may have a problem with the morphemic aspects of syntax (function words and inflections) in written language. In a previous piece of research, the current authors (Sterling et al. 1998) also found that dyslexic students in higher education produced shorter essays than controls, used more monosyllabic and fewer polysyllabic words, and their spelling error rate was much greater than that of controls.

The neglect of writing is probably due to a number of factors:

1. Writing is multi-faceted and performed for many purposes and many audiences. It is difficult to assess rigorously and consistently for the population of students in general (Gamaroff 2000). Different assessors place emphases on different aspects of writing and different disciplines have different expectations.
2. Given the emphasis in many studies of dyslexia on the central importance of the difficulties in reading and spelling and phonological deficits and the assumption that oral *language* is intact, it is not surprising that the written language of dyslexic students has been little studied.
3. There may well be an assumption in relation to the writing of students in higher education that, since these students have achieved access to higher education, they must be successful in the production of satisfactory written text, having presumably passed a number of assessments where writing is involved.

4. Investigations of adult dyslexia have not been greatly concerned with writing, since for the broad range of adult dyslexics from many walks of life this may not be an area that they find particularly disabling.

Students' perspectives on writing

Self-awareness and self-understanding are important elements in the development of competence as a learner. The more accurately one is able to evaluate one's strengths and weaknesses the more likely it is that one can make positive change (Riding and Rayner 1998). Given these considerations, a first premise in the assessment process might be that we need to understand the student's own perspective on his/her writing. Does the student perceive that s/he has a problem with writing? If so what is the nature of the problem? Is it to do with the mechanistic and formal aspects of writing such as spelling, grammar, punctuation and handwriting? Or are there problems related to the use of language or to the organization of essay material or text? In the study described above, the students were asked to complete a short questionnaire that aimed to investigate their perceptions of themselves as writers and their anxieties in relation to writing. They were asked to rate aspects of their perceptions on a scale of 1 to 5 where 1 signified 'always', 2 'usually', 3 'sometimes', 4 'rarely' and 5 'never'. The questions used and the results from the study are given in Table 3.3.

As can be seen from their responses to the first question in Table 3.3, students themselves, dyslexic and non-dyslexic alike, perceive the ability to write well to be very important. This response is augmented by the findings of Hatcher (2001) in an investigation of the needs and perceptions of dyslexic students from a wide range of disciplines in one university. Hatcher found that writing style was the principal area of concern for dyslexic students. In her study a highly developed writing style was also the competency most frequently mentioned as required and essential to the evaluation of the students' work by university tutors from all departments. In a recent survey of the perceptions of academic staff of the needs and difficulties of dyslexic students (described in Chapter 7) teaching staff were asked to rate the effects of the different aspects of writing on their evaluation of students' work on a Likert scale from 1 ('not at all') to 5 ('a great deal'). The average rating for the effect of spelling and grammar was 2.95. Twenty-nine per cent of staff gave a rating of 4 or 5 indicating that their marking was considerably affected by spelling and grammar. The average rating for the effect of fluency and clarity of expression was 3.89. Seventy-five per cent of staff gave a rating of 4 or 5 indicating that their marking was considerably affected by fluency and clarity of

Table 3.3. Means and standard deviations of ratings given by students in response to questions on their perceptions of writing

No.	Question	Controls		Dyslexics			
		Mean	SD	Mean	SD	t	p
	Rating for Q 1 Very important Not at all important 1 2 3 4 5						
1	I think it's important to be able to write well	1.73	1.10	1.93	0.70	.54	ns
	Rating for Qs 2–13 Always Never 1 2 3 4 5						
2	I enjoy writing	2.53	0.74	3.56	0.73	4.67	0.000
3	Thinking about writing makes me anxious	3.57	0.76	2.79	0.70	2.63	0.022
4	I put off tasks that involve writing	3.60	0.91	2.44	0.96	2.63	0.001
5	I avoid writing as much as possible	3.53	1.30	2.56	0.89	2.30	0.037
6	I worry about having to write when others are watching	4.07	1.22	2.31	1.01	4.67	0.000
7	I find it fairly easy to keep up with note-taking in lectures	2.40	1.12	3.47	0.99	2.19	0.047
8	I find it easy to hand in coursework in time for deadlines set by tutors	2.53	2.56	2.81	1.38	–0.32	ns
9	I am often unsure whether a word I have written is spelt correctly	3.40	0.63	2.00	0.52	7.36	0.000
10	If I am unsure how to spell a word I tend to avoid using it	4.00	.85	3.25	0.68	2.87	0.012
11	I have difficulty with punctuation when writing	3.13	.74	2.06	1.06	2.84	0.013
12	I have difficulty with the organisation of ideas in an essay	3.40	0.83	1.81	0.75	4.38	0.001
13	I make errors in the grammatical construction of sentences when writing	3.07	0.83	1.56	0.63	4.62	0.000
14	Compared to other students on my course my writing is	3.13	1.06	2.13	1.06	2.74	0.016
	Much slower...............Faster 1 2 3 4 5						
15	Please rate your writing skills (not handwriting) in comparison to those of other students on your course Much better Much worse 1 2 3 4 5	2.83	0.58	3.75	0.62	3.53	0.005

expression. The difference between these two mean ratings is highly significant statistically ($t(36) = -5.61$, $p = .000$). It can be seen therefore that most staff considered that both aspects of writing affected their evaluation of the work but that fluency and clarity of expression were rated as far more important than spelling and grammar errors. This suggests that if dyslexic students' problems are related to difficulties in the latter areas, as is traditionally perceived, then they may not suffer in relation to their peers when writing is evaluated. If, however, clarity of expression is affected by their difficulties in text production, then they may well be downgraded in assessment.

As can be seen from Table 3.3, in comparison with their peers, the students with dyslexia showed that they were more anxious about writing, avoided writing and were self-conscious about writing. In reply to all questions about different aspects of writing competence they showed that they considered their writing skills were poorer than those of other students on their courses. In effect, these self-perceptions and evaluations proved to be fairly accurate in that the students' self-ratings predicted aspects of writing skill as assessed in an essay-writing task and other assessments. Thus, there was a strong positive correlation between the students' perception of their writing speed and their total output of handwritten words; there was a strong negative correlation between lack of certainty about spellings and standard score on a spelling test; difficulties with the organization of ideas in an essay and perception of self as making grammatical errors in writing were correlated with the number of grammatical errors in an essay task (Farmer et al., in preparation).

The assessment of writing

As noted above writing is a complex activity with many facets. The processes and products of writing can therefore be assessed in many ways.

The candidates for assessment are the following:

- spelling (see Chapter 2)
- handwriting speed
- grammatical errors (such as omission or inappropriate use of prepositions, pronouns, determiners and suffixes)
- sentence construction problems (such as omission of main verb, switching of reference of subject of sentence, repetition/redundancy, inappropriate ordering of phrases/clauses)
- punctuation errors
- vocabulary use

- quality/clarity of argument and organization of ideas
- skill/ability in proofreading/revision of work.

How can these many aspects of writing be assessed? Should we construct a multiplicity of individual tasks, or is it possible or advisable to encompass all these aspects within one task? One way to identify the relevant aspects to assess in dyslexia is to compare the performance of students with and without dyslexia on candidate tasks. This type of investigation was carried out in the study described at the beginning of this chapter. In order to investigate the differences between dyslexic and non-dyslexic students in writing, Farmer et al. (2001) set the participants the following tasks:

1. *Free writing* The students were asked to write an essay for a university lecturer on the topic of the use of drugs by young people in modern society. The students were asked, in their essays, to comment on the information given in a histogram showing responses to a questionnaire on alcohol and illicit drug consumption by 2nd-year university students. The students were given five minutes to prepare their essay, ten minutes to write the first section and ten minutes to write the next section. One section was handwritten and one section word-processed. The students were then asked to read through their work and correct any errors. The word-processed section could be corrected using the spelling and grammar checkers available in Microsoft Word.
2. *Proofreading* Ability to detect and correct errors of spelling, grammar and punctuation in own free-writing was assessed from corrections made to the essay. A separate exercise also investigated the ability to proofread and correct a passage produced by another writer (see Figure 3.1). The passage contained errors of three types: spelling, grammar and punctuation.
3. *Speed of handwriting* The students were asked to write the sentence 'The quick brown fox jumps over the lazy dog' as quickly and as many times as possible for two minutes.

The following aspects of writing were assessed from the essay-writing task on both handwritten and word-processed formats:

- quantity of output (number of words)
- sophistication of vocabulary used (number/percentage of words of three syllables or more)

Instructions for participants

The passage below has many errors in it. There are different types of spelling, grammar and punctuation errors. Would you please read through the passage and correct any errors that you find. Please put a line through any incorrect word/letter/punctuation mark and write the correct version above. If a word/letter/punctuation mark is omitted, please put in an omission mark at the point at which it is omitted and write the omitted word/letter/mark above.

You will be given 5 minutes for this task.

e.g. Errors : In order to reed any passage the eyes must follow the print at the page.

e.g. Omissions: The eyes must move in a series pauses and jump

At university and collige, all of the following four skils in english is important: listening, for information in lectures seminars and tutorials; speaking, when taking part in seminars and tutorials; read of textbooks, jounrals and handouts; and writting, for essays and reports. Of these, reading is at least as improtant as the rest Stubents at tertiary level had a huge amount off Reading to do; some for core information and even more as background to the mane subject. it is therefore essential that it be done as efficiently possibel.

Written text has one distinct abvantage from spoken discourse: it is static. Whilst this means a text can de revewed as many times as the reader wishs, the rate to which any Text was read will dipend entirely on the speed of the readers eye movements. Given the amoumt of reading that most students has to do, It is cleerly in there interests to do so as quick and as effectively as possible.

Obviously students must understand what they reading. Less obviousley, reading slowly does not necesarily increases conprehension. in fact, increasing reading speed may actually improve understanding. One thing to bear to mind is that reading whilst being receptive skill, was most certainly not a passiv one. There must, be an intractive process between the reader and the text in order extract the meaning.

Figure 3.1. Proof-reading exercise.

- appropriateness of choice of words (number/percentage of words/phrases which were inappropriate/erroneous in a piece of formal writing, such as colloquialisms, dialect words, words lacking in explicit meaning or expressions containing redundancies, e.g. 'Okay'; 'ever so much'; 'doing bad things'; 'a few less'
- competence in spelling in free-writing (number/percentage of spelling errors + number/percentage of revisions of errors)
- grammatical competence in free-writing (number/percentage of grammatical and text construction errors + number/percentage of revisions of errors. These were divided into two types: Type 1 grammatical errors were errors in verb tense and number agreement, preposition and pronoun use and use of determiners; Type 2 grammatical errors were errors in other aspects of text construction such as

redundancy and repetition or words or phrases, omission of main verbs, incorrect ordering of clauses/phrases)
- competence in the use of appropriate punctuation in free-writing (number/percentage of punctuation errors + revisions).

The comparisons between dyslexic and control participants' scores on the measures of writing in the combined handwritten and word-processed sections of the essay are summarized in Table 3.4 as are the means for the other tasks.

Table 3.4. Means and standard deviations for measures of aspects of writing used by Farmer et al. (2001).

Measures	Controls (N=16)		Dyslexics (N=16)			
	Mean	SD	Mean	SD	t-test result	P value
Writing speed: No. of words	78	13	69	9	2.12	0.051
Measures derived from the essay-writing task.						
Total no. of words written	253	62	259	77	−0.27	ns
Percentage of words of 3+ syllables	13.86	1.76	10.63	2.42	3.49	0.003
Essay: Percent. spelling errors	2.39	3.01	8.56	5.58	−3.96	0.001
Essay: percent. grammatical errors. Type 1	0.26	0.32	1.09	0.89	3.30	0.016
Essay: percent. grammatical. errors. Type 2	1.32	1.00	1.42	0.36	0.22	ns
Essay: percent. punctuation errors	2.48	2.36	3.98	2.43	−1.16	ns
Essay: percent lexical choice errors	0.20	0.26	1.18	0.88	2.71	0.035
Measures derived from the proof-reading task						
Percentage of spelling errors detected and altered correctly	75.57	14.27	52.84	18.62	4.15	0.001
Percentage of grammatical errors detected and altered correctly	57.92	20.18	27.50	13.96	4.30	0.001
Percentage of punctuation errors detected and altered correctly	65.91	22.88	40.91	10.50	3.91	0.001

The differences between the mean handwriting speed for each group almost reached significance at the .05 level. Although on the whole the nondyslexic students wrote more quickly than the dyslexic students there was clearly no distinct separation of the groups on this task.

On the essay-writing task it can be seen that the mean scores for dyslexics and controls differed on a number of measures: percentage of polysyllabic words, percentage of spelling errors, percentage of Type 1 grammatical errors, percentage of lexical choice errors. There was no difference between the groups in the number of words written there was also no difference between the groups in Type 2 grammatical errors or on punctuation.

On the proofreading task the nondyslexic students were more success-ful than the dyslexic on every task. The order of difficulty of detection and correction for the types of error was the same for the two groups. Inspection of the data does seem to indicate that the grammatical errors were particularly difficult for the dyslexic group to detect.

These results will be discussed in relation to other research findings in the literature relating to dyslexia and in relation to their importance in the assessment of the strengths and weaknesses of students with dyslexia.

Discussion of assessments

Handwriting speed and output

There are no standardized assessments of handwriting speed (Sawyer et al. 1992, 1996). Generally, those who have attempted to measure hand-writing speed have chosen a task which does not involve short-term memory or semantic processing. Two well-known candidates are (a) the writing of one's own name at speed (Hughes and Suritsky 1994), and (b) the writing of the sentence 'The quick brown fox jumps over the lazy dog'. The former requires the production of an overlearned string of letters and the latter the production of all the letters of the alphabet. Although the former may be recommended owing to its low processing load, it may present inequalities in that some names are longer and more complex and may have several letters which are more difficult to produce.

Measures can be obtained as words per minute or as letters per minute. Hatcher (2001) found that dyslexic students when compared to controls had a significantly lower handwriting speed as measured in words per minute. Our study obtained similar results, although not quite reaching the 0.05 level of significance. Hatcher (2001) found an average speed of 27.65 words per minute for dyslexic university students and 33.06 for non-dyslexic controls on a sentence-writing task. In our study we found an average speed of 34.5 words per minute for dyslexic university students and 39 words per minute for controls in the 'quick brown fox' sentence-writing task. On a measure of word copying our dyslexic subjects therefore appear to be rather quicker than those in the Hatcher sample. Hughes and Suritsky (1994) found an average writing speed of 130 letters per minutes (SD = 20) for dyslexics and 157 (SD = 24) for controls. If our handwriting speed task is analysed in terms of letters per minute we find an average writing speed of 133 (SD = 18) letters per minute for dyslexics and 152 (SD = 24) for controls, very similar to the results from Hughes and Suritsky. Only two dyslexic students wrote more than 140 letters per minute. On the other hand, 13 out of 16 control students had a handwriting speed of more than 140 letters per minute. If we take the mean of the control students (152 letters per minute ± one standard deviation) then we find that the average range is from 124 to 176 letters per minute. Two of the controls and six of the dyslexics fall outside this category.

If we look at tasks which involve the additional load of the production of text as opposed to a copying-type task, McLoughlin et al. (1994) suggest that around 20 words per minute is a reasonable estimate for undergraduates; however, it is not clear on what type of task this estimate is based. Tasks which involve production of text and processing of information will clearly take longer than these simple tasks. As Singleton (1999) points out, speed of writing can be estimated from a free-writing task such as essay-writing (Singleton suggests asking the students to write for 20–30 minutes about the subject which they are studying). However, as he notes, in such a task some students may avoid using words they cannot spell, and this may give a misleading impression of their writing speed. In our study, when questioned after they had finished writing, all students with dyslexia stated that they had avoided one or more words in their essays because of their lack of certainty about spelling. Sterling et al. (1998) found that in a 30-minute free-writing task (writing an essay about life as a student, with guidelines as to content) in the first two 10-minute periods of writing dyslexics produced an average of 169 words (16.9 words per minute) and controls produced an average of 202 words (20.2 words per minute). In the more complex essay task described above in the current study it was found that dyslexic subjects and controls did not differ in the average number of handwritten words they produced per minute (dyslexics: 12.8; controls: 12.9; $t(15) = -0.07$, ns) nor in the average number of word-processed words they produced per minute (dyslexics: 13.1; controls: 12.3; t(15) = 0.49, ns). It must be noted that these essays were very short. The experimenter working with the participants observed a difference between the dyslexic and nondyslexic subjects in their approach to the task. He noted that the dyslexic participants did not spend much time thinking about what they were going to say but just wrote, whilst the other students were more reflective. The explanation for this is unclear but may well relate to the characteristic dyslexic ready access to ideas, but lack of consideration of organizational features. In a formal essay, where careful planning would pay off, these students might therefore have written down as many thoughts as possible without taking into account a framework. Their anxiety about their own rate of text production may also have caused them to 'rush into' writing in order to produce sufficient text. The other students, on the other hand, because of their greater fluency in writing and lack of concern in relation to this aspect, may have taken longer to produce rather better organized text. Hatcher (2001) found that students with dyslexia took significantly longer to complete the writing of a précis and included less information in the latter. Hughes and Suritsky (1994) also reported that, in a note-taking task, higher education students with learning disabilities wrote more slowly and noted fewer information units than controls. They found that there was a positive correlation between handwriting speed and amount of information recorded.

There does seem to be some contradiction here. It does seem that the essay task set in the current study was more complex for both groups of students and that both produced fewer words than students in other studies. It may be that when the generation of ideas is the more complex part of the writing task dyslexic students are not disadvantaged in terms of quantity of output, but their structure may be less adequate. On the other hand the essays produced were rather short for such a complex task and therefore may not give appropriate evidence of the students' writing competence. This needs further investigation.

Although quality rather than quantity should be the criterion in the assessment of essays, clearly if quantity is considerably decreased then fewer points can be made and less evidence cited. In order to achieve greater understanding of the predictors of output we carried out a regression analysis of the predictors of the quantity of output of handwritten words. The results of this showed that handwriting speed was one of the three predictors which between them accounted for 80 per cent of the variance (Farmer et al., in preparation). The other significant contributors were students' perceptions of their own speed of output of text (accounting for 23 per cent of the variance) and percentage of grammatical errors in the text (accounting for 35 per cent of the variance). A similar regression analysis carried out for the control group found no significant predictors of output apart from the students' own perceptions of their competence as writers. Hatcher (2001) also found that handwriting speed was one of three variables which best predicted the classification of students as dyslexic or non-dyslexic.

Handwriting speed is a mechanical, performance factor affecting the production of text. Rate of production of text will also be affected by the rate of production of ideas and the readiness with which these are translated into words. If we remove the performance factor of handwriting speed and look at the production of text by a different method, word-processing, our study of university students' essay-writing showed that there was a strong positive correlation between the number of words produced in this format and the number of words produced in the handwritten format ($r = 0.6043$, $p = 0.013$: Farmer et al. 2001). A similar result, comparing handwritten and word-processed output, was found by MacArthur and Graham (1987) working with 11–12-year-olds with learning difficulties. A regression analysis of the predictors of the quantity of output of word-processed words showed that 71 per cent of the variance in output for the dyslexic students is predicted by a combination of the students' own perceptions of their rate of production of writing and their ability to organize their ideas in writing and the percentage of grammatical errors and lexical problems in their essay. It would seem that in the production of text, when the performance factor of handwriting is removed the crucial element of difficulties in the production of grammatical text remains. Choice of vocabulary then comes more to the fore. Of course this is a small sample, and too many generalizations cannot be made. However, until further evidence is available, it seems that these aspects of writing are of key importance in assessment if we are to identify the extent of a student's difficulties. For further discussion of this topic see the section below titled 'Text output method'.

Since students cannot avoid, at times at least, the use of handwriting to produce text, for instance in note-taking, and since handwriting speed appears to be a factor which aids in discrimination between groups of dyslexic and nondyslexic students handwriting speed would seem to be an important aspect of the students' functioning to be included in any assessment battery.

Grammatical errors

Assessment of grammatical errors in text involves three levels of analysis: word, sentence and paragraph levels.

At word level, the types of errors to be noted are those where parts of words are erroneous or omitted or whole words are erroneous or omitted. The following types of error are common (Aaron and Phillips 1986; MacArthur and Graham 1987; Farmer et al. 2001):

- noun pluralization omission/errors
- possessive ending omission/errors
- verb tense and number omission/confusion errors (erroneous/omitted verb endings)
- pronoun omission/confusion errors
- determiner omission/confusion errors
- preposition omission/confusion errors
- suffix errors (e.g. stressful/stressed).

At sentence level, the types of error to be noted are those where the sentence construction is such as either to produce an incomplete sentence (by omission of a main verb) or to make meaning and reference unclear by disordered sequencing of clauses/phrases, inconsistency in verb subject reference or inconsistencies in verb tense within a sentence. Students may also produce redundancies and repetitions in their sentences.

At paragraph level, the types of error to be noted are those where the relationship between sentences is not clear owing to lack of clarity of verb subject reference (anaphoric reference), e.g. 'The students drink a great deal when examinations draw near. They are often stressful.'

In our study, there were significant differences between dyslexic subjects and controls in the number of grammatical errors produced. These were errors in such aspects of grammar as verb tense and number agreement errors, preposition and pronoun use, and use of determiners. However, in relation to other aspects of text construction such as redundancy and repetition, omission of main verbs, and incorrect ordering of clauses/phrases, there were no differences between the groups. Since these errors are predictive of output in both handwritten and word-processed text it seems that they are important elements to be considered in assessing the strengths and weaknesses of dyslexic students and also in considering the support and teaching which they may need.

Vocabulary and semantics

In our study we found that the dyslexic students were more likely to select immature or colloquial words/phrases from their lexicon, using words or phrases that are appropriate in colloquial speech but not in a formal essay (e.g. 'Okay'; 'ever so much'; 'doing bad things'; 'a few less'). The text constructed by students with dyslexia may be less sophisticated then that of the text constructed by controls. Farmer et al. (2001) and Sterling et al. (1998) found that, in essay-writing, nondyslexic students used a higher proportion of words of three or more syllables than dyslexic students. When asked about their choice of words, 14/16 dyslexic students in the Farmer et al. study said that they avoided using words that they were unsure how to spell – suggesting that a simpler, less sophisticated word may be selected.

It seems, therefore, that the texts constructed by dyslexic students may be more limited in terms of vocabulary use and it is possible that this may have an effect upon a reader's perception of the quality of the text. In a comparison of the mean WAIS vocabulary scores of the two groups of students a significant difference was found in favour of the non-dyslexic students ($t(15) = 4.92$, $p = 0.000$). Other studies of dyslexic students have not found these differences, however. Hatcher (2001) found no differences in mean WAIS vocabulary scores between dyslexic and nondyslexic students. It must be noted that Hatcher's study was conducted at an 'old', established university in the UK where, overall, the students come from more generally privileged backgrounds. 'New' universities in the UK have been developed from polytechnics which were higher education institutions where there was little emphasis on research and a great deal of emphasis on teaching. Many of the students who attend these universities are those who come from backgrounds where a university education was uncommon. Dyslexic students entering 'new' universities may have a rather different educational history from those entering 'old' universities. It may be the case that their difficulties in achieving educationally are compounded by environmental factors. Thus, their vocabularies may be less developed than those of their peers from similar backgrounds because, as a result of their difficulties, they are less able than their peers to compensate for environmental factors by picking up vocabulary from the reading of text and other sources. Singleton (1999) points out that the incidence of dyslexia in 'new' universities is slightly higher than in the 'old'. However, no analysis has been carried out of the demographic characteristics of the student groups. No definite conclusions can be drawn, and we can only suggest that this less developed use of vocabulary may be due to any one or a combination of any of the following factors:

- in writing, the students choose words that are easier to spell
- dyslexic students are overloaded in terms of information-processing demands when constructing text, finding the whole process more complex and taxing than non-dyslexic students, and they therefore find it more difficult to pick up the additional burden of code-switching from speech to writing
- some students with dyslexia come from less advantaged backgrounds where they have had little support in their school years, have left school early and have had little opportunity to develop a formal voice in writing
- similarly, these students may have had fewer opportunities to develop their vocabulary
- some students may feel that their identity is undermined by the adopting of the passive formal voice of some academic writing.

Organization of ideas and quality of argument

The process of essay writing is 'probably the most complex constructive act that most human beings are ever expected to perform' (Bereiter and Scardamalia 1983). Success in producing written discourse is the main goal of formal education (Gamaroff 2000). The rating of essays on these dimensions has not generally been considered in any of the literature on dyslexic writing. The rating of writing, as such, produces low inter-rater reliability and the criteria for so doing are disputed (Gamaroff 2000). A small sample of the essays produced in our study (four dyslexics and four controls) were rated by two raters on a grading scale of A to E but a low level of agreement was found. It must be noted, however, that this rating was carried out for a small sample and was performed on the basis of overall impression rather than a detailed marking schedule. Rater training and agreement of criteria are required in order to investigate this further.

The following are further points to consider in relation to the task used in assessing essay-writing. Our task was formal, devised in order to emulate the type of writing that might be required in examinations or assignments; however, the situation was a relaxed one where the students were made to feel at ease by a friendly young person. Some students may therefore have written their essay in response to the situation, rather than in response to the task as set. The exercise was also complicated by the fact that the students came from a range of disciplines, some of which would place more importance on the adoption of a formal style than others. The students were also at different levels in their university courses and no doubt therefore at different stages in their development of academic writing. All of these factors make it difficult to interpret the results. Possibly two writing tasks, one formal and one informal, would be more appropriate. This would enable the assessor to probe the student's ability to switch codes, use appropriate vocabulary and respond to the demands of different types of situation demanding writing.

Text output method

In determining the needs of dyslexic students, it is important to decide which method of text output would be the most appropriate for a student to use in assessment situations, particularly in examinations. The alternatives are handwriting, word-processing, dictation to a tape recorder or to a word-processor, or use of an amanuensis. How are decisions to be made about which form of output should be used?

The Singleton report (1999) found that virtually all higher education institutions allow extra time in written examinations for students with dyslexia. In a third of cases, a standard amount of time was allowed for all dyslexic students; in the other two thirds, the amount of time allowed varied, 'depending on the severity of the student's problems and other factors'. The Singleton report also gives a comprehensive analysis of attitudes in higher education to the use of different types of technology in examination situations. The majority of higher education institutions were reported to allow special arrangements in examinations, which included the use of an amanuensis or a word-processor. Only two thirds allowed the use of a tape recorder. It is not clear exactly how decisions as to the needs of students in examinations are to be determined. Singleton (1999) suggests that decisions as to the amount of time to be allowed should depend on the 'severity' of the effects of the students' dyslexia, and proposes a classification for the severity of dyslexia as follows:

Mild: the student has a high level of compensation and mild difficulties in a range of learning skills, or moderate difficulties in one learning skill area

Moderate: the student does not have a high level of compensation and has moderate learning difficulties in a range of learning skills, or severe difficulties in one skill area

Severe: the student has little or no compensation and has severe difficulties in a range of learning skills.

The Singleton report acknowledges the complexity and difficulty of applying this scheme in practice; it suggests that each case must be considered individually and ultimately the categorization of the severity of the student's problems must be the decision of a qualified assessor. They go on to recommend the following *minimum* amounts of additional time for candidates with dyslexia sitting written examinations:

Mild – 10 minutes per hour
Moderate – 15 minutes per hour
Severe – 15 minutes per hour.

No guidelines are given in relation to the use of technology.

These recommendations of course are based on an overall assessment of the severity of a student's dyslexia across a range of skill areas including the processing of auditory information, reading, writing, spelling, number work and memory. It may well be that some of these skills are not particularly relevant when assessing a student's needs in examinations. It is not really clear how a 'qualified' assessor would arrive at a decision. Nor do these areas take into account student stress and anxiety that may not be directly related to severity of dyslexia. Farmer et al. (2001) found that students with dyslexia had a generally higher level of anxiety than nondyslexic students (see Chapter 5) and that level of anxiety was negatively correlated with verbal IQ level ($r(16) = 0.5745$, $p = 0.02$). Students with lower verbal ability may be more generally anxious; however, other factors may also cause 'state' anxiety when students are taking exams.

Another accommodation that can be made is in the allowance of the use of different output methods. In order to investigate the usefulness of this, to some extent at least, we looked in our study at differences between handwritten and word-processed output (see the description above of the essay task). Comparisons between the dyslexics and controls for the two forms of output are given in Tables 3.5 and 3.6.

It can be seen from these tables that the students in the control group were generally more competent on every measure in both formats, except in number of words produced and in punctuation. When between-format comparisons were made for the two groups on these measures, before revision of the essays, it was seen that there were no differences between the two formats on any of the measures for either group. However, after they had completed the essays, the students were allowed time to revise what they had done. In the case of the word-processed essay the spelling and grammar checkers were switched on at that point. After revision, dyslexic students significantly reduced the percentage of spelling errors in both the handwritten and word-processed essays they had produced.

Table 3.5. Comparisons between means of dyslexic and non-dyslexic students on the measures of the hand-written essay

	Controls		Dyslexics			
	Mean	SD	Mean	SD	t-test result	p value
Essay : no. of words	129	44	128	36	0.13	ns
Percentage words with 3+ sylls.	13.91	3.47	11.32	3.98	1.79	0.095
Percentage of spelling errors	1.87	2.28	4.74	3.26	−3.29 **	0.005
Percentage of grammatical errors	0.89	1.41	2.34	1.54	−2.76 *	0.015
Percent punctuation errors.	1.34	1.50	2.35	1.63	−1.19	ns

Table 3.6. Comparisons between means of dyslexic and non-dyslexic students in the word-processed essay

	Controls		Dyslexics			
	Mean	SD	Mean	SD	t-test result	p
Essay: no. of words	124	33	131	49	0.49	ns
Percentage of words of 3+ syllables	14.07	2.93	10.03	2.34	3.52	0.003
Percentage of spelling errors	1.26	1.89	5.02	3.59	−4.10	0.001
Percentage of grammatical errors	1.22	.95	2.21	2.20	−2.76	0.015
Percentage of punctuation errors	1.06	1.18	2.24	1.85	−1.49	ns

Their word-processed work after revision had a significantly lower percentage of errors than their handwritten work. Control students, who, before revision, had produced significantly less errors in both formats, did not significantly reduce these errors after revision of the handwritten format, but did do so after revision of the word-processed format. Despite dyslexic students' success in reducing their errors, after revision they still had significantly more errors than control students in both formats. However the final word-processed work of the dyslexic students only contained 1.27 per cent spelling errors, a low rate, comparable to the percentage found in the handwritten work of non-dyslexic students (Sterling et al. 1998).

On the other hand, when percentage of grammatical errors was considered, it was found that dyslexic students produced more grammatical errors than controls, but very few of these errors were corrected. Control students also did not attempt to revise grammatical errors.

Dyslexic students did correct punctuation errors in their handwritten essays and in fact had fewer errors than control students in their final handwritten texts. Alterations to choice of words were not found.

It can be concluded that, at least in the case of spelling, dyslexic students find great benefit in the use of a word-processor to enable them to produce text of appropriate accuracy. However, these students are less likely to detect and correct other grammatical errors, such as errors of verb tense and number agreement, and appropriate use of function words such as prepositions and determiners,. It may well be that, given more time in the proofreading task, the dyslexic students may have been successful in detecting more errors; however, grammatical and sentence construction errors and errors of lexical choice may be more likely to affect a reader's critical evaluation of the text.

All this does not lead to a particular recommendation as regards technology, extra time and other support in examinations. However, the students' own perceptions of their ability as writers were an important predictor when output was considered; therefore it seems appropriate to conclude that the students' own perceptions of their needs in relation to examinations and other assessments should be to the fore when recommendations are made. Certainly if a student is a skilled typist and accustomed to word-processing work for assignments it would make sense that s/he should be allowed to use a word-processor in examinations. The down side to this may be that the student's examination script will then be readily identifiable to the tutor who marks it and so 'blind' marking will not be possible. A number of institutions are now adopting the policy of asking students to put dyslexia 'stickers' on their work in order that marking should not be influenced by spelling and other writing difficulties. This laudable practice will, of course, also detract from the blind marking procedure, unless there are several students with dyslexia in the student cohort.

As Singleton (1999) explains, there is a great deal of variability in the presentation of students with dyslexia in terms of the severity and type of difficulties they experience. As Singleton suggests, a blanket approach to dealing with dyslexic students' difficulties is improper and 'arrangements should be on an individual basis dependent on needs'.

Proofreading and the revision of writing

These are two related activities. Proofreading concerns the detection and correction of errors in text and generally concerns superficial aspects of writing such as spelling, grammar and punctuation. Revision of text is a wider-ranging activity which subsumes the more superficial activity involved in proofreading. It has been variously defined but most writers agree that it concerns more general detection of mismatches between what was intended and what was produced as text and includes the revision of meaning (Fitzgerald and Markham 1987). Compositional revisions are involved as well as issues of surface structure (secretarial issues). Proofreading is generally undertaken after the writing is completed. Revision may take place at any point in the writing process (Fitzgerald and Markham 1987). Successful detection of a text problem does not guarantee its appropriate revision and a writer may also detect a problem without being able to specify what it is (see review in Hacker et al. 1994). Rapp (1988) found that error detection in proofreading was a sensitive indicator of writing proficiency. She suggests that weaker writers have a higher processing load when proofreading text and therefore detect less errors. Butterfield et al. (1996) present a model of the text revision process that demonstrates that substantial amounts of information must be processed in working memory during text revision and therefore it is suggested that working memory limits will constrain revision. Most writers tend to revise their writing very little and those who do tend to 'act as proofreaders rather than as authors striving to convey clear and interesting meanings to an unknown audience' (Hacker et al. 1994). Detection of meaning errors requires comprehension of the text and comparison with meanings retained in the memory of earlier portions of the text. It is a more demanding task than detection of superficial aspects of the text such as spelling, morphology and punctuation. Studies have shown that the greater the demands on working memory in revision tasks the less likely the errors are to be detected and corrected (Hacker et al. 1994). The latter authors have shown that college students who have the ability to correct errors may yet have difficulties in applying that knowledge to the task of detecting text errors. They also found that the ability of students to detect errors of meaning was increased by giving increased time for revision.

Studies of the proofreading and revision competencies of students with dyslexia in higher education are singularly lacking. A few studies have looked at the developing competencies of small numbers of school students with learning disabilities in the United States. The results of these suggest that these students' abilities to detect and correct their spelling errors improve dramatically with the help of a spellchecker (Dalton et al. 1990; McArthur et al. 1996) and that, given some intervention to enhance strategies in the use of the spellchecker, high school students with learning disabilities are able to produce texts with spelling error rates comparable to those of their non-disabled peers (McNaughton et al. 1997). Some studies have directed their attention to evaluating intervention techniques to improve proofreading. The success of the outcomes from the latter is unclear (McNaughton et al. 1997).

The single published study to date that focuses on students in higher education investigated the effects of different proofreading conditions on the spelling performance of college students with learning disabilities (McNaughton et al. 1997). This study found that students who used a word-processor with a spellchecker corrected 81.9 per cent of their errors and the final draft of their work contained a 3.3 per cent spelling error rate. Students who handwrote their essays and had no access to spelling aids corrected 36 per cent of their errors and had a final error rate of 7.1 per cent. The mean time per error corrected was 52.5 seconds in the former condition and 180.8 seconds in the latter. However, Hughes and Suritsky (1994) found that in a similar writing task the mean error rate for non-LD students was 1.1 per cent and an error rate of 2.9 per cent was two SD above the mean. Therefore, even with the use of a word-processor and spellchecker, these higher education students with learning disabilities were not able to produce text that equalled that of their non-LD peers in terms of spelling accuracy. McNaughton et al. (1997) also note that 'it is not spelling errors alone that distinguish the writing of college students with LD . . . many of these students experience difficulty in producing fluent, coherent text.' They suggest that, 'given effective technology to address some of the more basic aspects of written composition', students' information-processing resources may be freed to deal with higher level aspects of text revision. A further study, carried out by Hatcher et al. (2001) found that students with dyslexia took longer to carry out a proofreading task than controls and detected fewer errors.

In our study of proofreading, students were studied in two types of task, one involving the detection and correction of spelling, grammar and punctuation errors in a set piece of text (see Fig. 3.2), and the other involving the revision of their own free writing (for discussion see the section on 'Text output method'). In the first task, spelling errors included the following types: letter sequencing; substitution of letters of similar form (m/n, b/d); vowel omission/substitutions/addition; and homophone substitution. Grammatical errors were of several types: verb tense errors; verb number errors; auxiliary verb errors; and function word (determiners, prepositions) omission/substitution. Punctuation errors included capitalization errors, stop and comma errors, and apostrophe errors. The students were given a time restriction of five minutes when carrying out the task. In this task, dyslexic students detected significantly fewer errors of all types than control students. Comparing the detection of the different types of error it was found that the dyslexic students were more likely to detect and correct spelling errors than punctuation errors and more likely to detect and correct punctuation errors than grammatical errors. Grammatical errors, therefore, seem not only to be the greatest barrier to the production of text but also the most difficult for dyslexics to detect and correct. The order of difficulty of the types of error was the same for control students as for the dyslexic group but, for the control group, the differences between the rates of detection of punctuation errors and grammatical errors and spelling errors were not significant. There was a highly significant positive correlation between the percentage of spelling errors corrected on the proofreading task and the standard score on the WRAT spelling test and the percentage of spelling errors made in a free-writing task for both groups.

Clearly our dyslexic students were less successful than their peers in all aspects of this task. It is possible that other factors over and above difficulties in detecting and correcting errors will have added to their difficulty. Thus, for instance, reading for meaning, not just for superficial characteristics of the words, was important in making some of the corrections. Therefore the reading of the text will in all likelihood have taken them longer. This increased demand will then have left them with fewer resources to bring to bear on the other aspects of the task. Some students adopted a strategy of writing out whole words or phrases, although this was not instructed. This also will have added to the time and workload involved. A future investigation should not restrict the amount of time allowed for the task. It may be, that under those conditions, dyslexic students' performance might be on a par with that of nondyslexics, although taking longer. As it is, we can conclude from the evidence of the two types of task that dyslexic students are able to correct at least some of their errors but that they are not as efficient at this process as their nondyslexic peers and it is likely that additional time for this would be helpful as greater time is needed for reading.

Demands of different disciplines and courses

Clearly the profile of strengths and weaknesses revealed by assessment must be related to the profile of demands of the course which the student will undertake. Singleton et al. (1999) state that 'it is essential that there is a realistic consideration of . . . the demands and delivery methods of the chosen course of study' and this may 'involve gathering information from academic staff delivering the student's course'. In relation to writing, this will involve the consideration of 'the amount and type of written work required and the length of time permitted; the balance of coursework, end-of-module tests and formal examinations; the level of technical writing accuracy required (e.g. spelling, grammar and punctuation)'. If all of this information is made available to staff involved in the assessment of the dyslexic student then a summary could be made of the student's strengths and weaknesses in relation to these demands. Thus a student with significant spelling difficulties and difficulties with grammar but relatively preserved oral skills will require a high level of support in relation to a modern languages course which has a high emphasis on accuracy of grammatical writing and spelling incorporated into assessments. The same student may require far less support if enrolled in an engineering or drama course. In a survey of staff attitudes to dyslexia in one university, Farmer et al. (2001) found that 12/40 respondents from across the range of disciplines said that errors of spelling and grammar markedly affected their evaluation of students' work. Two of the three staff whose marking was the most extremely affected by spelling and grammar taught modern languages. The third taught literature. On the other hand, 15/40 respondents said that errors of spelling and grammar had little effect on their evaluation of students work. Of these, two taught courses in the humanities and education, two taught social sciences, and the remaining eleven taught course in engineering, science, computing and maths.

It is not at present very clear that such a summary of the demands of individual courses is available for student assessors. Dyslexic students coming from a wide variety of courses present themselves to the central student services for assessment. The modules and course which they will be following will have published literature which gives some description of teaching, learning and assessment methods, but this will not necessarily have sufficient detail for the assessor and a complete picture may be difficult to compile from different sources. It would be helpful to central services if such information were readily available in collated format. On the other hand, Singleton (1999) also recommends that 'there should be a member of academic staff within each faculty and/or sub-faculty unit (e.g. school or department) with explicit responsibility for students with dyslexia within that area'. Some participants in the International BDA Conference at York (2001) also suggested that support tutors should be attached to specific departments within higher education institutions rather than being a centralized resource, thus facilitating dialogue, liaison and understanding and all aspects of assessment and support. Certainly the implementation of either of these two suggestions would facilitate the communication necessary to profile the demands of courses and the consideration of how these demands might affect an individual with a particular profile of strengths and weaknesses.

Summary: recommendations for assessment of writing

The following measures could be used in initial assessment and/or also in further diagnostic assessment for the provision of support and remediation:

1. Speed of text production: mechanical. A measure of both handwriting speed and word-processing speed would be useful. Recommended is the use of a measure of number of letters written per minute obtained from asking the student to copy the sentence 'The quick brown fox jumps over the lazy dog' as many times as possible for one minute.
2. Speed of text production: composition. The student could be required to write two short essays: one on a topic which does not require recall of information or complex ideas, such as 'Life as a university student'; one, as it might be written for a university lecturer, on a topic from their chosen discipline. The student could be given 15 minutes for each task and the number of words written per minute calculated for each.
3. Assessment of spelling errors: the number of spelling errors in the above tasks could be calculated as a percentage of total words written. The percentage error rate for our controls was 2.39 with a standard deviation of 3.01. Other studies report lower error rates for controls. McNaughton et al. (1997) found that an error rate greater than 2.9 per cent was two SD greater than the error rate for students without learning disabilities. Certainly an error rate of more than 5 per cent should be considered a serious problem.
4. Assessment of grammatical errors: the number/percentage of Type 1 grammatical errors could be calculated from the above tasks. These are errors in verb tense and number agreement, preposition and pronoun use, and use of determiners. The results of our study (see Table 3.3) suggest that an error rate of more than 3 per cent should be considered a serious problem.
5. Assessment of lexical choice errors: the number/percentage of words/phrases which are inappropriate/erroneous in the piece of formal writing, such as colloquialisms, dialect words, words lacking in

explicit meaning or expressions containing redundancies. The contrast between the demands of the two pieces of text should highlight these. Again, the results of our study suggest that an error rate of more than 3 per cent should be considered a serious problem.

6. Competence in proofreading could be assessed by asking the student to correct their essay work in red pen and calculating percentage of correct revisions. In addition, the example given in Figure 3.1, or something similar, could be used to assess length of time taken in proofreading work. It would also be helpful for support workers to assess the student's competence in the use of the spellchecker for revision work.

CHAPTER 4

Assessing and supporting numeracy

Badian (1999) points out that mathematics is a vague global term which encompasses different tasks and skills at different ages. A number of writers and researchers (Steeves 1983; Clayton 1994) would endorse Badian's view that it is important to distinguish between arithmetic and mathematics. Arithmetic involves number computation and is underpinned by the learning of number bonds and multiplication tables, whereas mathematics is made up of a number of elements including geometry, algebra, and calculus with a greater emphasis on the understanding of mathematical concepts. West (1991) suggests that this might explain why some eminent scientists and mathematicians were good at the creative, conceptual aspects of mathematics but relatively poor at simple computation or arithmetic. Steeves (1988) noted that among the dyslexic boys she taught some showed a talent for mathematics despite a lack of efficiency at computation.

Simple arithmetic involves a lot of repetition and rote learning of basic number facts. It is suggested (Lerner 1989; Brandys and Rourke 1991; Turner 1997; Adams and Hitch 1997) that for people with dyslexia limitations in working memory and with retrieval from long-term memory may underpin poor arithmetical performance. This impedes both the learning of basic number facts and the ability to hold numbers in one's head when carrying out mental arithmetic. Pritchard et al. (1989) and Turner Ellis et al. (1996) both found in studies of children's computation of tables that dyslexics have fewer number facts available to them than nondyslexics. In a sense dyslexics can end up being doubly disabled, in that their lack of number facts means they often have to do extra computation such as work out a times table before proceeding with the main part of the computation. In a mental arithmetic situation this is likely to increase the chance of overloading working memory. Hitch (1978) points out that even within arithmetic there is a critical difference between mental and written arithmetic, with mental arithmetic placing a greater load on working memory. Most of these studies were carried out with children, but recent studies have found that these same underlying deficits are present in adult dyslexics. Turner Ellis et al. (1996) found that, in a sample of 48 dyslexic adults, only 8 (16.67 per cent) could fluently recite their 6, 7 and 8 times tables. This is endorsed by our own and others' experience of the high number of dyslexic students reporting that they still do not know their multiplication tables. Miles and Miles (1999) argue that when the clinical and experimental evidence is reviewed it supports the thesis that the underlying difficulties in arithmetic are an integral part of dyslexia and it is unnecessary to use the additional label of dyscalculia. We would tend to endorse this view. Where a student's primary difficulty is dyslexia, it would seem more constructive and enabling to explain any number difficulties as part of underlying working memory limitations. Our experience was that the few students who received an additional label of dyscalculia were confused by this and tended to see themselves as doubly disabled: 'I would be very grateful if someone could explain exactly what dyscalculus is, I suffer from it but I don't understand' (female BA Business and Legal Studies, age 22).

Malmer (2000) also argues that the term dyscalculia should be limited to those students who just have difficulties with mathematics, whereas arithmetical difficulties in dyslexic students should be seen as an expression of their general underlying processing difficulties. He feels it is important to make this distinction because different forms of intervention may be needed depending on the underlying cause of the difficulties.

It is also important to stress that despite this evidence of some underlying difficulties dyslexic students can also have many strengths in the mathematical field. In our previous study (Riddick et al. 1997) of 16 dyslexic university students, one of the most successful students both academically and in terms of personal well-being was a BSc Mathematics student. There are also several accounts in the literature of successful dyslexic mathematicians (Joffe 1983; Jansons 1988).

What is unclear at present is if all dyslexics have underlying difficulties with some of the arithmetical aspects of mathematics. Gillis et al. (1995) in a review of the literature found that studies varied in their estimates from 50 per cent to 100 per cent of dyslexics also having some mathematical difficulties. Results may vary because different studies evaluate different aspects of mathematical performance and also have different criteria for selecting dyslexic or reading-disabled students. Their own conclusions, based on twin study data from the Colorado Reading Project, were that poor performance in reading and maths was the result of shared genetic factors. Alarcon et al. (1997) in a more recent twin study also conclude that genetic factors are important in mathematical difficulties but that environmental factors also make a significant contribution. Rourke has carried out studies with various colleagues over a number of years looking at whether different subgroups have similar or different types of mathematical disabilities. Rourke and Conway (1997) conclude that there are significant differences between those individuals who have just an arithmetical difficulty and those that have both reading and arithmetical difficulties. This conclusion is endorsed by Badian (1999) who also found some differences between children with combined reading and arithmetic problems (dyslexics) and children with just arithmetic problems. This later group were more likely to have encountered birth problems or serious illness. Badian argues that it is important to distinguish between these two groups because there are probably underlying differences in the nature of their arithmetical difficulties which are likely to require different forms of support or remediation. Ackerman and Dykman (1996) were particularly interested in speed of response across a number of domains (arithmetic, reading, coding and handwriting). They reported that slowness was more likely in adolescents with deficits in all areas than in adolescents with deficits in a single skill area. This again suggests an underlying deficit for dyslexic adolescents which affects their speed of performance across a number of areas. Ackerman and Dykman point out that slowness often leads to less practice at a task and this in turn means that there is less likelihood of responses becoming automatic. This fits with Fawcett and Nicolson's (1996) findings that dyslexics showed poor 'automaticity' over a number of tasks compared to nondyslexics.

As well as demands on working memory leading to computation errors, there are a number of other difficulties that some dyslexics may encounter. The first is simply the problem of reading accurately the words and or symbols that make up a mathematical problem. Coventry et al. (2001) point out that mathematical language is highly compressed with complete accuracy and low redundancy. Unlike ordinary English it is not possible to infer the meaning of an unknown word from the context it appears in. In more advanced mathematics, seemingly familiar words like 'evaluate' can have a specific and somewhat different meaning. Dyslexic students may need extra support to learn new or confusing terms. This is a problem for many students, and the provision of glossaries with notes, and repeated reminder of what specific words mean, can be of benefit to all students.

Some individuals both reverse and transpose numbers, and many find copying mathematics from screen, overhead or board difficult. The accuracy required in mathematics can be compromised by poor writing and layout and organization of work on the page. Although many of these difficulties ease with age some students find that they still make a number of errors in reading and recording calculations. Although calculators are enormously helpful in easing the working memory burden some dyslexic students report that they still make frequent errors when inputting information to their calculator. One student reported to her support tutor that she used three different calculators for inputting different types of mathematical information in order to reduce the errors she made. For some students the major difficulty seems to be that their early negative experiences of arithmetic have made them highly anxious about number work. Both Henderson (1998) and Chinn and Ashcroft (1998) have spent considerable time teaching mathematics to dyslexic children and adults. They both note the high level of anxiety experienced in relation to mathematics by a substantial proportion of dyslexic children and adults.

In assessing mathematical and or arithmetical difficulties five key areas need to be considered, although there will be overlap and interaction between them:

1. Input and output problems – the student has difficulty in some of the following:
- taking notes: accuracy and/or speed
- written recording of work; accuracy and/or speed
- organizing work on the page
- direction or sequencing of work
- inputting accurately to calculator
- listening to explanations whilst writing
- reading problems: accuracy and/or speed.

2. Working memory problems – learning/remembering number facts:

- learning/remembering procedures
- shorter than average auditory digit span
- shorter than average visual digit span.

3. Anxiety and low self-esteem – based on some of the following:
- stress of trying to 'keep up' in either input or output
- stress of trying to be accurate in either input/output
- stress of trying to comprehend whilst copying
- overload on working memory, exacerbated by anxiety
- stress of trying to learn/recall number facts
- negative feedback on speed/accuracy of work
- stress of trying to cover up difficulties
- stress of mental arithmetic type tasks

4. Gaps in mathematical knowledge related to lack of educational opportunity because of input/output or working memory difficulties.

5. When all the above are controlled for:

conceptual difficulties not attributable to any of them.

Assessment

Turner (1997) refers to arithmetic assessment as the Cinderella of basic attainments testing for dyslexics. Singleton (1999) in the Dyslexia in Higher Education report warns that focusing on a literacy framework rather than on the underlying processing deficits of dyslexia can lead to neglect of important areas such as numeracy. Despite this comment the report offers no specific advice on assessing numeracy under its guidelines.

Nearly all the students who returned our questionnaires said they were given an intelligence test as part of their overall assessment and certainly all those assessed at university were given one. The majority were given a WAIS assessment (Wechsler Adult Intelligence Scale) and this would have included a forwards and backwards digit span test and a test of arithmetic. The length of forwards and backwards digit span is a useful indicator of a student's auditory short term memory, although it has to be borne in mind that factors like anxiety or effective use of chunking strategies can decrease or elevate a student's digit span. The majority of students were also tested on the arithmetical part of the WRAT (Wide Range Achievement Test).

It could be argued that for those students taking arts-based subjects, where they do not expect to encounter any significant number work, this level of numeracy testing may well be appropriate. A similar difficulty to the one with literacy arises in that it can be difficult to ascertain the numeracy requirements of some courses, especially where there are diverse module choices and content. An arts course could have a module on business administration or management which requires a fair degree of numeracy. Where students are taking courses with a moderate to high degree of mathematics involvement, a more systematic assessment of numeracy would be indicated. Another important consideration is whether students report existing difficulties or anxieties with mathematics. Where students have attained good mathematics grades and express no concern over their numeracy there would be less need for additional assessment.

As well as standardized tests it is important to ask students about their own particular experiences of different aspects of mathematics. Some students have a global view of themselves as 'no good at maths' and careful questioning is needed to find out exactly what kind of difficulties they have encountered. One female student, for example, reported considerable difficulty with remembering numbers whilst trying to work things out in her head. When asked to describe exactly what she did, it became apparent that she had developed a wide range of good estimation and memory-load-reducing strategies and used her strong conceptual abilities to help her round her working memory difficulties. She had not been consciously aware that this was what she was doing and found it helpful to be aware of the strengths she had. The results from standardized tests backed up what she had reported and this information was fed back to her. She revised her opinion of herself and now describes herself as good at maths but poor at mental arithmetic. A male student reported that he was often first to understand a new concept or idea in his maths workshops but got frustrated because he would invariably make clerical errors if he was given a large number of examples to work through. He would accidentally transpose a number or forget to write a step down. He had not found working more slowly an effective strategy but had taught himself to check carefully through his work for errors when he had finished. He had always found writing things by hand difficult and laborious and it may be that checking afterwards was helpful for him because it eliminated the extra processing capacity involved in writing.

Where appropriate, students can be asked to bring along examples of present mathematical work they are having difficulty with and if they feel comfortable enough can be asked to work through some examples so they can talk about or explain where their present difficulties lie.

Support

The first step in the support process is for students to have an accurate understanding of their own strengths and weaknesses in relation to mathematics and to be aware of what coping strategies they already use and precisely what mathematical demands their present course is making on them. In deciding on the way forward it is also useful for students to review their previous educational experiences of mathematics. Because of past difficulties with tasks such as copying notes from the board or reading word-based mathematical problems they may have missed out on specific operations or rules. One student reported that because of her difficulties in copying from the board at school she often missed out on the accompanying explanation and as a consequence had never really understood how to work out fractions: 'I would very much like help with my maths as I find that more difficult than my spelling to understand.'

Support for number work has lagged behind that available for literacy, but an increasing number of dyslexia tutors are aware of these problems, and are offering appropriate support. Where students are unable to get such support there are now several helpful books available (Chinn and Ashcroft 1998; Henderson 1998; Miles and Miles 1992). Most of these were designed for children but where a student is having difficulties with basic number facts and concepts, many helpful strategies can be adopted. Chinn and Ashcroft found with arithmetic that a useful approach was to teach basic patterns or regularities so that students could use a logical approach and cut down on the amount of rote learning needed. As with literacy, students' individual motivation, experiences and learning styles will all influence how they progress. Chinn (2001) suggests that cognitive style is an important factor in mathematics although it is influenced by past teaching/learning experiences. He posits two contrasting styles – 'inchworm' and 'grasshopper'. Inchworms prefer a step-by-step, detailed, mechanical approach, whereas grasshoppers take a holistic approach with flexibility and use of estimation, but less attention to detail. Marolda and Davison (2000) have similarly suggested two broad learning styles. One involves a detailed, sequential, formulaic approach, whereas the other starts with the big picture and often uses visual or pictorial thinking. Ideally, it is useful to have a balance between two contrasting styles as both are needed for different mathematical tasks. Helping students to be aware of how they deploy these two styles, and where their current strengths and areas to develop are in relation to each style, should help them to gain insight and control over their learning. An important issue is how anxious and demoralized they have been made to feel by their past experiences of doing mathematics. Some students dread any formal number work and have very low expectations or self-efficacy: in fact, their main expectation is that they will fail. In this case it is especially important to make them aware of any informal number skills they already have and to start with a small and achievable task which builds on their existing skills.

Computers can be invaluable for teaching and reinforcing mathematics, but until recently programmes suitable for adults studying more advanced mathematics have been scarce. Because of concerns at the University of Sunderland about the number of students with numeracy difficulties there are now ongoing projects developing such programmes (Lejk 2000). Two recent examples of appropriate software are *Mathwise*, produced by NAG (numerical algorithms group) with HEFCE funding support, and *Mathematica for Students*, produced in the USA.

CHAPTER 5

Assessment and support relating to emotional adjustment and mental health

Students, with or without dyslexia, face many personal issues relating to adjustment and change when they enter a university. Rising numbers of mental health problems among students in general have been noted (Stanley and Manthorpe 2001). Young students who have recently left school enter a new phase of their lives at a time when they are still in adolescence and their understanding of their own identity is evolving and changing rapidly. University faces them with huge new challenges in relation to the re-evaluation of both their intellectual and their social competence. Some of them no longer live at home with their parents and the support a family can provide. For the first time they have to deal with issues of independent living, financial and social. For mature students, who usually study in the area where they have lived for some time with their families, there are other challenges: juggling the demands of family and study, returning to study after a period of work, taking up a challenge which they had rejected when younger or for which, at one time, they had been deemed insufficiently competent or intelligent. The students who face the least challenge in relation to social change are those young people who enter a university local to their home. They may, of course, have to contend with family strife in relation to the demands of their new lifestyle, but at least they are on familiar territory, can probably maintain some well-established supportive relationships and will suffer less financial stress if they live in their parental home. As we all know, for the majority of students, the burden of stress in relation to debt and the need to take on part-time work, in addition to studying, in order to cope with paying the bills and in order to be able to join in with student activities, has greatly increased over the last decade. This is a direct consequence of the abolition of the grant system and the introduction of student loans and tuition fees. Also, the new student social life which they are expected to join may seem carefree and irresponsible to an outsider, but it places great demands on the young person in that they feel the pressure to fit in, to get on with others from different backgrounds, to be seen to wear the right clothes, go to the right clubs, drink the right beer! Within their student accommodation these young people who may have lived with one small nuclear family all their lives will be thrust together with strangers to shake down and cope with the demands of communal living. All this when you are just starting a completely new course of study with much greater demand for independence in learning than was expected at school or college.

If we single out students with dyslexia for attention it is evident that, given their difficulties with study, personal organization and self-confidence, this new life as a university student will face them with some potentially overwhelming challenges. The HEFCE report (Singleton 1999) suggests that many students with dyslexia may bring with them a backlog of unhelpful coping strategies and damaged self-esteem. They may have excessive fears about being able to cope with academic life. Students with recently identified dyslexia may be struggling to reconcile their newfound identity as a dyslexic with their old identity as 'stupid' or 'lazy'. Students who enter university with as yet unidentified dyslexia may be striving to hide their difficulties and to cope, as they have done to date, without extra support or understanding, and indeed with the feeling that they are inadequate in many competencies required by university study. Students who have a long established identity as a person with dyslexia may well be more confident and comfortable with their identity and reconciled to their strengths and weaknesses than the two groups previously mentioned (Riddick et al. 1997). On the other hand, anxiety may relate not only to past history but also to coping strategies and other personality variables (Riddick et al. 1999) and also to the extent to which the demands of their chosen new course of study will emphasize their areas of weakness (Cowen 1988).

Studies of the emotional adjustment of students with dyslexia in higher education are not many. A few studies of the development of children and adolescents and adults with literacy difficulties have been conducted and these generally show low self-esteem and higher anxiety in these groups (see Riddick et al. 1999 for summary) The HEFCE report on dyslexia in higher education (Singleton 1999) identifies social and emotional factors as being among the 'other difficulties' experienced by students with dyslexia which merit consideration. The report points out that high levels of anxiety and stress have been identified as the most indicative behavioural correlates of dyslexia (Miles and Varma 1995). It also points out that people with dyslexia may experience panic reactions in academic situations and that the additional efforts required to cope with studying will undoubtedly cause tiredness which may well lead to stress, anxiety and depression. Miles and Varma also note that individuals with dyslexia can have 'good' days and 'bad' days. 'Bad' days are days when they make many mistakes, misread information, cannot find materials and forget appointments. Case study evidence does point to the long-lasting effects which dyslexia can have upon self-esteem. A study by Edwards (1994) clearly illustrates the loss of confidence. Evidence given by students in interviews in our previous research also shows the anxiety and stress created by educational experiences for many in this group (Riddick et al. 1997).

The case of higher education students with dyslexia should be considered rather differently from the case of adults with dyslexia in general. Boetsch et al. (1996) in a series of four studies of the psychosocial functioning of children, adolescents and adults with developmental dyslexia found that children and adolescents with dyslexia reported lower global self-worth and more depressive symptomatology than normal achievers. In contrast, adult dyslexic men reported more generalized psychological distress than their peers but were comparable to them in terms of self-worth, depressive symptomatology and other indices of adult adjustment. The authors accounted for this change by suggesting that in adulthood the men were able to pick a niche for themselves in jobs which emphasized their areas of strengths and competence and allowed them to de-emphasize their poor literacy skills. As a result they were no longer being constantly confronted with their weaknesses at the level they had experienced at school. Students at university, on the other hand, may be still in late adolescence, on the threshold of adulthood, or already mature adults. In contrast to adults entering the world of work they are still in a situation where much of the assessment of their competence depends on the use of their literacy skills. They have, of course, chosen voluntarily to enter into a higher educational setting and put themselves in this challenging situation. However, the hugely widening access to higher education puts far greater pressure on this group to attempt to obtain further educational qualifications after school. There will be many reasons for this choice of career path (peer and social pressure, desire for fulfilling employment, the necessity to acquire a university qualification in order to pursue a career in their area of strength).

Some quantitative research relating to the adjustment of students with dyslexia was carried out by the authors of this book in a previous study.

This showed that, using Battle's Culture-free Self-esteem Inventory (Battle 1992), a group of dyslexic students were lower in general self-esteem than a matched control group (Riddick et al. 1999). Their levels of personal and social self-esteem, however, did not differ from the levels of their peers. According to the CFSEI manual, general self-esteem refers to individuals' overall perceptions of their worth. Social self-esteem is the aspect of self-esteem that refers to individuals' perceptions of the quality of their relationships with their peers. Personal self-esteem is the aspect of self-esteem that refers to individuals' most intimate perceptions of self-worth. It therefore seems that, although these students were able to perceive themselves to be as valuable and worthy as their peers in terns of their personal and social adjustment, in their overall ability to deal with life they felt less adequate, less successful, less confident, and more ashamed of themselves than their peers. In the study, only one dyslexic student out of 16, as compared to ten out of 16 of their peers, reported high or very high self-esteem. Nine out of the 16 dyslexics reported low or very low self-esteem but only three of the nondyslexics did so. The two groups were also compared for levels of anxiety on the State-Trait Anxiety inventory (Spielberger et al. 1983). The differences between the two groups on Trait Anxiety showed a strong trend towards greater anxiety levels in the dyslexic group. A recent study conducted by Farmer et al. (2001), the methodology for which is described in Chapter 3, used the same inventory. Significant differences were found between a group of dyslexic university students and matched controls for trait anxiety ($t(15) = 2.22$, $p = 0.042$) but not for state anxiety ($t(15) = 0.07$, $p = 0.943$). In other words, the endorsement by the dyslexic students of items about their general state of mind indicated that they had higher everyday levels of anxiety than their peers, but in the assessment situation, where they were carrying out these tests, they did not feel more anxious than their peers, despite the fact that they were asked to do a number of tasks involving reading, writing and spelling. This may possibly be attributable to the fact that the assessor was himself a dyslexic individual and was good at relating to others with dyslexia and putting them at their ease. However, it is important to note that their chronic anxiety levels were much higher than those of their peers. In the same study, it can be seen that students with dyslexia had higher levels of anxiety generally about their competence as writers (see Chapter 3, on the assessment of writing) and lower levels of writing self-efficacy. The study by Riddick et al. (1999) showed that, though dyslexic students rated their academic competence as lower than that of their course peers at university, this did not produce significantly more anxiety about their work (although there was a strong trend for this difference to be significant). Other factors may mediate here. Our study showed that there was a significant correlation between level of anxiety and level of Verbal IQ (see Chapter 3). Dyslexic students with lower verbal IQs showed that they were more anxious in both state and trait questionnaires. The same relationship did not hold for the nondyslexic students. It must be noted that only small numbers of students (n = 32 in all) participated in this study and further investigation is needed. It is, however, possible that the dyslexic students with lower verbal IQs were those whose dyslexia was more severe in that language or severe memory difficulties were present. It is not, of course, clear whether the students are anxious because they have lower IQs, or whether being more anxious lowers your ability to perform in test situations such as an IQ test and/or your cognitive competence in general, or whether some intervening variable mediates both scores.

Emotional state has been found to have a strong effect on cognitive performance. Studies of test anxiety show that this is an important factor influencing performance (e.g. Dutke and Stoebber 2001). Stress has been shown also to affect many aspects of cognition and coping in everyday life (Matthews et al. 2000; Cassidy 1999). Gaudry and Spielberger (1971) have shown a strong relationship between anxiety and educational achievement in school-age children. Eysenck (1988) argues that the cognitive style which underlies trait anxiety determines one's vulnerability or resistance to external stressors. People who are high on trait anxiety tend to attend to threatening information more than people who are low in the same trait (Cassidy 1999). Thus, a dyslexic individual with higher anxiety may give more attention and attach more significance than other students to throwaway remarks, negative feedback, and criticisms of time-keeping or self-organization.

A study by Chemers et al. (2001) stresses the importance of self-belief and confidence in university adjustment of students. They suggest that confident students work harder, persist longer and use better learning and problem-solving strategies. They also suggest that students with high self-efficacy manage their learning environments more efficiently. Self-efficacy is the belief in one's capabilities to organize and execute a course of action required to produce given attainments (Bandura 1997). Self-efficacy beliefs are related to achievement in educational settings. We measured our students' writing self-efficacy by asking them, before they started writing, to rate on a scale of 1 to 5 how well they thought they would be able to write the essay in the essay-writing task described in

Chapter 3. The dyslexic students rated their ability to write the essay significantly lower than did the controls (t(15) = −3.31, p = 0.005). The writing self-efficacy of the dyslexic group was considerably lower. Since self-efficacy or self-belief is an important factor in educational achievement, regardless of level of academic competence, this is clearly an area in which the students with dyslexia will require support.

Nearly 60 per cent of academic staff (see Chapter 8), responding to a questionnaire on staff views of dyslexia, said that dyslexic students they taught showed anxiety and lack of confidence. Many of the academic staff who were interviewed personally (for example, the Fashion Marketing tutor) described in more detail the stress experienced by dyslexic students due to the extra work which they needed to put in to keep pace, the resulting fatigue, the problems they had with organization and their generally higher levels of anxiety. Support staff in their interviews also commented on the anxiety and stress experienced by students with dyslexia (Chapter 9). They point out the isolation such students can feel, and the need to develop the self-esteem and confidence of some students. The dyslexia tutor suggests that, on entering a university, students with dyslexia may suffer a complete undermining of their confidence due to the change in the level of support they experience and the demands made on them.

What should be done in terms of assessment and support for this aspect of the student's functioning? Should there be some sort of screening of the emotional state and adjustment of these students? If we identify a student with high levels of anxiety and low levels of self-esteem should these indices act as warnings that this student will need more help than others? An important mediator between students' needs and the type of understanding and support they will receive seems to be their level of self-advocacy. Time and again in interviews with academic staff (Chapter 8) the importance of the role that this plays was emphasized. Support staff (Chapter 9) also discussed the fact that some students are able to take on the role of self-advocate, explain their needs and regulate their learning from the start, whereas others lack confidence and self-awareness and therefore need a great deal of support from student services before they are able to understand exactly how their difficulties arise and what they may need to do themselves or may need to ask others to do in order to resolve these difficulties. It seems important, therefore, that both these aspects of functioning should be assessed in some way: their level of self-understanding and their level of emotional adjustment. A quick screen of levels of anxiety and levels of self-esteem could be carried out using the questionnaires such as the Culture-free Self-esteem Inventory (Battle

1992) and the State-Trait Anxiety Questionnaire (Spielberger et al. 1983).

Of course, there should be no question of such screening being a demand made upon a student: it is utterly essential that students should as far as possible feel that they are in charge of the process of assessment, that they are seeking the information in question and that they will control the dissemination of information arising from the assessment. The assessments carried out by a psychologist as part of the initial assessment leading to 'diagnosis' will be carefully explained to students beforehand (see Chapter 9). Assessment of emotional state need not be part of this process and could be carried out by support staff at another time, perhaps when support staff discuss with a student the results of his or her assessment and the nature of his or her needs. A less formal approach could be taken in a semi-structured interview that contained questions relating to the student's coping, levels of anxiety and confidence. It does seem important that an understanding of a student's general levels of anxiety and confidence should be obtained so that counsellor, student and staff may be aware of any potential for greater interference from emotional factors on the student's performance and coping. Levels and types of support could then be adjusted accordingly.

Counselling support should, of course, be there for all students. But, in particular, a counsellor should be available who understands the problems and needs of dyslexic students. Gilroy and Miles (1986; 1996) stress the importance of the availability of 'instant help' for these students. They say 'dyslexics find it difficult at times to deal with pressure, and stresses may accumulate until the mind becomes befuddled and the various problems begin to seem insurmountable'(1986: 35). They recommend making available a telephone number or address where students will be able to 'get in touch with the tutor at any time if they feel depressed, muddled or unable to cope'. Many texts on support for dyslexia advocate counselling support, although there is little evaluation of different types of approach or the effectiveness of counselling as opposed to other types of support (McKissock 2001). Certainly the idea of helping an individual to reframe their experience seems a very valid approach (Gerber et al. 1996).

The HEFCE Working party report (Singleton 1999) recommends the following:

- Every higher education institution should have at least one student counsellor available who has specific knowledge and/or experience of dyslexia counselling.

- All counsellors with students in higher education should have some awareness of the impact of dyslexia on everyday activities as well as educational ones.
- Counselling for students with dyslexia should be
  - available for immediate crises and long-term problems
  - an integral part of the support service within the institution
  - available as a priority to students recently identified as having dyslexia.
- The student's confidentiality must be respected at all times and information exchange with academic or other staff of the institution should only occur with the permission of the student and always with absolute discretion.

These seem very important suggestions. However, my interviews with staff suggest that it may be important that within every department or course there is a member of staff who develops an understanding of the problems of dyslexia: students can quickly turn to this member of staff for help and support in relation at least to aspects of their coping with the course, and the member of staff can act to liase between the student and other staff who teach that student. This would provide such students with an important security or support within the environment in which their learning is taking place and should provide well-informed advice, at least in relation to matters relating to their course which may be creating stress and anxiety. Some universities also organize support groups for students with dyslexia in order to provide a forum for the sharing of information, problems and support which should act to diminish any sense of isolation the student may feel and to give them access to information on ways of coping which other students find useful (see Chapter 9). Overall, it must be considered that the area of emotional adjustment is the most difficult to assess but perhaps the most important to understand and support.

CHAPTER 6

Evaluating university students' experiences of assessment and support

The Dyslexia in Higher Education Report (Singleton 1999) uses the term 'identification' to describe the processes that are carried out in order to establish whether a student has dyslexia. This can include both an initial screening test and a further in-depth psychological assessment. As an outcome of this, an evaluation of needs can be arranged in order to recommend appropriate provision including technological support. In designing a questionnaire it had to be born in mind that some students would have been identified when relatively young and are being re-assessed whereas others have been identified for the first time. The aim of the questionnaire study was to find out about students' experiences of the identification process, assessment of needs and subsequent support.

In conjunction with student services at two new universities, questionnaires were sent to all students who had under gone a full dyslexia assessment. (To preserve the anonymity of students and staff, the two universities have been given the fictitious names of Southside and Northside.) Both questionnaires contained similar questions but there were some differences as questions were tailored to the specific circumstances and practices of each university. In addition, we wanted to see if asking for information in different styles of question affected the nature of students' responses. (See Appendices for copies of the questionnaires.) Students were given the option of remaining anonymous but only two students out of the 74 who replied chose to do so. Students at the University of Southside were asked for permission to look at a copy of their latest diagnostic assessment report: all gave their permission, and some kindly included a copy of their report with the returned questionnaire. In our initial letter to students, we explained that we were keen to hear about their experiences of assessment and support at university and that we wanted their voices to be heard. We said that we intended to disseminate their views in the public domain but that all information would be anonymized.

In both universities the response rate was relatively low (about 30 per cent), but it is unclear how far this was because of technical difficulties such as students changing address and therefore not receiving the questionnaire and how far it was due to students choosing not to respond.

Total number of students responding from both universities

| Males | 28 | Females | 46 | **Total** | **74** |

Numbers responding from each university

Southside

| Males | 19 | Females | 25 | **Total** | **44** |

Northside

| Males | 9 | Females | 21 | **Total** | **30** |

The questionnaires were piloted with two dyslexic students, and with the staff of both student support services, and amendments were made based on their comments. Particular attention was paid to the layout and wording of questions. A significant number of yes/no, rating scale or checklist type of questions were included so that students could answer the majority of questions without extended writing. Several of these questions asked students for additional comments or asked an appropriate follow-up question such as how or in what way something might be the case. There were a few open questions such as 'What did you think was the main purpose of the assessment?' We hoped by this combination to allow students the choice of how much free writing they wished to use in responding to the questionnaire. The questions followed a narrative chronological format starting with when they were first assessed, and ending with what they thought of their current support at university. Individual students tended to be consistent in the way they responded to the questionnaire, with some adding little written comment and others adding comments or additional information whenever it was requested. It might be supposed that the students with the severest literacy difficulties would write the least. However, some students, who clearly did have considerable problems with writing and spelling, filled in all the appropriate qualitative questions, often writing at length about their thoughts and opinions, whereas some students, who appeared to have relatively good writing and spelling, wrote less. Students differ in their response style to questionnaires and other factors such as motivation, time available and willingness to think through answers to more open ended questions will influence their style of reply.

The University of Northside was ranked among the top new universities on a number of measures of teaching and learning and attracted students from a wide range of socio-economic backgrounds. The University of Southside was rated as one of the top new universities in terms of widening access with a higher proportion of students from non-traditional or poorer socio-economic backgrounds. These differences in the overall student population are perhaps reflected in our dyslexic sample with a higher proportion of mature students at Southside, and a later average age of identification (see Tables 6.1–6.3).

Experiences of assessment

One of the dyslexic students who filled in our questionnaire noted that this was the fourth time her dyslexia had been assessed. Whilst earlier identification and high standard, detailed psychological assessments are to be welcomed, they do raise the possibility that some students will have been assessed several times by the time they enter further or higher education. Assessment is carried out at school not only for diagnostic and intervention purposes but also as a requirement so that students can receive special arrangements for public examinations such as GCSEs. The exam boards that grant such accommodations require an assessment to be 'up to date', usually specifying this as within the past two years. In higher education, assessment is required so that students can apply for accommodations such as extra time in examinations. Another key reason for assessment in higher education is so that students can apply for appropriate support via the disabled students allowance.

This does raise the question of how both children and students feel about having to go through the assessment process. In the report of the National Working Party on Dyslexia in Higher Education (Singleton 1999) it was noted that 43 per cent of dyslexic students were identified for the first time whilst in higher education. The report also stated that there was anecdotal evidence that some students found the assessment process quite stressful for a variety of reasons, including not having an explanation of what would be involved or being treated in a way that reminded them of their humiliating times at school. In other cases, they reported they were given no immediate feedback and/or written reports were difficult to comprehend. Our own formal study (Riddick et al. 1997), and our informal interviews with students and experiences as assessors, would endorse these concerns. In order to look more closely at the factors which led to a

Table 6.1. Data on responses by individual male students at the University of Southside

Stu	Age	First assessment	Age first identified	Own decision	Already suspected	Discuss with others	Impact on self-esteem	View of feedback	Changed study approach
1	18	no	23	no	no	no	4	positive	yes
2	36	no	7	yes	n/a	n/a	1	positive	no
3	36	no	32	no	yes	yes	n/a	positive	no
4	21	no	18	no	yes	yes	4	positive	yes
5	42	no	37	n/a	n/a	no	5	positive	yes
6	31	yes	31	yes	yes	yes	at 1st 4 now 2	positive	yes
7	51	no	47	n/a	no	no	5	positive	yes
8	31	no	27	joint	yes	yes	1	positive	yes
9	37	yes	36	yes	yes	no	3	positive	yes
10	23	yes	22	no	yes	yes	3	positive	yes
11	30	yes	29	no	no	no	3	positive	yes
12	31	yes	31	no	no	no	5	negative	yes
13	37	yes	36	joint	yes	yes	1	positive	no
14	29	no	26	yes	yes	yes	2	positive	yes
15	34	no	25	no	no	no	2	positive	yes
16	31	no	11	no	n/a	yes	3	positive	yes
17	20	yes	20	yes	yes	no	2	positive	yes
18	19	yes	19	yes	yes	yes	3	positive	no
19	22	no	12	yes	n/a	yes	1	positive	yes
av. age	31		26						

Key:

Stu = student.

First assessment = were they assessed and identified as dyslexic for the first time whilst at university (yes) or prior to university (no)?

Age first identified = age when first assessed for dyslexia.

Own decision = whilst at university did they decide to seek assessment (yes) or was it suggested to them (no)?

Already suspected = prior to assessment being instigated, did they already suspect they were dyslexic?

Discuss with others = did they discuss their intention to be assessed with friends or relatives?

Impact on self-esteem = had being told they were dyslexic had an impact on their self-esteem? range from 1 (raised self-esteem) to 5 (lowered self-esteem)

View of feedback = what they thought of combined verbal and written feedback after the assessment.

Changed study approach = have they changed their approach to studying as a result of their assessment and/or support?

Table 6.2. Data on responses by individual female students at the University of Southside

Stu	age	first assessment	age first identified	own decision	already suspected	discuss with others	impact on self-esteem	view of feedback	changed study approach
20	18	no	14/15	no	n/a	yes	4	negative	yes
21	27	no	25	yes	yes	yes	1	positive	yes
22	23	yes	22	yes	no	no	4 then 2	positive	yes
23	21	yes	21	yes	yes	yes	2	mixed	yes
24	37	no	30	no	n/a	yes	2	neutral	no
25	21	no	17	yes	yes	yes	3	positive	yes
26	18	no	16/17	yes	n/a	yes	3	positive	yes
27	20	no	17	joint	yes	yes	4	positive	yes/no
28	23	yes	22*	yes	no	yes	4	positive	yes
29	24	yes	15	no	no	yes	5*	negative	no
30	20	no	34	no	n/a	yes	1	hard	yes
31	34	yes	7	no	yes	no	4	positive	yes
32	20	no	18*	n/a	n/a	n/a	3	positive	yes
33	22	yes	20	no	no	yes	4*	negative	yes/no
34	21	yes	52	no	no	yes	2	positive	no
35	52	yes	45	yes	yes	no	3	positive	yes/no
36	45	no	17	no	yes	yes	1	positive	yes
37	20	no	38	joint	n/a	no	1	positive	yes
38	38	yes	10	joint	yes	yes	1	positive	yes
39	28	no	17	joint	n/a	n/a	3	positive	yes
40	20	no	19	n/a	n/a	n/a	1	n/a	yes
41	20	yes	17	joint	no	yes	4	mixed	yes
42	19	no	11	n/a	n/a	yes	3	positive	yes
43	21	no	42	yes	no	yes	1	positive	yes
44	43	yes	23	yes	yes	yes	2	positive	yes
av. age	27								

Key:
Stu = student.
First assessment = were they assessed and identified as dyslexic for the first time whilst at university (yes) or prior to university (no)?
Age first identified = age when first assessed for dyslexia.
Own decision = whilst at university did they decide to seek assessment (yes) or was it suggested to them (no)?
Already suspected = prior to assessment being instigated, did they already suspect they were dyslexic?
Discuss with others = did they discuss their intention to be assessed with friends or relatives?
Impact on self-esteem = had being told they were dyslexic had an impact on their self-esteem? Range from 1 (raised self-esteem) to 5 (lowered self esteem)
View of feedback = what they thought of combined verbal and written feedback after the assessment: hard = feedback hard to understand?
Changed study approach = have they changed their approach to studying as a result of their assessment and/or support?
* These two students were assessed but not identified as dyslexic

Table 6.3. Data on responses by individual students at the University of Northside

Stu	m/f	Age	Age first assessed	First assessment	Assessment stressful	Verbal feedback	Written feedback	Change perception	Change strategies
1	m	20	12	no	no	5	5	yes+	4
2	m	20	12	no	a little	none	1	no	2
3	m	20	19	yes	moderately	2	3	no	1
4	m	19	8	no	no	2	2	no	4
5	m	20	17	no	no	2	3	no	3
6	m	20	10/11	no	no	3	2	no	3
7	m	21	14	no	no	2	3	yes+	2
8	m	37	35	yes	very	2	2	yes+	5
9	m	20	8	no	moderately	3	1	yes+	5
10	f	22	21	yes	a little	2	none	*	2
11	f	21	14	no	moderately	1	1	yes+	4
12	f	29	28	yes	moderately	3	2	yes+	2
13	f	22	10	no	moderately	2	2	yes+	3
14	f	20	12	no	a little	1	1	yes+	3
15	f	35	35	yes	no	4	4	no	1
16	f	18	10	no	a little	2	2	no	4
17	f	20	20	yes	no	2	2	no	4
18	f	22	10	no	moderately	2	2	yes+	3
19	f	20	20	yes	very	1	1**	yes+	3
20	f	21	18	no	a little	1	2	no	2
21	f	21	19	yes	no	3	3	no	2
22	f	21	11	no	a little	2	2	no	4
23	f	19	17/18	no	moderately	3	3	yes+	1
24	f	30	29	yes	no	1	1	yes+	1
25	f	47	36	no	moderately	3	3	yes+	5
26	f	20	17	no	moderately	3	3	yes+	4
27	f	29	28	yes	moderately	3	3	yes−	1
28	f	20	7	no	moderately	3	3	no	5
29	f	22	8	no	moderately	3	3	yes+	5
30	f	21	11	no	unbearably	2	1	yes+	2
Av. age		29	16.5						

Key:

Stu = student.

Age first assessed = age at which they were first assessed as dyslexic

First assessment = assessed for dyslexia at university for the first time

Own decision = did they decide to seek assessment at university or did someone else suggest it?

Assessment stressful = circle one of 'no' 'a little' 'moderately' 'very' 'unbearably'

Verbal feedback = Range from 1 (very useful/interesting) to 2 (not useful/interesting)

Written feedback = Range from 1 (very useful/interesting) to 2 (not useful/interesting)

Change perception = did being assessed as dyslexic change your perception of yourself, yes+ positively, yes− negatively

Change strategies = did being assessed as dyslexic change the strategies you used to cope with your difficulties; Range from 1 (not at all) to 5 (a lot)

* assessed as not dyslexic

** assessed as dyscalculic

more positive or negative experience of assessment, we designed questionnaires which focused on issues prior to, during and after the assessment. In considering students' experiences of assessment for dyslexia, an important point will be whether this is their first assessment or not. In addition, a number of other factors also needed to be taken into account:

1. first or subsequent assesssment (if subsequent, prior assessment experience)
2. self- or other-initiated
3. self-identity prior to assessment (Did they already suspect they were dyslexic?)
4. students' views of dyslexia prior to assessment (positive, neutral, negative?)
5. students' views of how significant others regard dyslexia
6. whether the nature and content of assessment is explained in advance
7. location, timing, pacing and content of the assessment
8. interpersonal factors (How does the student perceive the assessor?)
9. the nature and timing of initial and any subsequent feedback
10 the consequences of the assessment.

At both universities more females than males responded. This may be partly because of a tendency for females to be more willing to respond to social requests, but there may be other factors such as males being less willing to give information on their difficulties. This higher female-to-male ratio also goes against the underlying ratio of more males to females (5:1 to 3:1) being identified as dyslexic according to the literature (Miles and Miles 1999). The Dyslexia in Higher Education Report (Singleton 1999) gives no figures on the relative prevalence of identified dyslexia in male and female students. This may be an important ratio to monitor because of recent concerns over the possible under-identification of females and reporting of a ratio much closer to 1:1 (Shaywitz et al. 1990; Lubs et al. 1993). In a relatively recent large-scale British study, a ratio of 1.7:1 in favour of boys was found (Miles et al. 1998). The researchers suggest that some of the differences in ratios that are reported by different studies may be related to the particular way in which dyslexia is defined. What is of note is that the reported ratio of males to females has reduced in recent studies, which does suggest that there has been some under-identification of girls in the past. Anderson (1997) reviewed a number of USA studies on gender differences in numbers of males and females referred for special education services. She concluded that gender bias in referrals, especially by teachers, was a major factor in the predominance of male to female referrals for learning disabilities. A recent concern has been the under-identification of dyslexic bilingual children, the erroneous assumption being that their language difficulties are either attributable to having English as a second language or a general learning difficulty

(CRE 1996; Deponio et al. 2000; Everatt et al. 2000; Landon 2001). This would suggest that students from a bilingual or multilingual background may be at particular risk of being under-identified as dyslexic:

> I believe that identifying students who have dyslexia is difficult especially within the ethnic minority group. Mine is an example – it was put down as a second language problem then dyslexia. Not only has the system failed to recognise such students at university it also failed them in school.
>
> (Female, 29, Media Production)

It was only at the end of her second year at university that a lecturer suggested to this student that she was assessed for dyslexia.

Because of the relatively low response rate and the gender bias in the respondents our questionnaire data has to be interpreted cautiously, but the data did indicate that a slightly higher percentage of females to males were being assessed for the first time.

	N	First assessment	Subsequent assessment
Males	28	10 (35.7%)	18 (64.3%)
Females	46	19 (41.3%)	27 (58.7%)

Anderson (1997) has suggested that in circumstances like higher education where females can refer themselves there might be some redress in gender bias.

Prior experience

Especially where students come forward for dyslexia assessment for the first time it is important to investigate the reasons for them doing so. In order to investigate this we asked several questions:

What made you decide to be assessed whilst at university?

Own decision	If so, why?
Suggested by someone	If so, who?
	And why?

(If not assessed before university) Had you already suspected you were dyslexic?

No   Yes

Did you discuss your intention to be assessed with friends or relatives?

No   Yes

How did you feel about having to be assessed?

At Southside, the figures for the 44 students responding to the question of whether they were assessed or not assessed before university were as follows:

Assessed before	Not assessed before
25 (57%)	19 (43%)

Overall, 40 students replied to the question of whether seeking assessment was their own decision or was suggested by someone else:

Own decision	Both	Suggested by someone else
13 (32.5%)	7 (17.5%)	20 (50%)
	(Self +	(Lecturer/tutor 11
	Lecturer/tutor 6	Parents/school 4
	Dyslexic friend 1)	Student services
		– for update – 3
		Employment services 1
		Friend 1)

Out of the 30 Southside students for whom it was relevant to ask if they had already suspected they were dyslexic before they were first assessed the replies were as follows:

Already suspected	Did not suspect
20 (67%)	10 (33%)

Some commented that they had suspected for some time and similar comments were made by some of the Northside students: 'I always had bad spelling and reading and I always thought that I was dyslexic.'

Students were also asked if they had discussed their intention to be assessed with family or friends. As can be seen from these figures, where applicable around two thirds of students do discuss their intentions to be assessed:

	Discussed	Did not discuss	Not applicable/no answer
Female	18 (82%)	4 (18%)	3
Male	9 (50%)	9 (50%)	1
Total	**27 (67.5%)**	**13 (32.5%)**	**4**

Students were simply requested to circle *Yes* or *No* for this question but it would be useful in future research to investigate this in more detail. Who do students usually discuss their intentions with, and do these discussions have any effect on their decision to be assessed, or help them if they are anxious or apprehensive? A few hints of possible issues and influences appeared in various parts of the questionnaire. A mature student put next to her *Yes* response: 'Husband and a few close friends, not relatives'.

Another student commented later in the questionnaire that her father had reacted badly to the idea of her being dyslexic and saw it as a 'disease'. Whereas in some cases students see their family as very supportive, in other cases they have the added responsibility of trying to explain something that their parents or relatives have little understanding of.

In this sample 82 per cent of females said they discussed their intention to be assessed with friends or family whereas only 50 per cent of males said they discussed their forthcoming assessment with anyone. Students had widely varying reactions to the idea that they should be assessed for dyslexia. This included both students who had been assessed previously and students who were being assessed for the first time.

Answers from the 44 students at the University of Southside could be divided into four main categories:

Positive	Apprehensive	Negative	Ambivalent	No answer/not appropriate
17	17	3	3	4

Students who were categorized as apprehensive comprised 17 who said they were anxious, nervous, scared, fearful or worried, and three who described themselves as embarrassed or feeling stupid or daft:

Nervous

Apprehensive

I felt confused scared, what if there wasn't anything wrong with me then I'd just be thick. If there was something wrong how could anyone help me now.

Three students raised the concern that the assessment might indicate that they were not dyslexic but simply 'thick'. This is a concern informally expressed by a number of students who are considering dyslexia assessment.

In some cases students expressed mixed feelings: 'Trepidation, OK'; 'nervous and pleased'.

Students who said they were embarrassed or negative about having to be assessed were more likely to say that someone else had suggested it and there was a feeling that this had come out of the blue.

Both of the following two students said their parents had organized assessment when they were 14/15 years of age:

I was very embarrassed and very aware of being different from other people
Grudgingly went along with it

Another student responded that a university lecturer had suggested she might be dyslexic because of the difficulties she was having in completing a project. She had not already suspected that she might be dyslexic and on being asked how she felt about having to be assessed replied:

Why now at my age?

Answers that were classified as positive could be further divided into the following categories:

Fine/no concern	Relief/happy	Pragmatic
8	7	2

Several answers expressed relief or happiness that the problems a student had could be explained:

I had no problems with being assessed it was quite a relief
Happy there was a reason that I had problems studying

Others simply said they were not concerned about being assessed:

I had been assessed 4 times in my life it's no big deal.
Fine (the assessment was done with my best interest in mind to help me)

Some gave replies which suggested a pragmatic point of view that assessment was needed in order to obtain the help or support they required:

Need it!

Perhaps not surprisingly, the majority of students who had not been assessed before were likely to express particular concern and apprehension about their first assessment:

Very, very worried (I thought the assessor would tell me I was stupid, that's what I had been told at school)
Very nervous, not sure of what would be expected

But this was not always the case – some students who were being assessed for the first time reported that they were relatively positive or unconcerned about it:

Didn't concern me

In a similar vein, although the majority of students who had been assessed before were relatively positive or unconcerned about being assessed again, there were some students who expressed concerns:

fearful
I felt I was a bit stupid

The context surrounding students' former and present assessment needs to be taken into account. Some students had received only partial or idiosyncratic assessments in the past and were worried that their present assessment might show them not to be dyslexic:

My dyslexia was identified but not properly assessed at 6th form college I wanted to be sure I was dyslexic.

Even where students had been assessed before, for some there were doubts and uncertainties as to what the current assessment might recommend. Some had hoped that they had overcome their difficulties sufficiently not to need to seek help at university. Assessment practice for adults with dyslexia has developed and moved forward, and some students saw the assessment as a chance to evaluate their degree of literacy difficulties relative to the demands of the course they were taking. For others, having to have their assessment updated was seen more as a bureaucratic necessity. For some students, the whole process of assessment and feeling they were being judged reminded them of negative aspects of their school experience. For those students who were being assessed for the first time, it raised important issues about their own identity and competence. In many cases, these students first realized they had a problem when they or one of their lecturers/tutors noticed they were having difficulties with written work:

> I knew I had a problem with spelling but after receiving an exam paper back from a tutor, she marked my spelling with the lowest mark, that was when I knew I needed help.

For all the students the assessment was critical in determining whether they should apply for the disabled students allowance and if they were likely to be successful. It also had implications for the kind of support they were entitled to receive.

By considering such factors as whether students already suspected they have dyslexia, discussed their intention to be assessed, and took the decision to obtain assessment, it can be seen that the circumstances leading up to each student's assessment are different.

Practical issues

Another important area leading up to assessment is the practical or organizational one. If a student decides he or she wants an assessment or it is suggested he or she should have one, how easy is this for the sudent to arrange, who pays and does the student know what to expect? In the Dyslexia in Higher Education Report (Singleton 1999) it was estimated that about three-fifths of higher education institutions pay for assessment, and that about half carry out the assessment 'in-house' with others referring or expecting students to make their own arrangements. Where assessment is not paid for by the university, many students are advised to apply to their LEA (local education authority) for funding. LEAs vary in their funding policy and some students end up with no funding. The report notes anecdotal evidence that some unfunded students are deterred from being assessed because they can not afford it. From personal contact with students we would endorse this point. The two universities we investigated varied in their provision at the time the study was carried out. The University of Southside has a relatively well resourced and highly organized student support team (see Chapter 9 for further details). Assessment is an integral part of the support offered to students, with close liaison between support service staff and the assessing psychologist. Students are initially screened by the disability adviser and referred on for full psychological assessment when appropriate. The university automatically pays for assessments and arranges them within the university. The University of Northside was at the time still developing its services, although since then many of the recommendations of the HEFCE report have been put in place. The support of the disability adviser was much appreciated by students but as a sole operator it was impossible for her to deliver the breadth of integrated services available at Southside. Assessments were not automatically paid for by the university and were not arranged in-house. This inevitably leads to extra stress or concerns for some students and makes it more difficult for a coordinated support service to be delivered:

> It would have been easier if my university could carry out the dyslexia test. I had to travel back home to Leeds.
> When there was a disabled student worker it was difficult to get an appointment because of the amount of people she needed to see.

As already suggested many of these difficulties were to do with organizational and resourcing factors beyond the control of the disability adviser. And several students were very positive about the support she provided:

> Sarah was brilliant she sorted out the disabled student allowance quickly and was very easy to talk to.

Students at Southside University were asked if their latest diagnostic assessment was straightforward to organize. All 44 replied: 40 said 'Yes' and four said 'No'. These four assessments all took place outside the university set-up. They were also asked how long the assessment had taken to organize. The average time was about one month, with a range from two days to three/four months. Within the Southside system, students were usually assessed within two to three weeks of their initial contact with student services. Only three students, who had been taken for assessment by their parents when school had refused, reported paying at that time for their own assessments.

Prior information on assessment

The Southside students were also asked if they were given information on what their assessment would involve and, if so, who by:

No	Yes
16 (37%)	27 (63%)
	19 Southside student support
	5 adviser FE college/other university
	1 educational psychologist – Dyslexia Institute
	1 parent
	1 disability officer – Job Centre

It would be useful to know in future research whether those students who receive information about the assessment find it helpful, particularly if they are being assessed for the first time or are feeling anxious about the assessment. Students who said they had not been briefed before the assessment were assessed in a variety of settings including LEAs, colleges, employment services and a hospital.

The assessment

The discussion so far has been on the factors involved leading up to assessment. It can be argued that these may well have a bearing on how students perceive the assessment and its outcomes. Students at both universities were asked questions about what they recalled the assessment entailing and how they felt during the assessment process. In addition, the psychologist who carried out the majority of assessments at both universities was also interviewed about the assessment process (see Chapter 9).

At Northside University, students were asked to rate how they felt during the assessment on a verbal scale:

Did you find the experience of assessment stressful?

	No	A little	Moderately	Very	Unbearably
Female (21)	4 (19%)	5 (24%)	10 (48%)	1 (5%)	1 (5%)
Male (9)	5 (55%)	1 (11%)	2 (22%)	1 (11%)	0 (0%)
Total (30)	**9 (30%)**	**6 (20%)**	**12 (40%)**	**2 (7%)**	**1 (3%)**

Overall, 50 per cent of students rated the assessment as not or only a little stressful, whereas the other 50 per cent rated it as moderately to unbearably stressful. Conclusions can only be tentative from a small sample size like this, but do suggest that it would be worthwhile investigating whether there are any consistent gender differences with a larger sample.

If students did rate the experience stressful, they were asked if they could explain why. Not all students explained why they found the assessment stressful, and some, as in the following two examples, gave more than one reason:

> It was an unfamiliar environment. I felt worried in case I didn't have dyslexia and I felt very alone and scared.
>
> (Female, 20)

> * Embarassed when I could not answer simple questions.
> * Through doing art on previous courses I had not really put pen to paper or read out loud since GCSE.
> * Really nervous, heart beating, voice goes.
>
> (Female, 21)

Although some of the following categories overlapped they gave some indication of the aspects of assessment that students reported as stressful:

Getting things wrong	7
Feeling tested	3
Time pressure	3
Unknown/unfamiliar	3
Reading aloud	3
Alone, scared, anxious	3
Focusing on inabilities	2
Reminds of past failure	2
Feeling stupid	2
Might not be dyslexic	1

Several students mentioned embarrassment or shame at getting things wrong or not knowing the answer to questions:

> I had to concentrate very hard. I was worried that I was doing things wrong and found it frustrating when I didn't know the answers.
>
> (Female, 22)

> Knowing that some questions which I found very hard other people wouldn't think twice about.
>
> (Female, 22)

While students are being assessed they are not given any indication as to whether or not they have answered individual items correctly, since to do so would invalidate the test, although the assessor does offer general encouragement to the student. There were no comments suggesting that the assessors had added in an interpersonal way to the feeling of being 'tested' or getting things wrong. The majority of students appeared to accept that the assessment was carried out with their best interests in mind and that, even if stressful at the time, it would hopefully lead to long-term benefits. Others drew a distinction between the process of assessment and the person carrying it out:

> I felt a bit intimidated by the process not the assessor.

The problem for the assessors is that, however sensitively they carry out the assessment, students are being asked to perform some tasks that they find relatively difficult. Inevitably, students are being tested, however sympathetically this is handled. Unfortunately, for some of these students, testing has echoes of their past failures and humiliations in the education system:

> Although it had been stated that 'It's not an exam' I felt that I was being tested, which experience has shown I don't do very well at.
>
> (Male, 37)

Some students mentioned more specific aspects of the assessment process, such as the timed items, as a source of stress:

> Because I was constantly under time pressure.
>
> (Female, 21)

> My most recent assessment I found things harder and under pressure.
>
> (Male, 20)

Perhaps not surprisingly, three students specifically referred to reading aloud as a stressful experience. Both Riddick (1996) and Edwards (1994) have commented on the fear and humiliation experienced by some dyslexic children when asked to read aloud. Riddick et al. (1997) found that over half the dyslexic university students they interviewed recalled negative experiences of being asked to read out loud, leading in the worst cases to panic attacks and truancy:

> Found comprehension and reading aloud stressful – not confident at reading aloud.
>
> (Female, 21)

For other students, it was the uncertainty about what was going to happen or unfamiliarity with the surroundings which made them feel stressed:

> The tests were not what I expected. The environment was unknown.
>
> (Male, 20)

Three students reported that, although they had been nervous at the start of the assessment, they had relaxed as the assessment proceeded, with two specifically mentioning that the examiner had put them at their ease:

> Just a little because it was worrying being tested in the first place but the examiner was so nice I soon settled down.
>
> (Female, 21)

At Southside, based on our previous research and discussions with dyslexic students and support tutors, we drew up a list of words describing different possible feelings while being assessed. We included four terms deemed to be positive ('relaxed', 'interested', 'confident', 'curious') and four terms deemed to be negative ('anxious', 'stressed', 'nervous', 'on trial'). We also had a category of 'other' where students could add any additional feelings.

Students were asked to tick all the words that applied to them when they were being assessed for dyslexia. On average, students ticked four choices with a range from one to six.

Replies	25 females	19 males	Total 44	
	Female	Male	Total number	Total%
relaxed	1	5	6	14%
anxious	18	12	30	68%
interested	5	15	20	45%
stressed	12	10	22	50%
confident	1	1	2	4%
curious	9	11	20	45%
nervous	13	12	25	57%
on trial	12	2	14	32%

Out of the 44 students, 39 (89%) included some negative feelings in their choices, although 5 (11%), two female and three male, described only positive feelings. Four of these five students had been assessed before, and three had been identified at primary school age. Four males and ten female students (32%) described entirely negative feelings. Nine out of these fourteen students had not been assessed before, and another with only a partial previous assessment was anxious as to whether she was genuinely dyslexic. Additional comments added by some students endorsed the experiences reported by the Northside students:

> It mind mapped me back to all those times I was treated unfairly etc.

> I thought the assessor would tell me I was stupid that's what I had been told in school.

Other students described their experience in both positive and negative terms although the negatives tended to outweigh the positives:

> Female – anxious, stressed, curious, on trial
> Male – anxious, interested, stressed, nervous.

Some students pointed out that they felt varied sensations at different points in the assessment:

> Relaxed, anxious, nervous, curious – I think at different times I felt all these things.
>
> (Female)

For some students, there appeared to be a fluctuating balance between positive and negative feelings during the assessment. But, overall, it is clear that for the majority of students more negative than positive feelings are selected, with anxious, stressed and nervous feelings predominating.

It seems an unfortunate paradox that a proportion of dyslexic students have to go through a process which they find quite stressful in order to obtain the support they need. At present, there seems no viable way to change the nature of the actual assessment tasks. Computer-based tests may be a possible way forward in the future, although they still may not overcome the sensation of being 'tested' for some students.

At best, it is important that all the organizational and personal factors leading up to the assessment are carried out as efficiently and sympathetically as possible. Students should be briefed in advance as to what the assessment will entail and apprehensive students should have the chance to talk over particular fears and anxieties and be given reassurance where possible. Ideally, this initial briefing will take place in the location where the assessment will be carried out so students are familiar with the setting.

In order to understand more about students' experience of the assessment process those at Southside University were asked 'What do you think was the main purpose of the assessment?' Answers fell into two main categories of help/empowerment or assessing degree of dyslexia/problems with some students linking both together. Of the 44 students, 41 answered this question.

What do you think was the main purpose of assessment?

Help/empowerment			Both	Assessing dyslexia/problems	
11 (27%)			10 (24%)	20 (49%)	
help/empowerment/resources				assessing dys/assessing problems	
5	2	4		11	9

Answers that were categorized as 'help' or 'empowerment' were divided into those that spoke of general help or support, those that focused on specific help or resources and those that emphasized empowerment:

With a view to help. [General help]

(Male, 36)

So it gave me the means to achieve more and so people would acknowledge my disability. [Empowerment]

(Female, 20)

Some students linked together the need for their possible dyslexia or problems to be investigated so that it could be decided if they needed support, and if so what kind and level of support:

To see the level of dyslexia and how much extra help I would need to complete my studies.

(Female, 21)

The final major category comprised students who said the main purpose of the assessment was to assess their problems, abilities or dyslexia. Some expressed this in terms of finding out whether or not they were dyslexic, whereas others saw it as about the degree or nature of their dyslexia or difficulties:

To find out whether I was dyslexic.

(Female, 23)

To assess just how severe my dyslexia was.

(Male, 26)

Other students spoke of having their abilities, problems or difficulties assessed or investigated:

To assess my abilities.

(Male, 21)

To find out why I can not do things.

(Female, 24)

It is instructive to see the wide range of views students have about the main purpose of assessment and the diversity of ways in which students are already framing their differences or difficulties. It could be argued that some of this diversity is a quirk of the written format, with some students possibly avoiding words they cannot spell. What is striking is that, while some students are taking an empowerment perspective, others appear to have a deficit model of dyslexia, that focuses on their inabilities or weaknesses:

To find ones weak points. [Deficit model]

(Female, 24)

This assessment was done with my best interest in mind to help me at university. [Empowerment model]

(Female, 45)

Again, it would be helpful to know what factors influence students' initial perceptions and understandings of their processing difficulties and dyslexia. These may well have a bearing on how they view the purpose of their assessment. Does talking to someone well-informed such as a studies adviser change some students' perceptions of what the assessment is about in a positive way?

Students were asked if they thought their assessment was a fair reflection of their abilities and difficulties:

Yes	No	Mixed
34 (81%)	7 (17%)	1 (2%)

Evaluating the assessment process

A final question in this section asked students if they thought the assessment process could be improved and if so in what way. Despite 50 per cent of students rating the assessment process as moderately to unbearably stressful relatively few thought the face-to-face aspects of the assessment process could be improved in any way. Where suggestions were made these tended to be focused on organizational issues such as speeding up waiting times for assessment or receipt of the ensuing report.

At the University of Southside students were asked the following question:

Could the assessment process have been improved in any way? Yes/No
If 'Yes', how?

Yes	No	No answer	Don't know
18 (41%)	18 (41%)	6 (14%)	2 (4%)

At the University of Northside students were asked:

What if any changes would you recommend for the assessment procedure?

Changes suggested	Suggest no changes needed	Do not know	No answer	Unclear
9 (37%)	4 (13%)	3 (10%)	12 (40%)	2 (7%)

As students were only asked to comment on changes they would recommend, it may well be that several students who did not answer this question were happy with the assessment process and therefore saw no need to comment.

Face-to-face aspects of the assessment process

In considering the recommendations for change, the responses from students at both universities have been combined. Four students (5%) commented on the length of the assessment, and suggested short breaks would be helpful. Only two students (3%) suggested any change in interpersonal conduct during the assessment: both would have liked a more relaxed and informal approach. A single student (1%) suggested a change in the assessment content to enable her to show what she could do and ask her what she was good at. Two students pointed out that they didn't know enough about testing methods to be able to comment on this aspect of the assessment process.

Factors before and after the face to face assessment

Three students (4%) would have liked more information prior to the assessment. At the University of Southside, students are usually briefed in advance by the disability adviser. Five students (7%) commented on the lack, or slowness, and/or difficulty of obtaining an assessment prior to university. Another four (5%) commented on various aspects of timing at university such as waiting a long time for an assessment, or waiting a long time for the recommended equipment to arrive after the assessment recommendations. Four students (5%) wanted more feedback, explanation or counselling after the assessment. Another two students who had circled 'Yes' said they didn't know in what precise way the assessment could be improved as they had been reasonably happy with it, but felt that most things can be improved in some way. What was encouraging was that where all aspects of the assessment process were working well students were usually happy with it, even if they had found the face-to-face assessment somewhat stressful. One student, for example, who gave the assessment a rating of moderately stressful, put under suggested improvements 'None – very good'. Most of the students who suggested improvements were either not assessed at the University of Southside/Northside or had missed out on an aspect of the pre- or post-assessment support for a variety of reasons. Some were in exceptional categories, such as attending a college with courses franchised by the University where preparation and follow-up work related to the face-to-face assessment were not as comprehensive. The Dyslexia in Higher Education Report (Singleton 1999) notes that follow-up counselling 'is often a neglected part of the diagnostic assessment procedure'. A student who was assessed outside of the university commented on her assessment feedback:

> A lot of information was given at one session and there was no follow up from the actual Institute.

Under changes to the assessment process she put:

> Counselling after (the diagnostic assessment) or do a follow up session, there is a lot of information and it is an extremely stressful and emotional time.

Feedback

A vital part of the assessment process is the quality and nature of the feedback that students receive (Turner 1997). McLoughlin et al. (1994) argue that feedback is in fact the most important part of the assessment process.

Of the 44 students at Southside University, 42 said they had been clearly identified as dyslexic. One said she did not fully understand the feedback she had received and that suggestions for support were inconclusive, nor was it suggested she applied for the disabled students allowance. Another student said she was identified as dyscalculic and one-to-one maths support was recommended but she was not advised to apply for the disabled students allowance. Of the 30 students at the university of Northside, 28 said they were identified as dyslexic. One said she was not identified as dyslexic and another said she had been identified as dyscalculic:

> I was assessed as having problems with numbers and spacial awareness. I was very relieved to know what I had. I was assessed as having dyscalculia which is a specific learning difficulty very similar to dyslexia which means I suffer from poor spatial awareness and number blindness. I was given a scrap of A4 lined paper with my condition on it and I kept it with me everywhere because it helped me believe I wasn't stupid. It was worth more to me than anything else in the world.

Students were asked a series of practical and evaluative questions about feedback. The Southside students were first asked if they were given any verbal feedback at the end of the assessment session and/or at a later time, and if so what they thought of it. They were then asked what they thought of the written report they received. Students generally answered the questions about feedback in a composite manner, so they would, for example, answer 'very good' to both questions or just answer one of the questions. Two students commented that they found the written report confusing but that verbal feedback cleared this up. Because nearly all students treated feedback as a generic category, their overall response to feedback is given in the following table.

Response to feedback by Southside University cohort

	Positive	Negative	Neutral/mixed	Hard to understand	No answer
Male (19)	18 (95%)	1 (5%)	0	0	0
Female (25)	18 (72%)	2 (8%)	2 (8%)	2 (8%)	1 (4%)
Total (44)	36 (82%)	3 (7%)	2 (4.5%)	2 (4.5%)	2 (2%)

Comments such as 'very helpful', 'interesting', 'explained a lot', 'useful', 'gave me a better understanding', 'good', 'excellent', 'informative', and 'quite accurate' were all rated as positive. Two female students commented that the written feedback was for one 'a little hard to understand' and for the other 'rather difficult to understand'. In other parts of the questionnaire they were both very positive about the implications of their assessment and the increased confidence and understanding that it gave them. For this reason their responses were classified separately from those students who linked lack of understanding with more negative comments and outcomes:

> confusing, too technical for a lay person, dented confidence all deficiencies in black and white' (identified as dyscalculic).

Two of the three students who considered their feedback to be negative said they did not understand their feedback and they were not clearly identified as dyslexic. One was told she had dyscalculia and the other said her assessment was inconclusive and suggested no follow-up support. Perhaps it is not surprising that students who receive feedback that either contravenes their expectations or is more complex and/or equivocal than usual are more likely to be confused or disappointed by it. Like many universities the University of Southside initially screens students before recommending whether they should proceed to a full dyslexia assessment. The disability adviser uses the Dyslexia Adult Screening Test. Approximately two-thirds of students go on to a full dyslexia assessment; the other third are offered adult literacy and basic skills training as appropriate, the assumption being that in many cases lack of educational opportunity or practice has hampered literacy or study skills, especially for students from more non-traditional backgrounds. The difference in the quality of feedback is obviously important in how students evaluate it. But in some cases, where the same assessor had written reports of similar tone, content and organization, there were still sometimes marked differences in how these were perceived by different students. As individuals come to the assessment process with diverse backgrounds, experiences and expectations it is understandable that their reactions, even to seemingly similar feedback, can vary.

An important part of the feedback process is that students feel they are able to talk over the implications of their assessment sufficiently. This might also mediate to some extent what they think of their assessment feedback, as students often relied on this as a way of clarifying or having interpreted aspects of their written report. In most cases where the assessment was carried out at the University of Southside students' reports first went to the disability adviser. This was a planned policy because the support service thought it very important that students were initially taken through their report by someone who could effectively interpret it for them. For students who had assessments elsewhere the opportunity to do this was more variable.

Were you able to talk over the implications of your assessment sufficiently?

Yes 28 (65%)   No 15 (35%)

This is a relatively small sample, so caution is needed in interpreting the results, but it is of concern that over a third of students did not think they were able to talk over the implications of their assessment sufficiently. Again, depending on students' prior experiences, and their current understanding and needs in relation to dyslexia, their view of what constitutes 'sufficient' will inevitably vary. In some cases it was clear that no follow-up session was available after assessment, whereas in other cases it was the number, timing and accessibility of sessions that was at issue.

Students at the University of Northside were asked to rate both the verbal and written feedback they had received after their assessment on a 5-point scale:

Very useful/ interesting		Moderately useful/ interesting		not useful/ interesting
1	2	3	4	5

Over 70 per cent of students gave their written and verbal feedback the same rating and a further 25 per cent gave them ratings within one point of each other (see Table 6.3). This is perhaps not surprising as the initial verbal and subsequent written feedback is provided by the same person. This might suggest that the content of what is being conveyed is more important than the format in which it is conveyed. Alternatively, it may be that the nature of the verbal feedback influences how the written report is received, or that the written report retrospectively influences how the verbal feedback is perceived. This is not to suggest that either is dispensable but that they work in tandem to reinforce each other.

Feedback		Verbal	Written
1	Very useful/interesting	5 (17%)	7 (24%)
2		12 (41%)	10 (34.5%)
3	Moderately useful/interesting	10 (34.5%)	10 (34.5%)
4		1 (3.5%)	1 (3.5%)
5	Not useful/interesting	1 (3.5%)	1 (3.5%)

For both the written and verbal feedback, 93 per cent of students rate it as moderately to very useful/interesting. Some of the students who rated their feedback as moderately interesting/useful pointed out that they had been assessed before so their most recent feedback tended to confirm what they already knew. The female student who rated her feedback negatively had been assessed in Germany and had only received a one-page report with no follow-up support or recommendations. The male student who rated his feedback very negatively had been last assessed as a child and appeared not to have had much of the feedback directed towards himself; he commented that he was still relatively unaware of his diagnosed problem.

Perception of self and coping strategies

Self-perception

It could be argued that the ultimate purpose of assessment is to enable and empower dyslexic students. It is hoped this can be achieved by enhancing self-understanding and coping strategies as well as by providing appropriate support and accommodation within a dyslexia-friendly environment. It is therefore important to know what impact assessment and/or subsequent support has on dyslexic adults and children. Does it change their self-perception, their self-esteem or their coping strategies in a positive manner?

Because this was seen as a key issue it was addressed at several points in the questionnaires. Students at both universities were asked if being assessed as dyslexic changed the way they saw themselves and if so in what way. Answers to how it had changed their self-perception were classified as positive, mixed or negative.

| | Changed self-perception | |
	Yes	No
Southside	28 (67%)	14 (33%)
Northside	17 (59%)	12 (41%)
Total	45 (63%)	26 (37%)

| Direction self-perception is changed in | | |
Positive	Mixed	Negative
39 (87%)	3 (6.5%)	3 (6.5%)

Some students had first been assessed when relatively young, at seven or eight years of age, and had grown up with the idea that they were dyslexic, so it was therefore difficult for some to reflect back on what the initial impact of this had been: 'I was only 7!'

In part, it seems to depend on how this question is interpreted. Some students said that, no, it had not changed their perception of themselves but it had given them greater understanding of themselves:

> No, but it was a relief, I became more aware of my mistakes etc.
>
> (Male, 20, Drama)

Although some students gave several reasons for their change of self-perception there were some predominant reasons. One was that it countered the negative view they had been given of themselves especially at school:

> It finally put years of failure + misery + guilt behind me.
>
> (Male, 31, Biomedical Science)

> Relief, I was always teased at school for being stupid, now I could get help with my spelling (assessed at 8 years) I felt more confident after my spelling and reading improved, I was picked on less.
>
> (Female, 22, Finance)

Other students stressed the self-understanding that being identifies as dyslexic gave them:

> . . . accepted myself more.
>
> (Male, 51, Religious Studies)

That it wasn't my fault! People no longer thought I was lazy or stupid and I felt relieved that there was an answer to why I found the most basic things difficult.

(Female, 20, Podiatry)

It explained a lot of the difficulties I had, which was good.

(Female, 19, Sports Studies)

In other cases, students linked understanding to an increase in their confidence:

Yes I felt more confident about my abilities, especially reading as previously had thought I was stupid, didn't understand why I found it a problem.

(Female, 21, Human Organization)

Yes very much so, once I come to terms with having dyslexia. I became more confident and felt more able to understand my limitations and to be honest to others about my dyslexia. I had a reason for my spelling being poor.

For some students they felt it strengthened their resolve and increased their motivation and persistence:

If anything it made me stronger

(Female, 21, 3D Design)

I know if I want to achieve something I have to work hard at acquiring the knowledge and keep on at it to keep the knowledge.

(Male, 31, Computing)

Although some students who had been assessed before didn't think their recent assessment had influenced their self-perception, others indicated that it had updated and focused their understanding:

I knew I was dyslexic as I had been assessed before so the outcome was not too much of a shock. But it did focus me on what work I should be doing to improve myself. I am now working on my reading and my writing and working to do something to improve my maths.

(Male, 31, Business Studies)

It was a long time since my last test and this told me what problems were dominating now.

(Female, 28, Media and Culture)

The majority of students (87%) who said that being identified as dyslexic changed how they saw themselves described these changes as positive. But there were three students (6.5%) who saw their change in perception as negative.

I felt that I was 'labelled' (disabled in some way)

(Male, 21, Business Studies)

Less than who I thought I was previously

(Male, 31, Law)

Made me think what is the point of studying hard when my English hinders my career. Especially when I have been told it cannot be solved.

(Female, 29, Media Production)

Because of the wide range of experiences and opportunities that each student has encountered, it is hard to pick any outstanding factors which led to students having a more negative view of themselves after being assessed. It was tentatively noted that negative students were critical of the feedback they received and were not given an opportunity to talk it over sufficiently. But these factors also applied to several other students whose self-perception changed in a positive direction. Three students felt that their change in self-perception was mixed:

I knew I had problems before but not 'officially' this made me feel quite inadequate. But I quite liked the fact that I had an IQ in the 'superior range' therefore Good + Bad.

A limitation of a questionnaire study like this is that students are being asked to reflect retrospectively on events and experiences with very variable time scales. A few students pointed out in response to this question (and another one on self-esteem) that their self-perception changed over time depending on circumstances:

It changes with time.

(Male, 20, Quantity Surveying)

This student was first assessed when he was eight years old and was relieved to be told he was dyslexic. Now he feels less sure because he reports he is taking a course where he is made to feel that dyslexia is a 'poor excuse' for any difficulties he is encountering.

Three students commented in various parts of the questionnaire that being aware of their dyslexia also made them more aware of their mistakes:

Not myself but my work (Question If so in what way?) Ah that must be the dyslexia – made me more frustrated than when I didn't know, because I knew if I didn't have it I could do better – Ignorance is bliss?

(Female, 18, Electronic Media Design)

Acknowledging or using a label which denotes a disability or difference can be a complex and sometimes contradictory process for the person concerned (Low 1996). Changing life circumstances and experiences can make the process sometimes an ambivalent one, with both positive and negative outcomes attached to using a particular label (Quicke and Winter 1994). Riddick (2000, 2001a) has argued that labels may have a particularly important role to play for people with 'hidden disabilities', in that they can explain why it is not appropriate to judge certain individuals negatively against cultural norms for specific skills such as accurate spelling:

> So many people had told me I was a bit thick and lazy without realising just how hard I would try to do the work.
>
> (Male, 26, Computing)

> It sounds better than left handed, clumsy, useless, thick, gorpy under achiever, I have been led to believe I am . . . Its definitely not a learning difficulty, it's a difficulty learning. these words can be mixed up and be upsetting.
>
> (Female, 47, MA, Art)

Many practitioners would argue that self-knowledge and effective coping strategies often start with identification. But for a small proportion of dyslexic individuals this does not seem to be the case. Without following such individuals over time we do not know if they will eventually develop a more positive view of themselves. Nor do we know if lack of information or support in developing a constructive view of dyslexia has played a significant part. One of the students who was negative about being identified as dyslexic had received regular support from student services and her department, and, although very positive about this support, still saw dyslexia as a 'disease'. Some people who meet the criteria for dyslexia prefer not to see themselves in this way. Especially where their disability is relatively mild and their circumstances relatively benign they may choose to concentrate on their strengths and ignore their weaknesses.

It has been argued that a drawback of this approach is that when life circumstances and demands change these tactics may no longer be adequate as a way of coping. Although there are documented examples where this is the case, there are other examples where adults who fulfil the criteria for dyslexia have successfully coped with changing life demands without consciously limiting their goals and aspirations. An experienced teacher who was head of department in a comprehensive agreed to take part in some research on the coping strategies of dyslexic teachers (Riddick 2001b). He clearly met the criteria for dyslexia, had a brother who had been identified as dyslexic and openly acknowledged his spelling difficulties. But in his interview he said he 'hated' the word dyslexia and never used it either in relation to himself or children with literacy difficulties. Despite this, as a chief examiner he had insisted on the exam board reviewing the readability of exam questions and at school was committed to approaches that enabled children with literacy problems. He stressed the importance of turning any literacy difficulties he had in relation to studying and teaching into a positive, and clearly had a number of effective coping strategies. It could be argued that he studied and trained at a time when there was little support for dyslexia and this was a rational strategy to adopt in such circumstances. On the other hand, three other teachers who trained and studied at a similar time had all come to acknowledge themselves as dyslexic, and saw this as a positive development.

It is difficult and ethically problematic to gain access to individuals who meet the criteria for dyslexia but choose not to view themselves in this way, so we have little information on their self-perception and the coping strategies they use. It does suggest that we need to be open-minded about the range of coping strategies people use when they have a cognitive difference, and should not be overly prescriptive about what the optimum strategies might be.

Self-esteem

Students at the University of Southside were also asked to describe their reaction to being told they were dyslexic and to rate on a 5-point scale the impact that this had on their self-esteem.

Raised self-esteem	1	2	3	4	5 Lowered self-esteem

1	Raised self-esteem	11 (27%)	49% raised self-esteem
2		9 (22%)	
3		11 (27%)	27% self-esteem remained the same
4		6 (17%)	
5	Lowered self-esteem	3 (7%)	24% lowered self-esteem

As with the question on self-perception there were considerable variations in students responses and some pointed out that their self-esteem had become more positive with time and understanding, whereas they were initially quite shocked and frightened to be told they were dyslexic. Two students, for example, ringed 4 on the rating scale with an arrow and a ring round the 2 explaining that their initial rating would have been 4 but now it is 2:

> At first shock, would I be able to do my course.
>> (Male, 31, Environmental Studies; self-esteem rating, at first 4 but now 2)

A selection of responses to the question 'What was your reaction to being told you were dyslexic?' are listed below, along with students' rating of its effect on their self-esteem. A few students said their initial reaction was one of shock or horror:

> Terror at first (I am a freak)
>
> Realization at the end (This must be why I act the way I do!)
>> (Male, 26, Computing; self-esteem rating 4)

Some of those who had been identified as adults said that their main feeling was one of anger or frustration at not being identified and supported at school:

> Cried on the way home, anger, frustration.
> (Male, Education; self-esteem rating no answer, but writes 'I have always lacked confidence')
>
> Shocked/ annoyed that it took so long to be diagnosed and relieved in another sense
>> (Female, Early Childhood Studies; self-esteem rating 4)

Others linked their upset or confusion to relief at also understanding more about their strengths and weaknesses:

> Upset but relieved as I always thought I was stupid and now I knew what the problem was.
>> (Male, 21, Business Studies; self-esteem rating 4)
>
> Confused and relieved to find out I have ability in writing.
>> (Male, 42, Community Studies; self-esteem rating 5)

This student, in the next part of the questionnaire, said he was:

> more confident in asking for help in reading and writing.

He had also responded to the previous question about whether the outcome of the assessment changed the way he saw himself:

> I realized that I was not thick as I had been told throughout my schooling.

This underlines the importance of caution in interpreting answers to individual questions without seeing them within a dynamic and narrative context. The precise wording of questions will inevitably influence answers. As suggested before, an important factor is the particular point in time that the student is being asked to comment on.

Some students who had been identified when young felt that more recent assessments had therefore had much less impact on them, so they tended to give their self-esteem a rating of 3, indicating that it had not changed as a result of their more recent assessments:

> I had known for many years so it was no shock.
> (Female, 28, Media and Culture; self-esteem rating 3. First assessed at 10 years of age)

Other students who had not been assessed when younger had strongly suspected they were dyslexic, so the assessment endorsed what they were already thinking:

> Relief that what I thought was correct.
> (Male, 29, Community Work; self-esteem rating 2)

> I already knew 99 per cent or knew I had some problem.
> (Female, 27, Community Work; self-esteem rating 1)

Others expressed themselves as happy or glad to be identified as dyslexic:

> Happy it explained a lot especially my troubled years at primary school.
> (Male, 22, Geology; self-esteem rating 1)

Some students seemed to distinguish between their immediate response to being told they were dyslexic and the longer term effect on their self-esteem, which may explain the seeming disparity in their comments and rating:

> Scared, confused.
> (Female, 20, Performing Arts; self-esteem rating 1)

This student had commented in response to the question of the outcome of assessment on her self-perception:

> I was less afraid to be different and my confidence began to soar again.

In summary, almost 50 per cent of students said that being told they were dyslexic raised their self-esteem; just over a quarter said their self-esteem remained the same; and just under a quarter said it lowered their self-esteem. All the students who said it raised their self-esteem also said that if it changed their self-perception that was in a positive direction. Some of the students who rated their self-esteem as lowered also spoke of improved self-perception or more confidence in other parts of the questionnaire, illustrating the complexity of this issue and the need to interpret individual questions cautiously. Does this depend on how individual students define or construe self-esteem, or does it say more about the subsequent support and environment they have been trying to cope in?

How important a role do support tutors or disability advisers play in helping some students to develop a positive sense of what dyslexia means for them. One student who described herself as 'shocked' when she was first told she was dyslexic and rated her self-esteem as lowered was followed up. She had been assessed 2 years previously and had initially been ashamed of her difficulties and very wary of letting other students and tutors know about them. She had received one-to-one tutoring and a range of computing equipment since her assessment, and had written her final dissertation on dyslexia in children. She was asked how she now felt about the term 'dyslexia' and what it meant for her:

> Over the last couple of years I have come to terms with my difficulties and I've been much more open about them especially with my job as a student ambassador.
> I feel that the label has helped me understand what is wrong with me and that I am not thick. Before being identified with dyslexia I had not heard of it. Now I would tell people not to be embarrassed about the problem and that with the right help they should get what they want.

Amy is now pursuing further study at university to enable her to move towards her goal of working in the field of dyslexia, which she says she is determined to do. Many students, and particularly those who are assessed as dyslexic for the first time at university, have to construct or come to terms with a new identity. Some feel secure in who they are and see dyslexia as fairly peripheral, whereas for others it is (for a time at least) at the core of their identity. Some like Amy have turned what is initially a source of anger and shame into a strong motivating force that gives them the drive and determination to succeed.

Support and coping strategies

Students at both universities were asked a number of questions about the outcome of the diagnostic assessment. First they were asked if there was a follow-up assessment of their learning needs and if they were recommended to apply for the DSA (Disabled Students Allowance). They were then asked to identify what support had been recommended for them and how much of it they had actually received. Finally they were asked to rate on a five-point scale how supportive course tutors and student support services had been. Students were also asked what types of support and coping strategies they had found most effective so far.

Coping strategies – Northside

Students at the University of Northside were asked 'What strategies do you currently use to help you cope with your difficulties?' The overall responses to this question are given below, followed by examples of responses to each category. Some students listed several strategies so they are included in the overall numbers for several categories:

Specific study skills	10 (36%)
Organization and planning	6 (21%)
No answer	5 (18%)
Ask/accept help	4 (14%)
Computer or other equipment	4 (14%)
Subconscious strategies	2 (7%)
None	1 (4%)
Work harder	1 (4%)
Self-understanding	1 (4%)

Just over a third of students gave examples of specific study skills, often listing several in their answer:

> When reading textbooks, make short notes as I read, tape some of the more complicated lectures. Try and make notes of the important points that will enhance the tapes.
>
> (Male, 37, Computing)

> Spider planning, brain storming for essays, repetitive learning, lessons in spelling and grammar when in school, spellcheck on the computer.
>
> (Female, 18, Travel and Tourism)

In many of these accounts of specific study skills, a degree of organization and planning is implied. Other students explicitly mentioned organization, time management or planning, either on its own or in conjunction with other strategies:

A lot more planning.

(Male, 20, Sociology)

Give myself more time with assignments.

(Female, 21, Human Organization)

Implicit in many of the students' accounts was the use of a word processor and especially a spellchecker, but again some students highlighted the computer as their key coping strategy or one of their main strategies:

A laptop computer has greatly helped my studies . . . and essay writing and I recommend where possible everyone should be granted one.

(Female, 21, History of Art)

Computers.

(Male, 21, 3D Design)

The main coping strategy reported by a few students was to ask for help when they needed it:

I ask for help a lot more now.

(Female, 20, Health Studies)

I OPEN MY MOUTH WIDE – I ask questions (sometimes considered disruptive). Write down numbers I need immediately. I read different books on Dyslexia to understand my limitations.

(Female, 47, MA Art and Cultural Management)

This was one of the few responses which mentioned actively seeking self-understanding as an explicit coping strategy, although other students may have been doing this without formally recognising it as a coping strategy.

Although working harder could be seen as part of good organization and planning, it is not necessarily the case. It is possible to work hard without being well-organized or structured in what you are doing. It also possible to be well-organized but not particularly hardworking. For this reason, working harder was classified in a separate category:

WORK HARDER.

(Male, 20, Quantity Surveying)

Some students reported that they had subconsciously developed a number of coping strategies which were so much part of their life that they were largely unaware of them or had difficulty in explicating them:

Nothing specific, I had 3 years of tuition, so I deal with it subconsciously.
(Male, 19, Marketing and Retail Management; first identified at 8 years of age)

Friends, spell checks, the strategies are now engrained within my character, they are hard to explain.
(Male, 20, Drama)

Five students (16%) gave no answer to this question. Caution has to be exercised in interpreting the meaning of no answers in the context of this questionnaire. Three of the students tended to answer the yes/no and rating scale parts of the questionnaire and leave a fair proportion of the open-ended questions blank. There was no indication from their hand-writing and spelling that these three were the severest students in terms of impaired writing and spelling ability. Other students who left the question of coping strategies blank had replied to most open-ended questions, suggesting that this did signify something in the context of their overall responses. Perhaps they lacked awareness of what coping strategies they were using, or felt they were not using effective strategies, or they were unclear what is meant by coping strategies.

Coping strategies – Southside

It would have been possible to combine the responses from the two universities but, given the differences in the average ages of the two cohorts and also the higher proportion of students from non-traditional backgrounds at Southside, we were interested to compare the coping strategies that students at the two universities said they used.

Students at the University of Southside were asked 'What have you found the most effective coping strategies so far?' Many students listed a number of different strategies. For the purposes of classification these were put under the following headings (figures refer to the number of students mentioning this strategy out of 42):

Specific study skills	23 (55%)
Organization, planning and time management	13 (31%)
Using equipment	11 (26%)
Emotional regulation	6 (14%)
Enlist help from others	4 (9.5%)
Work hard	2 (5%)
Avoid difficult course or module	2 (5%)
Not coping or do not know	2 (5%)
No answer	2 (5%)
Subconscious strategies	1 (2%)

As with the University of Northside, coping strategies fell into a number of main categories with many students giving several strategies in their answer.

> I try to use them all (coping strategies) to get the best results.
>
> (Male, 30, Business)

> My computer spell check
> IBM via voice
> and my wife (proof reader)
>
> (Male, 36, Education)

Specific study skills were again the most widely listed strategy, followed by planning and organization:

> Word process everything, constantly read fiction/fact, edit and re-edit work on computer, proof read.
>
> (Male, 22, Geology)

> Time management, deal with one thing at a time, prioritise.
>
> (Female, 18, Social Science)

Again, several students listed their computer. An interesting point raised by the first comment below is how far coping strategies evolve with time and circumstances and the support available:

> Personal computer, tape recorder, ask me in a months time, I've only just stated using them.

> I find that using a computer I produce better work.
>
> (Male, 29, Community Work)

For nearly 10 per cent of students, asking for help or receiving help outside of the specialist support services was an important coping strategy:

> Family and friends.
>
> (Male, 42, CYWSD)

> Ask for help.
>
> (Male, 34, Computer Studies)

A coping strategy detailed by six female students was some form of emotional regulation, three specifically mentioning keeping calm as part of this:

> Coloured sheet acetates, memory prompts with colours. being more calm and organized for each task instead of panicking.
>
> (Female, 43, Social Work)

Trying to keep calm.

(Female, 23, Politics)

My own – learning the meanings of words; reading my work out loud: taking time out then going back; keeping calm; using a word I have problems with a lot; not letting it get to me; having a sense of humour.

(Female, 20, Social Sciences)

Whether this is particularly a female strategy or more a case of women having a different style of expression which is more willing to articulate strategies such as this is uncertain. It may be a quirk of relatively small sample sizes but it is also notable that no female students at Northside University claimed this as one of their coping strategies. Perhaps the high level of support at Southside may help students to develop a better level of planning and self-regulation based on a wide range of effective study skills. It has been suggested that the more confidence students have in their own skills the more likely they are to develop a calm and thoughtful approach to their learning and the higher their self-efficacy is likely to be (Zimmerman 1989; Bandura and Jourden 1991; Chemers et al. 2001). Self-efficacy is a measure of how sure or confident someone is in his or her ability to succeed at a specific task. The important point about self-efficacy is that when you take individuals with the same level of ability for a particular task those with higher self-efficacy will be more likely to succeed. It has also been demonstrated that individuals with higher self-efficacy show more persistence and determination in completing a task.

A few students, like the last one quoted above, also talked about having developed their own coping strategies over the years prior to being offered support, and did not want to have to discard or drastically change these.

Seven students at Southside had taken a specialist dyslexia module called 'Get Sussed'. This is a module open to all first-year dyslexic students, with the credit points counting towards their course marks for the year. The aim of the module is to give dyslexic students greater insight and understanding about dyslexia, with a focus on specific study skills and effective coping strategies. All seven students were very positive about the module: six of them listed it under the support they had found most helpful so far, and one student put it under the coping strategies he had found most effective:

The Dyslexia module offered to all first year students is very, very good.

(Male, 31, Biomedical Science)

The literature on coping strategies often distinguishes between what it judges to be positive and negative coping strategies. Strategies which involve denial or avoidance are invariably deemed to be negative. But, as argued elsewhere in this chapter, we know relatively little about such strategies and under what circumstances they may be judged as either positive or negative in outcome:

> Giving up things I'm not very good at.
>
> (Female, 18, Electronic Media Design)

> I do plan my work much better now and I stay on top of all my work. I have also picked modules that I know I can do well in. For example theatre production as 40 per cent of the mark is practical.
>
> (Female, 21, Performance Art)

Cowen (1988) lists appropriate course selection as a positive coping strategy, so in this context giving up or not selecting course modules that do not suit your learning style could be seen as a positive strategy.

In considering the experiences of dyslexic students it is important to place these within the wider context of the general student population. Issues related to social and economic factors affect many students, but particularly those from non-traditional backgrounds who are more likely to enter university from access courses or further education (Tinto 1987). Widening participation has led to a much broader spectrum of students with a wide range of needs. Student loans and the need to work to finance their way through university are a fact of life for many students. Dyslexic students are equally vulnerable to the range of pressures and concerns facing students overall. One area of particular concern is that, as they generally have to spend considerably more time on their coursework and assignments in order to keep up, they have less time available for other activities such as paid work, childcare or other family commitments:

> I have tried many (coping strategies) but I am poor with almost two-year-old twin sons who cry all the time and I am not coping at the moment.
>
> (Male, 26, Computing)

This student had already listed a number of specific study skills, such as memory maps, colour-coding and taping lectures, in answer to a previous question on whether he had changed his approach to studying as a result of his assessment/support. He had attended the 'Get Sussed' module and was receiving specialist one-to-one tuition and rated the student support services as very good. This underlines the point that even seemingly well supported and motivated dyslexic students can struggle because of a range of social, emotional and economic factors. Brunsden et al. (2000) argue that Tinto's model of not coping and attrition based on broad institutional factors is too vague, and needs to be supplemented by more research on specific individual factors such as finance and childcare. They also call for more research based directly on students' perspectives.

> No specific strategies have worked.
>
> (Male, 21, Business)

Because of the relatively small sample size, and the complexity of the factors influencing students at both universities, any comparison of their coping strategies has to be tentative. It was notable that a higher percentage of students at Southside claimed to use the two most commonly mentioned strategies: specific study skills, and organization and planning. This may reflect the higher percentage of students at this university receiving one-to-one tuition on specific skills and strategies. In considering coping strategies, what was striking was the wide range of reported strategies used by different students. In total, over 50 different strategies were mentioned, ranging from highly specific study skills to more pervasive organizational and attitudinal strategies.

In addition to being asked about their coping strategies, students at the university of Southside were also asked 'What kind of support have you found most helpful so far?' Some students listed several forms of support, whereas others did not answer the question at all:

> One to one tuition and all of the following, . . . computer, printer and scanner, text help, pocket spell checker, thesaurus, dictaphone, training on equipment.
>
> (Female, 23, Early Childhood Studies)

Answers from 42 students (some students have answers in several categories):

Computer	23 (55%)
One-to-one tuition	11(26%)
Extra time in exams	7 (17%)
'Get Sussed'	6 (14%)
Support team/group	3 (7%)
Family or friends	3 (7%)
Dictaphone	2 (5%)
Lecturers informed	2 (5%)

Amanuensis for exams	1 (2%)
Yellow spld stickers	1 (2%)
No answer	5 (12%)

Several students named their computer plus one-to-one tuition as the most helpful form of support:

> My computer and one to one.
>
> (Male, 36, Education)

> My own computer and the assistance of a tutor.
>
> (Male, 21, Business Management)

As in previous research (Riddick et al. 1997), some students underlined that for them a computer transformed their ability to cope and was a vital piece of equipment:

> The computer, this helps me do my assignments much easier than before.
>
> (Male, 31, Environmental Studies)

> My computer – my life has improved 100 per cent since getting it, so has my work. 20 per cent extra time in exams is very reassuring and helps me relax.
>
> (Female, 20, Social Science)

Extra time in exams was important especially for those students assessed as having particularly slow writing speeds. An important element of extra time, as in the example above, is that it can help reduce anxiety and give people the confidence that they don't need to rush things.

> Computer, spell check etc.
>
> (Male, 37, Engineering)

Spellcheckers were often mentioned in relation to computers, although some students also mentioned small handheld spellcheckers. These were particularly important for on 'the spot situations'. One dyslexic trainee teacher always carried one in her bag so she could use it whilst teaching children.

For other students, one-to-one help was the key form of support that they valued. Within the category of one-to-one support, students itemized a range of different skills and needs that were addressed. These included improving basic literacy skills, maths, proofreading, structuring of assignments, organizing of study time, note-taking, memory, etc. In addition, for many students the social support offered by one-to-one tuition was important. They could talk over particular worries or anxieties they had about coping with their course, and tuition was usually tailored to meet the particular study or assessment demands that the student was currently encountering.

Some students also sought advice from their specialist tutors on how to ask for help or seek entitlements from their course tutors. More general discussion on the nature of dyslexia and how to deal with it effectively, plus encouragement and support from someone they saw as on their side were all-important elements of the support for some students:

> One to One tuition.
>
> (Male, 23, Biology)

> 1–1 tuition to organize thoughts into assignment plans to expand and work from
> (Female, 18, Social Science)

Approximately 50 per cent of the students who named most helpful forms of support, listed more than one. These are instructive in getting a flavour of the individual range and balance of support that particular students value. The first example below shows a combination of technical support and social support both at home and university:

> Having my computer – so I don't have to hand write assignments three or four times.
> Scanner – getting book out of the library and scan pages that I need.
> Support group – I am not alone
> My husband, when I ask how do you spell the same word for the sixth time.
> (Female, 38, Social Studies)

In this next example, there is again a combination of specific practical support plus social support and back-up support or advocacy in helping this student communicate his needs to his academic department:

> Yellow spld stickers
> Someone there when I have a problem
> Having my lecturers e-mailed about what is happening
> (Male, 20, Chemical and Pharmaceutical Science)

Students can put stickers on their assignments to remind tutors that they are dyslexic when it comes to marking them. This can be seen as part of the wider issue of how students communicate about their dyslexia with their academic department. An important aspect is giving students the confidence or skills to advocate for themselves, starting with the ability to effectively communicate their difficulties and needs. Most students gave permission for the support team to notify their academic department of their dyslexia and the support that they will need. For some students, this is the first step in learning to communicate with their department. The aim of the support team is to move from a position where they advocate for students to one where they enable students to be effective self-advocates. Our interviews with academic staff illustrated that even with interested and sympathetic staff it was much easier for them to offer support when students were open about their difficulties and ensuing needs and coping strategies. A small number of students had had such aversive experiences in the past or perceived their tutors as so unsympathetic that they did not want their academic department notified of their dyslexia.

A number of students emphasized in various parts of the questionnaire the importance of support being there when you need it.

As described earlier in this chapter, the University of Southside offers a module to dyslexic students in the first year called 'Get Sussed'. Brunsden et al. (2000) suggest that initial orientation plus study skills modules or programmes are important in reducing general student drop-out rates. 'Get Sussed' can be seen as a specialist orientation and study skills module for dyslexic students which ideally enables them to get off to a positive start at university. It also enables dyslexic students from different courses to meet and support each other. An important point about this module is that it is an integral part of students' studies, in that it gains them credit points and is not additional to their usual coursework assignments. Given what is known about the considerable amount of extra time that dyslexic students have to spend on their course work and assignments it seems important to find ways of delivering support that do not add to the overall time burden. One issue at present is that a fair proportion of dyslexic students miss out on the 'Get Sussed' module because they are only identified as dyslexic some way into their university career, or because timetabling clashes make it impossible for them to attend.

In looking at the questionnaires it was important to take a holistic approach as well as a cross-sectional one. In the following example, logical connections could be seen between the answers this student gave to several questions:

What kind of support have you found most helpful so far?

Get sussed was very useful. Dyslexia was explained along with ways of attempting to improve.

Have you changed your approach to studying as a result of your assessment and/or support?

> When I have to study or write essays I am much more organised. I use a plan with a logical structure. I have learnt to take better notes and write more clearly.

What have you found the most effective coping strategies so far?

> To plan everything step by step
> To allow myself time to write and rewrite
> To make my written work content as clear and logical as possible through planning.
> (Female, 21, Communication Studies)

For most students, but particularly those who responded in more detail, there was a 'narrative' running through their answers. It is important not to over-interpret this but, equally, it would be remiss to ignore it completely. In some cases, answers to one question helped to clarify or validate answers to other questions, or explain exceptions, or put in provisos.

Students' evaluation of support

A final part of the questionnaire asked students at both universities to evaluate the support they had received and to add further comments on anything they thought important.

At Southside students were asked to rate the reaction of their tutors/lecturers to their dyslexia on a scale of one to five, and space was left for additional comments:

Very helpful		Moderately helpful		Totally unhelpful
1	2	3	4	5

The average rating was 2.6, with 45 per cent of students rating lecturers as moderately to very helpful and 28 per cent of students rating lecturers as fairly to totally unhelpful. Some students pointed out that it was difficult to give an overall rating because there was wide variation between lecturers and tutors within their departments.

One student put '1 to 5' for her rating and commented:

> most helpful
> some very helpful
> a few totally unhelpful

Another student gave no numerical rating but commented:

> some excellent
> some dreadful

Several students reported that most staff were helpful apart from one.

The University of Northside students were asked whether they had discussed their dyslexia with their personal tutor/course leader and, if so, were asked to rate how helpful they found this:

If 'Yes', was this helpful?

Very helpful		Moderately helpful		Totally unhelpful
1	2	3	4	5

Of the 29 relevant responses, 65.5 per cent said they had spoken to their course leader and/or personal tutor and 34.5 per cent had not done so. Of those who discussed their dyslexia, none rated their tutors as totally helpful, 21 per cent rated them as fairly helpful, and 47 per cent rated them as fairly to totally unhelpful. As with Southside, some students reported mixed experiences with some very helpful tutors and some indifferent or unsympathetic tutors:

> One really helpful offering support but another said it was my problem not hers and it had better not affect my work in the classroom.
>
> (Female, 20, Education)

Those students who reported they had not spoken to academic staff were not specifically asked to explain why they had not spoken to anybody, although a number added comments Some students clearly would have liked academic staff to know about their difficulties but saw this as the responsibility of the support services and departments to arrange:

> I would prefer it if my lecturers did know.
>
> (Female, 19, Sociology)

> I was surprised to find that lecturers were not made aware that one of their students was dyslexic. I think it is important that they are made aware.
>
> (Female, 20, Psychology)

How far students should be responsible for making staff aware of their difficulties, and how far this is the responsibility of specialist support staff, is an important issue that needs clarifying. One difficulty is that, even when support staff do inform the academic department, this information does not always reach the right members of staff. The usual policy is that, with the student's permission, the relevant course leader is informed. One student gives her lecturers a rating of 3 and comments:

> There are so many students on the course it is hard for the lecturers to remember if you are dyslexic or not, so you end up having to remind them constantly so they can understand your difficulties.
>
> (Female, 21, 3D Design)

Carron (2001) questioned dyslexic students at the University of Southside about the nature of support from tutors/lecturers. She asked students if they had ever been made to feel uncomfortable about approaching tutors and obtained the following results:

No 44%   Yes 53%   No answer 3%

These results reinforce the idea that there is considerable individual variation between staff within departments or subject areas in terms of their understanding and response to dyslexia. Within an inclusive whole-institution framework these results are of concern. Particularly for those students who have had past experiences of disbelief, humiliation or negative attitudes, even one negative person in a department can undermine students' self-belief and best efforts to put the past behind them. There are reports that negative experiences may prime some dyslexic children and adults to become especially sensitive to criticism (Edwards 1994; Riddick 1996; Gilroy and Miles 1996). Some staff may unintentionally give offence because of lack of understanding about the nature of dyslexia or lack of awareness that a particular student is dyslexic:

> I have received feedback with comments about spelling and sentence/language use which I found to be inappropriately presented. I feel that if this lecturer was aware of the situation this feedback could have been presented in a more useful way.
>
> (Female, 20, Psychology)

In some cases, feedback which is intended to help a student improve their work will be perceived simply as criticism. In other cases, staff still dispute the existence of dyslexia or see any accommodation for it as a threat to academic standards (Gilroy 1995):

> Some just shrug and say you're on a degree course now get on with it.
>
> (Male, 37, Computing for Business)

There still seems to be a lingering, although thankfully diminishing, problem of making a hidden disability both visible and legitimate in the eyes of some individuals. From either a disability rights or an equal opportunities perspective, it is unacceptable for any members of staff to denigrate a student because of his or her disability. It is the responsibility of the institution and the departments within it to make this policy clear to all staff.

Carron (2001) also asked students whether they minded other students finding out about the support they received: 59 per cent did not mind, and 41 per cent said they did mind.

One approach is for academic tutors to consult students in private about how open or discreet they wish to be in a general sense about their dyslexia and how, ideally, they would like specific support such as lecture notes delivered to them. Because for practical or organizational reasons this may not always be possible, it would seem desirable for all lecturers to adopt a discreet approach in delivering support unless a student clearly signals otherwise.

Students at Southside were finally asked to rate and comment on the support services for dyslexia provided by the university:

Very good		Moderate		Very poor
1	2	3	4	5

The average rating was 4.5, with 75 per cent of students giving a rating of 5. Many added positive comments to their 5 rating:

Very willing to help, understanding not patronising.

They will make time for me whenever I need it.

Student services have given me a lot of support and the determination to carry on.

The support supplied by Southside University is brilliant. The team they have are very good, they are approachable and bend over backwards in order to help you, no matter how little or big the problem, if it were not for them I would have given up long ago.

(Female, 22, Biomedical Science)

Several students commented in one form or another that it was the support of student services that had enabled them to carry on, and that without it they may well have dropped out. As well as the practical support offered by student services for many students, it was clear that they also valued the emotional support and the feeling that there was a team of people who understood and believed in them:

> Being able to talk to them, their understanding of how I felt . . . Being assessed brought back unpleasant memories of school. The support I was given by the team at Southside was excellent, after many years of carrying the hurt with me I was able to pass it over. In some ways being assessed was the start of a healing process and the start of HE life.
>
> (Female, 38, Social Studies)

The Dyslexia in Higher Education Report (Singleton 1999) stresses the need for counselling for dyslexic students, to help them deal both with past negative experiences and also anxieties or frustrations engendered by their current studies.

Negative ratings of 1 or 2 were given by 12.5 per cent of the students: some of these were on courses franchised to colleges, while others were on satellite campuses; some were on part-time courses (sometimes in the evening), with little spare time at university to attend support sessions – especially if they had no transport and it involved travelling to another campus. The overall message was that where students could access support it was evaluated very positively. Where criticisms were made, these focused on reported lack of access to support.

For the University of Southside students, the views and reported practices of many of the key support staff are available in Chapter 9 of this book.

CHAPTER 7

Profiling the student's course: which aspects of a course cause difficulty for students with dyslexia?

One of the key functions which an assessment should perform is the profiling of the individual student's strengths, weaknesses and learning style. This profile should then be considered in conjunction with the demands of the particular course that the student is undertaking. The Singleton report (1999) recommends that the evaluation of the learning and support needs of students with dyslexia requires understanding of:

- the nature of the student's problems of literacy and learning
- the nature and strengths of the student's learning style
- the demands of the student's higher education course
- the type of technology and other support available
- the procedures for the DSA application.

Singleton also suggests a realistic consideration of the following matters:

- The demands and delivery methods of the chosen course of study should be evaluated in terms of the student's individual strengths and weaknesses. This may involve gathering information from and liaison with academic staff delivering the components of the student's course.
- The student's cognitive strengths, learning styles, attitudes and preferences should be taken into account – students with dyslexia are often very inflexible in the ways in which they are able to learn.
- How the support will be financed.

And Singleton recommends that, in relation to the course requirements, the following should be considered:

- The mode of course delivery, such as emphasis on lectures or practical work.
- Lecturing style (e.g. with or without handouts and/or OHPs).
- The amount and type of written work required and the length of time permitted.
- The balance of coursework, end-of-module test and formal examinations.
- The level of technical accuracy required (e.g. spelling, grammar and punctuation).
- The amount and type of reading required and time available to undertake it.
- Whether oral presentations are required.
- The extent to which any learning strengths of the student can be brought into play.

Singleton's excellent and comprehensive recommendations are based on a national survey of dyslexia provision in higher education, requiring institutional responses, consultative meetings with representatives from interested parties, including higher education institutions, and working party meetings. On the whole, however, the views of academic staff themselves who teach the students are lacking.

In order to develop an understanding of the meaning of the recommendations and to illustrate what may be involved in this assessment of course demands, a survey of the views of academic staff from a range of disciplines was carried out in one university to obtain an understanding of their attitudes to students with dyslexia, their knowledge of the types of difficulty these students encountered with their courses and their own needs for support in relation to the education of these students. A questionnaire was sent out to a sample of 100 staff, including course leaders, in each faculty (see Appendix to this chapter for copy of the questionnaire). Thirty-eight replies were received from 16 different departments. These covered a wide range of courses with very differing demands. The respondents had substantial teaching experience, the average number of years being 13 with a standard deviation of 8.5 years. Only two respondents had less than four years experience. At the other end of the range, seven respondents had 20 or more years of teaching experience. Staff were asked if any students with dyslexia took their courses currently or in the past. Ninety per cent (n = 34) answered yes to this question. Those who answered yes to this question were also presented with a list of difficulties which dyslexic students may show when studying and asked to endorse those difficulties which the dyslexic students they taught had shown. The results of this are given in Table 7.1.

As can be seen from Table 7.1, virtually all staff considered that dyslexic students had problems with spelling. Grammar and clarity/fluency of writing were also noted as problems by many staff. Here again, as observed in Chapter 3, we see the important role that the written productions of students play in staff perceptions of students' competence. A restricted vocabulary used in writing was much less commonly perceived but was still endorsed by a significant number of staff. Handwriting difficulties were rather less prominent than might be expected, undoubtedly due to the omnipresence nowadays of opportunities for word-processing. Slow reading and difficulties in the comprehension of reading matter were noted by about 60 per cent of staff. These difficulties, which are common to nearly all adult dyslexics, are not therefore so visible to staff as are the problems of writing. In all likelihood, this is due to the fact that there is much less of a demand on students to read during staff–student contact time, and the reading of substantial quantities of material is not so commonly part of the assessment process as is the production of written work. Almost as many staff who noted the reading problems of students also noted their problems in note-taking. Again, this is generally a problem for students with dyslexia, although the mode of course delivery in some modules may mean that for some students note-taking is not a frequent activity. Staff generally will not be aware of

Table 7.1. Frequency and percentages of staff responding to question on problems of students with dyslexia

Problem area for students with dyslexia	No. of staff endorsing	% of staff endorsing
note-taking	20	58.8
spelling	33	97.1
grammar	27	79.4
clarity/fluency of writing	28	82.4
handwriting	11	32.4
restricted vocabulary in writing	13	38.2
slow reading and reading comprehension	21	61.8
meeting deadlines	13	38.2
finding/organizing materials	13	38.2
timetables	7	20.6
group discussions	4	11.8
numeracy	9	26.5
confidence and anxiety	20	58.8

slowness in note-taking unless students draw this problem to their attention by asking for lecture notes or asking to tape-record a lecture. Many staff will provide substantial handouts which obviate the necessity for extensive note-taking (see Chapter 8). Equally as many staff observed that dyslexic students taking their courses may be anxious and lack confidence. It is interesting to note that such a high proportion of staff were aware of this aspect of the dyslexic student's problems. Clearly this is a significant area of concern of which all university staff should be aware. Anxiety may be increased and self-esteem decreased by comments made by staff who are unaware of the dyslexic student's problems. Difficulties in meeting deadlines and other aspects of organization such as finding materials were noted by a significant number of staff. These difficulties no doubt contribute to the anxiety felt by many of the students. The research carried out with dyslexic students and controls by Farmer et al. (2001) shows that the dyslexics as a group have a significantly higher level of anxiety than non-dyslexic controls (see Chapter 5). Riddick et al. (1999) also found lower levels of self-esteem in their group of dyslexic students. Problems with numeracy also figured as a difficulty that a smaller number of staff had observed. Obviously, not all courses will have numeracy demands, but it is important to note that numeracy problems should be considered in assessment. Relatively only a few staff noted that dyslexic students may have problems in contributing to group discussions, but this is still an item to consider when profiling a student's strengths and weaknesses and relating them to course demands.

Problems related to specific disciplines

Semi-structured interviews were conducted individually with nine tutors from different disciplines across the University who volunteered to help (see Appendix for format of the interview). The interviews were tape-recorded and later transcribed. Points made by the tutors are summa-rized below. Edited verbatim extracts are also reproduced as these often give a stronger impression of the involvement and understanding of the tutors than is represented in a summary.

In these interviews the following were discussed: staff attitudes and strategies relating to the identification of students with dyslexia; the nature of the difficulties which individuals with dyslexia studying their courses might encounter and staff perceptions of the student's needs in relation to these difficulties (reported in this chapter); staff accommoda-tions and support for dyslexic students; and the type of support which the staff themselves would like to receive in relation to the support of dyslexic students (reported in Chapter 8).

Clearly any course in higher education will make demands on students' competencies in many areas. Reading and writing will be demanded in all courses whether they are related to a science or an arts-based subject All courses will require students to organize their time and their materials, follow timetables, find rooms, hand in assessments to a timetable, use libraries, discuss information and ideas with others. In addition, however, courses will clearly have greatly different approaches to teaching and learning, depending on the skills and competencies they hope to develop in their students and the concepts and ideas which are the content of their teaching. Thus, Engineering will differ from Drama, Education from Media Studies, History from Computing. Through the interviews we hoped to throw light on the nature of those demands as perceived by the staff and also on the types of support which staff had found necessary and/or effective to enable dyslexic students to succeed. In conducting these interviews, it was also hoped that from the answers received it would be possible to distil a set of questions which in future could be asked by dyslexic students in deciding which course would be appropriate to them and which also would be useful to support staff in assessing the needs of dyslexic students and endeavouring to inform tutors about these. The answers given by staff to the questions on student identification, course demands and student needs are summarized below.

Academic staff views of course demands, student identification and student needs

Not all tutors gave information on procedures for identification of students. If the numbers of students with dyslexia entering a course had been few in the past, courses did not usually have specific procedures in place. When asked about the demands of the courses they taught, it is also interesting to note that tutors frequently mentioned aspects of the course which quite a number of students found taxing, but which they thought might be even more demanding and stressful for students with dyslexia. Many staff indeed seemed to see a continuum of need rather than to clearly identify students with dyslexia as an entirely separate and different group.

Computing and Maths: courses on databases, programming and systems analysis

Reading

The tutor teaching these courses explained that texts on database design, theory of relational databases and relational algebra are densely written and contain many technical terms. Students with dyslexia may have particular problems in recalling the meaning of the terms and then comprehending the meaning of the text. Their short-term memory problems will create problems in the storage of enough information in working memory to enable them to relate all the ideas together.

Skim-reading to find information is also needed. This tutor reported of one student: 'He couldn't skim-read, he couldn't quickly run a finger down a page and find what he was looking for. He had to read in detail in order to be able to understand what the glossary terms were.'

Spelling

The syntax of programming and database languages may cause dyslexic students problems as individual terms must be spelled absolutely correctly and the words have to be in the correct order.

Organization of thoughts

Computing demands logic in any sort of discussion. Dyslexic students may seem to be following several different threads of thought at once and to jump from one to the other. They may jump from one topic to another without any apparent logic. In this discipline the tutor said: 'We start at step one, then we move through step two and three and eventually reach step four. Some dyslexic students' thoughts seem to dance all over the place.'

Memory

Problems with short- and long-term memory also interfere with the development of a logical programme or text. The tutor said: 'Problems with memory cause problems in a logical subject area where we require people to start at step one.' She also commented on how short-term memory difficulties affected the ability of one particular dyslexic student to produce well-organized text. She said: 'When he'd written it took him a long time to go back and re-read what he'd written because he couldn't remember, he couldn't remember. The short-term memory problems were the worst thing about it.'

Sequencing

Problems in this area were seen as a major hurdle. This tutor said: 'Computing is very sequential. I think it's a difficult subject for people with dyslexia . . . If students are determined to do computing one of the new degrees in multi-media computing might be a better area. There we're looking at sound, pictures, video and all those aspects of computing. If students are visually more in tune with what's going on they may be able to bring some independent thought to that area and be successful.'

Writing

A difficulty in structuring one's thoughts and therefore in structuring text was again seen as a significant problem in computing. As noted above, writing needs to be very logically structured in this subject. The tutor explained: 'It's this multi-threading and the fact they're thinking of all different things at the same time . . . it all comes out on paper the way it's going through in their mind . . . they do find it difficult to gather together their thoughts.'

Numeracy

The study of computing requires a high level of numeracy. This tutor remarked: 'Students with dyslexia may also have difficulties in numeracy which they may not have recognized. They may have been assessed in relation to their literacy problems, but numeracy may not have been considered. There is a need for assessment in this area.'

Assessment

Assessment on this course is mainly by assignment though there are a few exams. Students may have a reader or use a word-processor in exams.

Education

Reading and memory

The fact that a great deal of information must be read and remembered was seen as a difficulty for students with dyslexia. The tutor commented: 'Students with dyslexia will have difficulty with the amount of information they have to assimilate. If you're doing an education course you do have to take on board an awful lot of knowledge if you're going to do well . . . subject knowledge, child development, an awareness of how children learn and the ways children learn . . . a huge amount of knowledge for a students to actually access in a way that makes sense to them.'

Writing

On the initial teacher training courses, apart from the assessment of practice as a teacher, assessment is through written assignment. So a great deal of assessed written work is required. The tutor commented: 'It's quite a heavily assessed course for the number of units.'

Organization

Teaching requires many different types of organizational skill. Within the course there are assignments to produce and teaching practices to organize which require a great deal of juggling with materials and time. She said that task and time management could be major hurdles: 'I think . . . the load of assessments, organization, organising yourself for the submission of work. I think all that would be challenging for somebody who is dyslexic . . . [Also] organization of time . . . in terms of their own block of placement that's explicit, that's something they have to be able to do on placement . . . The school day is very, very structured. So the time element has become a very visible part of the day . . . that's problematic for students as well.'

Oral language

There is a demand for teachers now to be able to model standard English for their pupils. A general language difficulty may be part of the dyslexic person's difficulty. Dyslexic people with difficulties in word-finding or other aspects of oral language may have problems in making some of the modifications that are required. Lack of self-confidence may affect their ability to adopt more formal speech and change their everyday mode. This tutor reported that: 'We are assessed on our students' ability to model standard English. That has implications, if you think if people are speaking in a dialect that isn't standard a lot of the time and it's fairly well established and it hasn't been picked up and identified earlier. A lot of our energy is going into the assessment and identifying areas of the students' language that are non-standard and identifying a standard version of that and practising it.'

Other demands which may cause problems for dyslexic students.

Initial Teacher Training courses are evaluated largely on the quality of the performance of the student teachers they produce. So, for instance, this tutor also remarked: 'If an inspector came in and they were in a class and a student was seen to be putting up spelling mistakes then this could well be seen to be a failure of the course to support and train the student appropriately.' She said: 'Increasingly teachers will have to have higher degrees of English knowledge. At primary level they need to have much more in-depth knowledge about language and about numeracy.'

Dyslexic students will also have difficulty with the tests introduced to audit their own subject knowledge in numeracy and literacy: 'At the end of their courses they have to go through these skills tests, which if they don't pass they don't become qualified teachers.' These are proving problematic for a number of students, but for dyslexic students it is likely that these may be a major hurdle and a source of stress. This tutor said that many staff are now wondering whether 'it's possible or fair to take dyslexic students onto Initial Teacher Training (ITT) courses because of the amount of pressure they are put under and the fact that they are being assessed on their weakness and their strengths aren't taken into account . . . that's a very big issue in ITT at the moment.' The admissions procedures had recently been altered on this course in order to try to ensure the appropriate quality of entrants. The tutor reported: 'We have a course reliant on its student intake . . . Obviously we are assessing students now on entry. Last year we introduced a written test to pick up grammar and spelling problems.' So, as this tutor suggests, admission to an ITT course may well be becoming increasingly problematic for candidates with dyslexia, and, even given success in overcoming this hurdle, ultimate success in obtaining the final qualification will remain an issue given the current situation.

Engineering

Reading

Although this tutor described the course as demanding a lot of reading he said that this was reading from textbooks rather than current papers and articles, in which case it was possible sometimes to direct students to books that were more clearly written and therefore easier to assimilate.

Writing

There are quite heavy demands on writing in written assignments in the second and final year and students also have to write lab reports. He said that you may see the problems of dyslexia in terms of sequencing and organization 'in more protracted written bits of work. You can see that the structure isn't what it ought to be and it doesn't flow the way it ought to, and they may come to what they perceive to be a conclusion, but it isn't, it's just hanging there.'

Note-taking

The provision of extensive handouts was not standard on this course. The tutor reported that he did not provide handouts unless a student specifically asked for this. He also said: 'A lot of them are quite reluctant to come forward, whether it's a macho image, or whether it is this self-esteem problem that they don't want too many people to know about it.' He said: 'I know that keeping up with notes is a real problem.' He considered that some dyslexic students may have to spend a lot more time than other students in the evening writing up their notes.

Problems with spatial organization

This tutor considered that students with spatial organization problems would not be likely to choose engineering as a course to follow since spatial awareness was essential to the engineer. He said that problems with spatial organization were something that were not seen in engineering: 'Maybe it's the type that comes in, because in engineering you do need to have a very good spatial awareness because if you don't have spatial awareness, three-dimensional vision, you can't be a very good engineer.'

Sequencing

Students with sequencing problems would also have great difficulty with an engineering course, he suggested: 'So much of our work is numerate rather than literate so, from the point of view of working though numerical problems and getting answers to them, you have got to go in a particular sequence. There's no way you can put paragraphs in the wrong order so that they don't flow . . . So that discipline is required. And that discipline forces itself upon you because you may not be able to do B until you have got the answer to A . . . so they've got to go that way.' It is likely that dyslexic students who have sequencing and related numeracy problems would not attempt to become engineers since the patent demands to be competent in these areas and the admissions criteria for such courses would mean that students with such problems would not perceive engineering as an area to which they were attracted, or would not be successful in achieving the necessary prerequisite qualifications for entry to the courses.

Other considerations

This tutor considered that the main difficulty for dyslexic students who required additional help and support might be in obtaining access to tutors: 'I think that the main problem that they have is the time constraint. An hour lecture is over in an hour. You can't find additional time for them. If they are free at a different time of the week you aren't. So you've got a certain amount of material that you must get through for the benefit of everyone else. If they don't go out of their way to come to you, then there's not a lot you can do.' The great majority of students on engineering courses are male, and this tutor considered that there may well be a problem for males in asking for help. They feel that they should be strong and independent, cope on their own, and being open about problems is taboo. As quoted above, he said: 'A lot of them are quite reluctant to come forward.' He was not sure about the cause of this but suggested that it may be to do with the required macho image that seems to be necessary for males working in groups of males. Certainly, developmental studies of male conversation and social interaction suggest that dominance and competitiveness are important elements in establishing social identity in male groups (Maccoby 1988, 1990).

This tutor (and others such as the Health Studies tutor) stressed the feeling that if students, for whatever reason, do not want to stand out and be different from the rest they will not receive the help they may need and to which they are entitled. This tutor said: 'In many ways, until they come to terms with it . . . I suppose they must come to terms with it and be comfortable with it sometime . . . until they come to terms with it they probably are their own worst enemy in some ways, not taking advantage of concessions that people realize that they need.' (See also comments on self-advocacy in Chapter 8.)

Drama

Evidence here is given from two interviews, one with the course leader for the drama course, a Performing Arts course within the School of Art, and one from the Tutorial Adviser for the School of Art. Both of these tutors made positive comments about the admission of students with dyslexia to the courses within the School. The course leader said: 'We have a number of students who have dyslexia. Apparently it is something that can be quite common in arts. So it is something that we are very aware of and we have a number of students who I have to say are very, very successful in completing their degree and actually do extremely well.' The tutorial adviser also explained: 'We don't really see it as a major problem. If the student takes advantage of the extra money which is available to them and if they get the computer and software and if they use it, if they take advantage of preliminary discussion with tutors about essays before they do them, then they shouldn't really have a great deal of problems.'

Reading

The course leader said: 'Academically it's not a soft option. Although we're practice-based there's a lot of reading and it is demanding for a dyslexic student . . . There's learning lines, reading scripts, sight-reading . . .' The tutorial adviser added: 'The area which a lot of people don't tend to think of is that we do work quite a lot of the time from text. And sight-reading is obviously a problem.' He explained: 'What we'll do is, we'll give out an extract from a play for instance and we'll read it round in the group and we'll take it away and work on it, and it can obviously be very embarrassing if you have a problem and you can't sight-read. Obviously what you're seeking in drama students is to read text intelligently with some kind of grasp of meaning from the first time they pick it up really . . . because it's quite important often when you work on a text to get the sound of it in the air first before you work on it.'

Writing

The course leader said: 'I think in comparison to other courses, the amount of written work the students have to complete will be considerably less because the units are practice-based . . .' On the other hand, writing is demanded in some activities: 'One of the things . . . we ask our students to do, because the course is practice-based, is to keep a journal . . . and they hand in a synopsis of that journal for most units. This is partly because one of the key things to develop in drama is the ability to develop the skills of the reflective practitioner . . . And in the third year, in the drama course, their dissertation is a documentation and evaluation of practice of a research project in the arts. That can be very difficult for a dyslexic student because of the sheer volume of writing required.'

Assessment

In this type of course students with dyslexia are less stressed by a quantity of written work and examinations. The tutor reported that 80 per cent of the assessment of a double unit in practice-based work is actually on the practice:. 'I've just finished doing site-specific work in Year 2 for example and there are three practical units and although the synopsis of the journal has a weight of 20 per cent, there's a very small weighting in that. The vast majority of the assessment in those units is purely on process, contribution to the sessions, taking part in devising, the research for the role and then actually the performance itself so that is very much a practice-based assessment. And that's the same across drama and performance. They're very heavily practice-based.'

Self-confidence

Clearly, if you are to be a performer or a facilitator of drama the ability to speak out in groups is essential. Students with dyslexia might therefore find a drama course very demanding. However, this tutor said: 'Thinking of some students who I know are dyslexic, a couple of them are quite shy and quiet.' She added that, despite the clear demand for coping with exposing yourself to others in a fairly extroverted way, 'You do get a surprising level of students who are unsure of themselves.' This, however, could actually be compensated for through the medium of drama. She said that it may be different when you give them a part: 'As themselves they can be quite unsure of themselves, but with a role, being someone else, it's a very different process.'

Health Studies

Course size and structure

There are two overall points about these courses which are very relevant to students with dyslexia: (a) the size of the course and the staff–student contact; (b) their inter-disciplinary nature. In Health Studies, the tutor taught on two small courses taking in 30 students a year and, as the tutor said, 'We don't get huge numbers wanting to come on our courses so we are keen to keep the students we get.' This tutor also stressed the fact that as these were interdisciplinary courses, (a) a student could do well in some aspects and not on others depending on his or her strengths and weaknesses, and (b) a difficulty might be hidden because of the number of disparate units that were taken and the fact that communication and feedback between tutors of the different units might be more difficult since they were dispersed through different departments or even different faculties. 'Our courses are very inter-disciplinary across the board, so in many ways students can almost hide . . . some learning difficulties can be hidden because of the diverseness if you like. We have IT for example which requires numeracy more than literacy in some of the work . . . A group of our students also learn a foreign language which takes them even to another faculty . . . and then of course they do research and then there's Health Studies. So you can get a poor mark perhaps in one area, or a poor sort of general kind of position in the group, but then do well in something else, which tends to sort of perhaps distract any real focus on what is happening to this learner . . . But in a couple of cases, three cases in the last three years, we've actually identified quite serious learning difficulties in students who, themselves, were aware that they were struggling in different areas. But they've managed to get through school, they've managed to get into a university. And you think . . . *how do they do it?* All credit to them . . . but in all cases it wasn't because they didn't have an ability, in fact they were clever to disguise their disability you know in ways, by demonstrating that they had strengths in other areas.' She described one extreme case of a dyslexic student as follows: 'One lad who we picked up at the end of year one, he was brilliant at IT and quite sharp on anything numerical and he wrote quite well – what he wrote – but there was just not enough and no references whatsoever. And he came to see me for a talk, I said "You're not reading" and he sat there and said "I can't read" . . . I couldn't believe it. He actually said "I can't read".'

Reading

This tutor stressed the importance of a breadth of reading and the use of a range of references in students' written assignments in what is essentially a social science discipline. She said: 'In marking the students' work it seems there's a marked difference between those who have read the class notes and then give you it back as an essay and those who have gone and done further reading. And it's the lack of reading that's been the biggest difficulty we have found for our students who do have some reading or dyslexic problems. They're not reading so there's no referencing . . . the work may be nicely written . . . they've looked at their spelling and their grammar . . . they've been to perhaps study skills, they've used Microsoft Word which has a grammar check, but there's no backing from their reading.'

Writing

There is an emphasis on the production of written work for assignments, and also exams, but it appeared that the students received a great deal of support from their tutors in the process of the production of their assignments and the development of writing skills (see Chapter 8). The most daunting piece of written work is the final year research project report. Students go away from the University on a research placement, carry out their empirical research and then report on it. 'There's this huge piece of written work, whether it's quantitative research or not it doesn't matter or . . . it's all got to come together in a big 12 000 word report. So some students just freak out. I mean their biggest essay will have been 3 000 words, then suddenly they're onto this.' However, again, a great deal of support is provided by tutors and by the central support services (see Chapter 8).

Numeracy and quantitative skills

There is a demand for a reasonable facility with numbers and understanding of numerical data on this course. This tutor said: 'Well we do ask for at least a Grade C in Maths to get onto the health development course because there's a lot of quantitative work in epidemiology . . . projections, mortality, morbidity, fertility rates and trends over time. You've got to know whether that's bigger than that, whether the aggregate makes it different . . . all that kind of thing . . . so we have some weak students, but by having that filtering [the demand for a grade C] it does mean that we start from a reasonable basis.' She qualified this by saying that ' there are some students who struggle with it . . . we tend to guide them when it comes to their own project.' By this she meant that a student who struggled with quantitative analysis could be directed towards a qualitative approach in their final year project. She considered that difficulties with numeracy were not as problematic for students on this course as were difficulties with reading.

Organization

The tutor considered that, although using word-processors is a boon for dyslexic students, other aspects of computer use could raise some problems in terms of spatial organization and sequencing demands. She said: 'One issue that is becoming more apparent is moving between computer labs . . . although the University students' access labs all have the same front end, the actual access to certain programmes – and our students use special programmes – is not possible in some labs and in others it's quite convoluted . . . certain bits of software are only available in one lab which is specialized . . . but the computer access screen still has the same front end as in all other labs. So they go to another lab and look at something which looks exactly the same and they spend an hour trying to find a programme which isn't there.' She also said: 'The other thing I find problematic is the faculty web site. It takes about seven steps to get to our course. There is often just one word or phrase which has a certain meaning which you have to click on . . . but the chosen word or phrase may not be particularly meaningful.' For a dyslexic student with 'problems in placing things in a sequence and remembering where they have come from' this may raise some problems. She considered that 'Some of the flexible e-learning will disadvantage a lot of learners, not just dyslexic learners, but adult learners who are computer illiterate, having to shift to the world of e-learning.'

Another big organizational demand is the setting up and conducting of their final year empirical research project: 'They have to go off . . . they leave the University for two months to carry out the research for which they've been well prepared over the three years, two and a half years by this stage. They gather data . . . They have to set up the placement. That's part of the learning.' So students are expected to conduct all the communication in relation to this project, contacting an organization, possibly abroad, explaining their position, their aims and objectives and methods and getting the necessary permissions, etc. and also sorting out any other practical aspects such as travel, visas, accommodation, etc. Of course, tutors will support and advise but the onus and responsibility is the student's.

Oral communication skills

The students are expected to be able to work as part of a group in Year 2 on an assessed oral presentation of their research work at that stage. In Year 2 there is an assessed group presentation. They also have a research viva in Year 2 in front of a small panel of lecturers. But probably the most demanding element of the course in terms of oral communication comes in the setting up and conducting of their third year project. The tutor commented in relation to this: 'Of course the big thing is communication. They have to set it all up . . . And many of them go abroad . . . so you know they're having to develop their personal verbal skills as well as their written and analytical ones.'

History

Reading

History is a subject where a great deal of reading is expected; however, the tutor here, who only had experience of one student with dyslexia, said that difficulties with reading had not been a major concern raised by the student. He said: 'I suspect that he doesn't read as fast as some of the other students, but considering the circumstances he's done a reasonable amount.'

Writing

This was the principal area of concern for this tutor. There is a high level of demand for essay production on the course. Assessment is mainly by coursework. Students might be required to produce three different essays for different units by mid-November in the first semester of the academic year. Of the particular student who he knew well he said: 'I think the fairly heavy workload in terms of producing the essays for different courses perhaps meant that the work wasn't always as well polished as it should have been.'

One of the main things he mentioned in relation to writing was not simply the problem of formulating correct sentences but also, more significantly from the point of view of historical work, the necessity of formulating an argument. He said: 'The real problem is the formulation of the argument because this is absolutely crucial to what we expect from our the students . . . Where students get penalized is, and this is a general point, if their expression's poor and that affects the quality of the argument . . . accordingly, then they will not get as good marks.'

Assessment

Assessment is a mixture, but predominantly by coursework. If several essays are required at or around the same point of time a great deal of time management and management of materials is required. The main feature of concern to a dyslexic student in relation to this, apart from the stress of the necessary reading and writing, is the fact that there are deadlines, and although the tutor said that there could be leniency in relation to these, it was not encouraged since a student might build up a backlog of pieces of work to be handed in. And, as the tutor commented: 'If people are under pressure to produce essays for three different units by the middle of November, it creates a certain pressure. Some people can reel these essays off very quickly but obviously someone in this situation [a student with dyslexia] cannot, and there's always the possibility that one of the essays might suffer quite badly through being rushed out. Another big demand on writing occurs in the third year where there is a dissertation weighted with 30 credits in the second semester. This is a research-based project in which the student must use primary sources of information. As the tutor noted: 'It's a big project and it's something that people if they're well organized and they decide, as this student did, what they want to do at an early stage then . . . it's a chance for people to really shine, if they've got the commitment.'

Oral communication

The main emphasis of the course is on written communication but the tutor did say that there was one unit in the third year where there are oral assessments which the tutor tapes and the tapes are made available to the external examiner. A student with lack of confidence or problems in word-finding or other aspects of oral language might have difficulties here. The tutor said: 'I think that's something we need to take into account. It's quite easy to make the assumption that because someone has difficulty in putting words onto paper then oral presentation will be better for them, but that's not always the case.'

Note-taking

On this course the giving of handouts was not standard practice. The tutor said that members of staff varied in their approach to this and it was 'a case of individual practice'. He said: 'What I tend to do is simply put down names and anything I intend to emphasize on an overhead. And because of my style of lecturing those tend to be written the night before. But . . . there's a principle here, that the students' note-taking should involve their judgement as to what they think is important. We perhaps need to give them more direction about this as part of the general skills package at the beginning. But I do feel by the time the students are in second year they ought to be less mollycoddled.' Clearly, history is a matter of interpretation and opinion rather than scientific 'fact' as found in engineering. Here, the tutor was emphasizing the importance of the development of a particularly important competence in dealing with historical material. He did, however, add later, when considering the whole process of learning, that 'perhaps we should pay a bit more attention to how the dyslexic students deal with the earlier stages of this process starting with the lectures'.

Course structure

History can be allied to a number of other subjects such as politics, economics or sociology in Joint Honours courses. The tutor pointed out that there might be a number of pitfalls for a student with dyslexia in attempting a Joint Honours course. The two subjects will probably have different approaches to the teaching and learning process. He considered the History and Sociology Joint Honours course that they offered. He said that, in Sociology, they tend to have short thin [one semester long] 10 credit units. History has short fat [one semester long] 20 credit units.

Other courses may have long thin 20 credit units spread out across two semesters. The workload for a semester in one half of their Joint course may consist of three 20 credit units and in the other half six 10 credit units. On the former the students may have more time to get into the work in depth and do sufficient reading if they are dyslexic. In coping with the contrasting approach taken on the other Honours course, the student with dyslexia may find it difficult to adjust their study mode to the different demands. The tutor also noted that different courses will have different requirements in terms of presentation of work, handing-in of work, attendance at seminars, amount/type of reading. This demands a high level of awareness and organization on the part of the student. Another contrasting consideration on two joint courses may be in the style of writing required. Discursive, descriptive or personally expressive writing may be welcomed in one subject but frowned on in another (See Chapter 3 and discussion of writing and writings by Crème and Lea 1997; Lea and Street 1998; Pollak 2001.)

Psychology

Reading

In psychology, students are required to do a great deal of reading, not only of textbooks, but also, particularly in the second and third years of the course, of original journal articles. In the case of textbooks, it is possible to point students towards the texts which are more clearly written, but this is not usually the case with journal articles. Students will have to be able to read quite dense texts in which there may well be a large number of jargon, subject-related words.

Writing

This tutor said that, in Psychology, 'We are aware of the difficulties of dyslexic students in the assessment context, rather than in the teaching context.' The bulk of assessment is by timed examination. He said: 'Within this faculty we must have the highest ratio of exams to coursework assessments.' In the first year, many of these examinations are of the multiple-choice type but thereafter the main demand is for timed essay responses to unseen papers. He also said that within psychology there was a support and guidance unit in the first year, where essay-writing in psychology was addressed as an issue, but thereafter no particular guidance was given. Students also have to write lab reports on their empirical work, regarding which there are quite rigid and precise expectations of structure, layout and writing style. This constitutes the other main strand of assessment, leading up to the report of their third year individual research project which is a 30 credit unit seen as the cumulative point of their development. The demand is for a particular type of writing and this is seen as integral to their competence as psychologists. Dyslexic students who struggle to produce written text for a number of reasons (linguistic and mechanical) may find it more difficult than the average student to adopt the appropriate voice and formality required. This may be penalized.

Organization and sequencing

A great deal of organization is required in order to produce adequate lab reports and the third year dissertation: 'Of course, these come under elements of key skills management and planning, which is all about sequencing. Expectations of lab reports I don't know . . . that's an element of dyslexia I'm unaware of, of course we have quite rigid expectations. Some individuals in lab reports in year one struggled to grasp the format that's expected of them, the overall configuration of what might be expected. In terms of deadlines these are carefully staggered across units so that students are not expected to hand in two major assignments at the same time, but in the second year particularly many students find it hard to keep to the timetable of demands for the completion of coursework.'

Numeracy

A fairly high level of numeracy is required. A 'C' in Maths at GCSE level is a minimum entry requirement. There are four experimental design and statistics modules, plus assessments in other modules requiring the understanding and use of experimental design and the quantitative analysis of data using statistical packages.

Note-taking

All tutors give handouts in psychology modules, but the style of these will vary. Some may give several pages with their complete lecture notes, others will give abbreviated versions. Many lecturers will give glossaries with definitions of terms in addition to their main handouts.

Fashion Marketing

This course was one of several design courses within the School of Art and Design, which included the following courses: Fashion Design,

Transportation, Graphics, Industrial Design, Three-dimensional Design, Multi-media and Jewellery Design. As in the Drama department, so in the School of Art and Design, dyslexia was fairly commonplace and not seen as a particularly intractable problem. The tutor reported: 'We seem to have a number of students who have it mildly and we seem to have one each year who has it quite badly and we had a student who left not last year but the year before who was so bad that he'd been in special schools all his life.' Later, she added: 'We get so many of them into Art and Design . . . because . . . from what I've read about it, they do tend to be very visual in the way that they see things. And it's an obvious route for them, especially if they're not very academic as well. They get channelled into us, early on from school.'

Organization

This tutor commented that one of the main problems for dyslexic students was the necessity for a high level of organization of self, materials and tasks. She said: 'The students actually have to work incredibly hard on a course like this, because they might have four projects on the go at once as well as the written side which actually is extremely time-consuming. I think it's taxing . . . We have different types of work that the students hand in and most of the kind of work that we're expecting from students is probably drawn project work, but it's quite complex in the way that they put that together. There's a research and development stage, there's a design and development stage and then there's an actual outcome, which could be two-dimensional or three-dimensional and it's . . . form if you like. The students actually find that *kind* of work much easier, which is why they're here, which is why we've got a large amount of dyslexic students. In a sense, that they can do as well as any other students. Where the problem comes is in the organization of that material, time management and the sorts of skills that dyslexics find incredibly difficult such as ordering things. That's where they need extra support . . . I wouldn't like to have to do it again! It's actually really quite hard work and I think that in terms of organizing your time to get through those tasks and understanding how long it takes to do those. I think the time thing [is a major problem] . . . Their understanding of time is completely different.'

Organization of thought and ideas

This tutor considered that creativity was a strength for dyslexic students following the design courses; however, this very fluency with ideas might also cause organizational problems. She said: 'They find it very difficult to actually sometimes to come to conclusions as well or, when we're asking for concepts, they can come up with lots of ideas, but it's making decisions, deciding what they want to do and then progressing that in an orderly way, in a logical way shall we say, that can prove difficult. So I think they need extra support, and understanding that they might not find that as easy as other students.'

Writing

Clearly, in a design course writing is not the major focus, but this is a degree course and the production of written work is demanded. The tutor said: 'Obviously there is an academic side, a theoretical side which has to be fulfilled and it's fairly rigorous and I think that's where the difficulties come in. They have to do . . . well there are written reports right through the course. They have to do a marketing dissertation which is very rigorous and they do a market planning unit as well afterwards. That's in the final year and . . . so they have as much as anybody . . . It could be five to seven thousand words. It's a very rigorous intense piece of research. Also we have an industrial placement report which counts for ten per cent of their final degree and is done in-house. So, we do have elements within the course and there are other written assignments. We have contextual studies and production studies and business environment lecture series which run right the way through which have written assignments as well.'

This tutor however felt that writing and spelling were an issue for a large number of students on their courses, not just for those who were identified as being dyslexic. She said: 'I think, in a way, that we've got a dumbing down of everybody's English at the minute. They're feeding through to us and the standard has definitely dropped. You don't get anything that doesn't have spelling mistakes in it. We try and stamp that out. We try to be as strict as we possible can and it's something that we pick students up on. But I think in the environment there are lots of things that aren't helping like email, text-messaging, shortening of things. I think we're going through a big language change at the moment.' The standard of demand for entrance qualification was quite high for these extremely popular courses. However the tutor said: 'We get students in here and on the whole they've got three to four A Levels . . . but they still can't spell very well. The grammar's not quite right. They make up words. They join words together to form new words you've never heard of before. They do all sorts of weird things . . . and in the context of that . . . I think that in a way we provide quite a good service for the dyslexics!'

Numeracy

Since this course was not purely about design but was also about market-ing, there was a need for competence in numeracy. The tutor explained: 'The thing is you see they have to do market research which involves statistics. We ask for GCSE maths . . . It's a bit easier now but they used to have to do quite complicated work on that. Now computer programmes just do it all, but they still have to be able to analyse that information . . .'

General considerations re matching students to courses

Some staff did not see dyslexia as a major barrier to students taking their courses as long as they were prepared to take advantage of the services available. Some courses might indeed be helpful and some courses talked about positive aspects of students with dyslexia. On the other hand, other courses such as Computing and Maths saw many real problems endemic in their discipline, which would play upon a dyslexic student's weaknesses. It was evident that there was an element of channelling taking place in the developmental path of students in that their difficulties with words might cause them to develop skills in other domains such as the spatial and visual. On the other hand, not all students with dyslexia followed such a course and some, albeit a few, chose subjects which required facility with words and the manipulation of written text. Several tutors, from across a range of disciplines, talked about students who had been extremely successful in gaining first class and upper second class honours degrees despite all their difficulties. Others, such as the Health Studies tutor, talked about the fantastic achievement of some students who had very severe difficulties in gaining any higher education qualification.

Summary

This range of courses does not, of course, represent every type of course within a modern university. These examples are cited to give a flavour of the different approaches taken by courses and the types of pitfalls which tutors have observed or which they foresee as possible for dyslexic students in tackling their courses. Of course, whether or not they occur as pitfalls, in fact, will depend on a number of factors, including students' individual profiles of strengths and weaknesses, their awareness of their own needs, their willingness to take responsibility for addressing these, their confidence in coming forward and discussing their needs with tutors and the responsiveness of tutors in responding to teaching and learning needs which are identified, either by themselves or by support services or by the students in question.

The issues raised by the tutors cited above suggest that, in choosing a course and in considering where they may need particular support, dyslexic students or those seeking to support them might ask the questions listed below. This is not an exhaustive list but could prompt or flag up for students and their tutors an awareness of pitfalls. Forewarned is forearmed. Awareness of difficulty may allow strategies to be adopted which will overcome or circumvent the problems arising. Chapter 8, which follows, looks at some of the strategies and supports which have been adopted by academic staff teaching students with dyslexia.

Course size

How many students are enrolled on the course?
What is the staff:student ratio?

Course structure

Does the course involve the study of modules in more than one division/department/school or faculty of the University? If it does then the following questions need to be asked in relation to all departments teaching modules within the course.

Reading: amount/type

Are tutors able to indicate core texts which are accessible in terms of language and style?
What emphasis is placed on reading a wide range of texts independently?
Is the reading of papers from academic journals required?

Reading: contexts

Is reading of texts at sight required for work within seminars/workshops/placement and training activities?
Is reading aloud required within seminars/workshops?

Writing: amount/type

How far is the main assessment of students' work dependent on the production of written work in exams and in assignments?
How important is the organization of logical argument and ideas in the assessment of that writing?

Writing: contexts

Do students have to produce writing as part of workshops/seminars/placement and training activities?
Are alternative outputs to handwriting possible?

Spelling/grammar

Is competence in the use of correct spelling and/or grammar integral to success in the course?
Is correct spelling and/or grammar an important consideration in assessment?

Assessments: balance/type

What types of assessment are used?
What concessions are available in examinations?
Is dyslexia considered to be an 'extenuating circumstance' in marking?

Teaching methods: note-taking demands

If lectures are used, are handouts provided?
How extensive are these?
Are they made available to the student prior to the lecture?

Use of e-learning

Are support materials available on the internet?
Can students email tutors re aspects of the course?

Organizational demands

Are deadlines for the submission of work staggered?
If not, will dyslexic students be allowed concessions in relation to these?
Are there some aspects of the course that require a great deal of the student in terms of self/time/task management?

Numeracy demands

Do aspects of the course require competence in activities involving numeracy?

Oral presentation/ communication demands

Is confident communication with others in public demanded/assessed?

Memory demands

Are there particular activities within the course which stress the use of short-term memory?

Sequencing demands

Are there particular activities within the course which stress the importance of accuracy in sequencing?

Appendix A

Questionnaire on Dyslexia in HE for University Teaching Staff

This is an anonymous questionnaire. Your name is not required.
Would you please fill in or ring the appropriate answer or tick the appropriate box.
University. . . . .
Department/division . . . .
Subject/s taught . . . .
No. of years as University teacher . . . .

1) What do you understand by the term 'dyslexia'?
. . . .
. . . .
. . . .
. . . .

2) Do you personally know anyone with dyslexia (apart from students that you teach)?

YES   **NO**

If the answer to (2) is YES please go to (3). If the answer to (2) is NO please go to (4).

3) What sort of difficulties do the dyslexic people that you know have?
. . . .
. . . .
. . . .
. . . .

4) Do any dyslexic students take your courses/modules – or have they in the past?

YES   **NO**

If the answer to (4) is YES please go to (5). If the answer to (4) is NO please go to (12).

5) Have dyslexic students shown any of the following problems when studying your modules?

Difficulties in keeping up with note-taking in lectures etc.   ☐
Spelling errors in written work   ☐
Grammatical errors in written work   ☐
Lack of clarity/fluency of expression in written work   ☐
Illegible handwriting   ☐
Restricted vocabulary in written work   ☐
Slow speed of reading and comprehending texts   ☐
Difficulties in keeping to deadlines   ☐
Difficulties in finding/organizing materials/themselves   ☐
Difficulties with timetables   ☐
Difficulties with contribution to group discussions   ☐
Difficulties with numeracy   ☐
Lack of self-confidence and anxiety   ☐

6) Are any of the following allowances/types of assistance given within your department for students with dyslexia?

Extra time in examinations
Extra time to complete assignments   ☐
Amanuensis in exams   ☐
Reader in exams   ☐
Use of word-processor in exams   ☐
Support tuition/training in skills such as essay-writing,   ☐
    note-taking etc.
Advice on study strategies and skills   ☐
Counselling on coping with dyslexia   ☐
Other (please specify) . . . .   ☐

Comments. . . . .
. . . .

7) In your opinion is it appropriate for universities to admit people with dyslexia as students to courses in your discipline?

YES   **NO**

Comments . . . .
. . . .
. . . .

8) Are you circulated with a list of students with dyslexia on your courses/modules?

YES   **NO**

9) (a) Has any dyslexic student ever requested specific types of support or concessions from you?

YES   **NO**

(b) If Yes, were these types of support/ concessions granted?

YES   **NO**

(c) If Yes, could you please give examples of types of support/concessions granted.

....

....

....

....

10) Have you, personally, made any changes to your teaching or taken any particular steps to help dyslexic students access your modules?

YES   **NO**

If Yes could you please explain what changes you have made or steps you have taken?

....

....

....

....

....

11) Have you encountered students with difficulties similar to the difficulties of dyslexic students who have *not* been identified as being dyslexic?

YES   **NO**

Comments...

....

....

12) How far do errors of spelling and grammar affect your marking of students' work?

(Please rate the degree to which your marking is affected by circling one of the numbers below.)

Not at all   **A great deal**
  1   2   3   4   5

13) How far does fluency/clarity of written expression affect your marking of students' work?

(Please rate the degree to which your marking is affected by circling one of the numbers below.)

Not at all   **A great deal**
  1   2   3   4   5

14) Have you ever received any in-service training on dyslexia and the needs of dyslexic students?

                        YES   **NO**

15) If training were available would you avail yourself of this?

                        YES   **NO**

16) Ideally what, if any, further information would you like to receive about students with dyslexia on your course?

Information about their
Reading ability
Spelling ability
Reading speed
Writing speed
Organizational difficulties
Other. Please explain . . . .
. . . .
. . . .
. . . .
. . . .

17) Have you any further comments you would like to make about the teaching of students with dyslexia? . . . .
. . . .
. . . .
. . . .

Appendix B

A semi-structured interview was conducted individually with each member of staff based on the following questions:

What experience have you had in the past of teaching students with dyslexia?

What particular problems with your course might a dyslexic student who has the following difficulties experience:

- reading: slow speed, inaccuracy, slow comprehension
- writing: deficits in grammar, handwriting, organization of ideas, use of appropriate writing style, writing in public, slowness in production of written work
- spelling
- organization of time
- organization of layout
- following timetables
- spatial layout of buildings, etc.
- lack of fluency in expressing ideas orally
- difficulties in pronouncing/finding words
- short-term memory – difficulty in remembering instructions
- taking longer to read and produce written work
- difficulties with multi-tasking, e.g. listening, understanding and taking notes.

What types of assessments are used on your course/s?

What concessions are made in assessment?

Have you referred students for assessment who you have suspected might be dyslexic?

What information do you think would be particularly helpful in relation to the students needs and the accommodations that you might make?

What support would you like?

What do you think are staff attitudes to students with dyslexia?

CHAPTER 8

Views of academic staff on support for students with dyslexia

The Singleton report (1999) recommends that the evaluation of the learning and support needs of students with dyslexia requires, amongst other things, the understanding of the demands of the student's higher education course and the type of technology and other support available. Many universities nowadays have available not only support for students struggling with the development of their literacy and numeracy skills but also specific support for students with dyslexia. This support is supplied by central student services and aims to meet many of the needs of these students regardless of their disciplinary affiliation. However, these central services, although clearly of enormous importance to students, are not the only possible sources of support. Academic staff within students' courses may be able to provide subject-specific support which responds directly to the issues arising in related to the development of discipline-specific knowledge and skills. So, not only may many tutors on a student's course give concessions in relation to examinations and other assessment, but they may also provide modified or additional materials and advice on learning strategies, and they might also take other courses of action which will facilitate the learning and coping of students with dyslexia. In order to investigate this aspect of support, two types of data were collected from staff in one university: first, questionnaire data (see Chapter 7 and Appendix) and, second, individual interview material (see description of interview in Chapter 7).

In the questionnaire, staff were asked if any of a list of allowances/types of assistance were given within their department for students with dyslexia. The answers are summarized in Table 8.1 below.

As Singleton (1999) reported, virtually all higher education institutions allow extra time for students with dyslexia in examinations, although the amount allowed is variable. The lower percentage of staff

Table 8.1. Frequency and percentages of staff responding to questions on types of support provided for students with dyslexia within their departments

Type of support	No. of staff giving	% of staff giving
Help: extra time in exams.	26	76.5
Help: extra time for assignments	13	38.2
Amanuensis in exams	3	8.8
Reader in exams	3	8.8
Use of word processor in exams	11	32.4
Support tuition/training in skills such as essay-writing, note-taking, etc.	10	29.4
Advice on study strategies and skills	15	44.1
Counselling on coping with dyslexia	8	23.5
Other:		
Advice to go to central support services	3	8.8
OU tutor: OU provided extensive information and support and advice on helping individuals with dyslexia	1	2.9

reporting the allowance of extra time in this survey merely reflects the differing types of assessment required by different courses. Quite a number of university courses do not have an examination requirement but use continuous assessment by assignment, observation of practice and other means. It can be concluded therefore that 33 per cent of tutors who responded to the survey taught on courses that were not assessed by examination. One might have expected that extra time for assignments might be a more common practice but only 38 per cent endorsed this as a practice. Extra time for assignments can of course be seen as a mixed blessing. If the course has a number of assignments with staggered deadlines then later submission of one assignment will have knock-on effects for the time available to the student for the submission of subsequent pieces of work. On the other hand, if the work is a one-off cumulative piece within a course which demands finding and organizing materials, competing for reading material, etc., or if several deadlines fall together (as may happen with Joint Honours courses) then extra time may be helpful to a student with dyslexia. Extra time may also be helpful if deadlines are not staggered and several submissions are required at the same time. In particular this may occur in a multi-disciplinary course or combined/joint honours courses.

Of the other supports that might be provided in examinations the use of a word-processor was most commonly endorsed (32 per cent). Clearly, if a student has difficulties with the production of legible hand-writing or in writing with sufficient speed then if they are proficient in the use of a word-processor this will be a great benefit – to both student and tutor. The use of a word-processor also gives access to spellchecking and this again can be a great benefit to the reader. Over and above the use of a spellchecker, other more sophisticated packages are available to assist in the production of text, such as Text-help (word prediction software), voice-input software and text-to-speech software. Ideally, the recommendations as to the necessity for a student to use these should be included in the initial assessment of the student's needs.

A small proportion of staff also endorsed the use of a reader and/or an amanuensis in examinations. These supports will be necessary for a small number of students with severe difficulties. The fact that a relatively small number of staff endorsed their use within the department does not mean that other departments would not countenance their use, but merely signifies that the staff in this survey had not experienced the practice of the use of these supports.

Less than half the staff in this survey had given specific advice to students with dyslexia on study strategies and only 29 per cent reported tutoring the students in relation to their essay-writing, note-taking, etc. Some staff had sent students to the central support unit for students with literacy and numeracy difficulties and a few reported counselling students in relation to their coping as a dyslexic person. These results suggest that many of the respondents to the survey had little direct contact with students with dyslexia in relation to their learning and studying problems. It must be noted of course that the response rate to the survey was low (38 per cent) and it seems likely that those who responded were those who were generally sympathetic to the needs of dyslexic students. Indeed, all the respondents replied in the affirmative to the question 'In your opinion is it appropriate for universities to admit people with dyslexia as students to courses in your discipline?', though some added a reservation about certain courses, e.g. 'Certain disciplines such as typographic design would not be appropriate for a sufferer' or 'However, they may find getting a job difficult'. On the other hand, many lecturers commented on the intelligence, creativity and high levels of achievement of some dyslexic individuals. It seems possible – though not tested – that some of the staff who failed to reply might be less understanding and supportive in their attitudes. Therefore, we can tentatively conclude that, even within a supportive group of staff, less than half had direct contact with students with dyslexia regarding their learning needs and, if responses were available from all academic staff, we might well find others who were less supportive and constructive in their approach.

Some ways of supporting students with dyslexia

As described in the previous chapter, semi-structured interviews were conducted individually with nine tutors from different disciplines across the University who volunteered to help. In these interviews the following were discussed: the nature of the difficulties that individuals with dyslexia studying their course might encounter, and staff perceptions of their needs (reported and discussed in the previous chapter), staff accommodations and support for dyslexic students and the type of support which the staff themselves would like to receive in relation to the support of dyslexic students. The latter are reported and discussed in this chapter.

Computing and Maths

This tutor had also worked as a tutor for the Open University and the ways of supporting students she describes here are based mainly on that experience. She explained that, as one might expect, as a centre for distance learning, the Open University catered for the learning needs of a much higher proportion of students with disabilities than might be found in location-based universities. She also explained that the Open University carried out a careful assessment of the needs of these students, advised tutors in relation to these needs and resourced the support that it gave to disabled students by paying tutors to give individual tutorials to these students and to develop resources which met their individual needs.

Reading

This tutor had worked with one student who had been fairly recently identified as dyslexic. This student had difficulty coping with the reading demands of the texts provided since, as noted in the preceding chapter, texts on database design, theory of relational databases and relational algebra are densely written and include many technical terms. She said: 'My student at the OU, I ended up writing a glossary for him with every month's work that he was given to do, the material that he was given . . . I did it electronically and emailed it, put it on a computer conference form for the rest of the students as well. It was all in alphabetical order. If a term just required a one sentence explanation I would include it in the glossary, whereas if it was something that required more than that I would put in a reference to the actual book, chapter or page that he had to look at to find the information . . . I colour-coded it as well, so that anything . . . anything to do with programming was blue so I just highlighted it and gave it a blue background. Everything to do with the theory behind programming was pink. So we just picked a different colour for each . . . sort of theme . . . and we colour-coded the glossary to match. So that if he was looking for something to do with programming and he wanted some practical examples he would look at all the blue things and it meant he didn't have to skim through the whole glossary . . . He couldn't skim read, he couldn't quickly run a finger down a page and find what he was looking for. He had to read in detail in order to be able to understand what the glossary terms were. It was a mixture of an index and a glossary. If the term in the glossary was a complex one and needed some examples then I would index the notes rather than actually including it. I might put the definition there and then say for examples colour-coded yellow please go to Unit 3 page 12–13 and I would actually put paragraph headings as well. With a normal student if you sent them to a page they would just look at the paragraph headings and say "Oh this is the one that I want", but with him you actually had to direct him specifically to the bit that you wanted him to read . . . to save him time because otherwise he wouldn't get through it."

She went on to explain that the syntax of programming languages and database languages also causes difficulty to dyslexic students because everything must be spelt absolutely correctly and the words must also be in the correct sequence. She found that dyslexic students often had difficulty with syntax, more so than the other students. She suggested the following approach to helping students with this problem: 'In the course material that we give them we tend to have examples and . . . some kind of index to the examples would be a help, so that instead of having to skim through weeks upon weeks of notes to find an example of what they're trying to do, if we could just index that directly . . . so if you want to do [a particular routine] this is exactly where you'll find it, Week 3 page 2. Because they're often a lot slower at reading than the normal students and I think they give up more easily when they can't find what they're looking for . . . And then we put all the materials on the Intranet any way. It should be relatively easy to create an index of that kind that takes them directly to the bit that they need . . . It's just time though isn't it . . . And it's time for every unit isn't it . . . it's not really just the programming unit or just the database unit. Most of our units have a technical content . . . so every time new unit material is developed it means remembering to update the index or the glossary.'

Organization

This tutor also described how she helped this Open University student overcome his organizational problems: 'The OU paid for me to do it.

They paid for me to go and give individual tutorials. Extra tutorials are given if the student asks for them. They used to pay me to go down to T . . . to do extra sessions with him to try and help him organize. He had a study with the computer in and all his colour-coded notes. He didn't leave things on the computer he used to print them out. He was more comfortable with hard copy than he was with soft . . . So he used to print them out with all the colour and file them away. He had plastic covers on his wall and the different colours went into the different covers, like a magazine rack . . . And he had to keep organized. Whenever we finished a session he would gather together all the papers we had discussed and code them himself and file them away before I left . . . If he left them and came back to them an hour or two later he wouldn't remember what we had been discussing and so he wouldn't be able to find his work. If we had a system like that . . . If we had a colour-coded index, or even one online that we updated every week, so that we added the new terms and colour-coded those. It wouldn't be a vast amount of work.'

Assessment

This student also had problems in following exam questions in these courses. These questions were more complex than the standard essay type question. He needed someone to read the question and re-read it whenever needed. She said: 'He said that he understood the spoken word a lot more easily than he understood the written word. And if I read the question out he said "Oh, that's quite straightforward" and if I reread the bits that were appropriate at the right time he seemed to like that because it jogged his memory as well. He might not have got back to the written word to try to reread it because of the problems he had.'

Within this department, if necessary, students might use a word-processor incorporating spell- and grammar-checkers rather than hand-write an exam. The tutor explained, 'You can get intelligent agents now for computers where if you type something in Word and click on the agent it'll actually read it back to you. It speaks to you and has a speech synthesizer that can recognize the written word. So if they were in a room on their own and had that facility as well that would surely help. You could have the paper on the computer and have it read to you.'

Additional suggestions for strategies to support students with problematic aspects of the course

This tutor also commented that many students had problems with the symbolic notation used in relational algebra and that this must be particularly problematical for dyslexic students. She said that 'one member of staff has been developing a textual version of the algebra in which the terms are written out as text'. She also mentioned other graphical tools they might develop to assist students in their use of notation and in programming. She felt that these would be helpful to all students but would be particularly helpful to students with dyslexia.

Education

This tutor considered that many of her students had problems with the literacy demands of the course and that dyslexic students were on the extreme of a continuum rather than isolated in their difference from others. This tutor saw many of her students as requiring support in writing and coping with their workloads, therefore she talked in a more general way about supporting students who were struggling, rather than addressing the specific needs of dyslexic students. Most of the tutors, at some point in our discussions, made the observation that the support provided for dyslexic students would probably also be helpful to other students who were struggling with aspects of the course, but were not considered to be dyslexic. She said: 'I think as a department we're very committed to supporting students in need and in terms of the support for those with more extreme problems, individual students might have a mentor specifically.'

Support for difficulties with all aspects of course

She said: 'We provide quite a lot of support, intersessional support for grammar and for spelling. We've tried to be responsive, I think – but less than we would like to be just because of the pressures we're under. But what we're trying to do now . . . we're changing really. We're having to change our whole teaching style. So we're looking actually at delivering notes to students beforehand . . . we're looking at ways of bringing in support materials for students . . . Actually we're planning a course for next year where we've started off with a reasonably traditional model and we've just swung it round and are looking at . . . students taking on much more responsibility, you know, for their own learning and taking on ideas. But, as always, when you're re-creating courses, you're looking more creatively at teaching and learning. So we're looking at accessing the students earlier to very specific aspects of the course – to viewpoints. So we're looking to actually highlighting the analytical aspect much earlier . . . Where we used to leave it to individual students to do . . . we're now building that into the courses in a much more structured way. And then we're looking for more presentation of ideas back from the students.' This tutor suggested that staff must take their students as they find them and attempt to provide sufficient support for all in entering a taxing profession. She said: 'We want to provide the support for the students who are coming through and we actually think that we're doing that primarily by the way that we're changing the delivery of the course . . . A lot more study support material that we're putting out by emailing, making available our lecture notes beforehand.' However, she did add that, despite all their efforts to provide support, students must be acquainted with a large body of ideas and knowledge. She said: 'I would imagine that one of the biggest pressures would be the amount students have to read in the future.'

Use of group support and feedback

She explained that students would often be given a task to do as a group and that their participation in carrying out the task, the roles that they took and the skills and competencies they showed would be monitored and assessed as part of a group, allowing the students opportunities to reflect on their strengths and weaknesses in comparison to their peers. She said: 'Now each of those directed intersessional tasks will go into a booklet and be explicitly monitored and assessed in each of the sessions . . . and this will actually highlight the skills involved, so the group's skills will be addressed within each of the directed tasks. What are your strengths in this situation? Which things do you find difficult? And then we're going to build that into tutorial support and look at how you would actually target steps forward in particular areas.'

Organization

When questioned about the burden of assignments and how dyslexic students might be supported with these she responded: 'I think all of us as tutors highlight to students at the beginning of the year that they do need to start planning for this now. I think once you're experienced and know your course, you know what will happen if you don't actually alert students to it. So we tend to have signpost points for them. Plan it in – this is what you're going to do. We actually have sessions on assignments, so any difficulties or misunderstandings about that can be cleared up . . . We used to find they would get mixed messages from one tutor to another. So what we do now is have a whole-year group session where we actually address that as a year group and talk through issues so people can bring up what they're concerned about . . . and their misconceptions.'

The identification of dyslexia

Because of this approach to student needs as a continuum there was no specific approach to identification of dyslexic students, although the problems of dyslexia were recognized. This tutor said in relation to the identification of dyslexia: 'We do sessions on dyslexia. Students will sometimes come through from that – or quite often to do with their children.' In other words, when students received information about the nature of dyslexia they sometimes recognized their own difficulties in the description. Students also sometimes found that a child of their own was struggling inexplicably with literacy and other aspects of life, and when their child was identified as dyslexic they realized that they themselves had similar problems.

Engineering

This tutor had experience of one or two individuals with dyslexia on his courses. He also spoke of an extremely successful young academic engineer with dyslexia who had won a highly rated prize.

Reading

The tutor explained how he had sometimes recommended to students with language problems texts which were more accessible in terms of their writing style. In this subject, therefore, it is possible to recommend simpler texts for those with dyslexic problems since the reading that is recommended is all found in textbooks. Research-based journal papers are not considered useful at undergraduate level.

Self-advocacy

This lecturer emphasized how important it was for the dyslexic student to seek out the lecturer and explain his/her difficulties: 'If they don't go out of their way to come to you, then there's not a lot you can do . . . So in many ways, until they come to terms with it – I suppose they must come to terms with it and be comfortable with it sometime – until they come to terms with it they probably are their own worst enemy in some ways . . . not taking advantage of these concessions that people realize that they need.' He was very sympathetic to the needs of dyslexic students, having a dyslexic son himself. However, he recognized that dyslexia is manifested very differently in many cases and therefore that one could not just make blanket arrangements for all students. He felt that it was important that the students should know that tutors were sympathetic to their problems and could be approached for help. He said: 'I would rather be able to talk to them face to face and get them to recognize that I am a human being and that I know what their problems are . . . that's in an ideal world.'

Identification

Along with several other members of staff who were interviewed, this lecturer said that there was a problem in that students who came to the course and had not previously been identified as being dyslexic had to pay for a full assessment if this was recommended by the support services. This was regarded as a discriminatory practice: students from more affluent backgrounds were able to call upon their parents to support them and pay the fee (£160 at the time of these interviews), but students struggling financially might well be put off by what would amount to perhaps one months rent, a substantial outlay. He added: 'Indeed the thought of going into higher education may have put you off with your disability because you might not have thought that this was available. So perhaps that should be made known in the early schooling years so that . . . If in fact you think your child is dyslexic and it's going to cost £280 up front to get a test done, if the result is negative then . . . good. If it's positive then . . . OK then it opens the door to all of these other journeys . . . the money's coming back on itself . . . but you know people do not know these things and I find it very sad really.'

Drama

Evidence here is given from two interviews, one with the course leader for the drama course, a Performing Arts course within the School of Art, and one from the Tutorial Adviser for the School of Art.

Identification

In drama, as in other visual and performing arts courses, dyslexia is regarded as relatively common. So, on the question of identification, the course leader said: 'It is something that we are very aware of and we try to pick it up as quickly as possible. I mean often we know because they tell us and they bring in their documentation, etc. and that information comes through to us. But what we also do is we have a guidance unit. We have an intensive two-week guidance unit at the beginning of the year which is a model which we have borrowed from our media colleagues. Actually that works extremely well because what that does is it allows us to give the students an induction into the course and combine it with elements of practice. Everybody goes to the theatre, we go to see a particular show . . . And part of the assessment for that is a critical review of whatever theatre visit we undertake as a group. And that's handed in within three or four weeks of the students starting . . . Partly that gets over the dreadful anxiety about completing your first university assignment, but that also enables us to pick up straight away anybody that we think might be struggling and see them and try and assess what the situation is in relation to it . . . Obviously we try to make sure that the right sort of support is put in place as soon as possible. So, in the feedback from their assignment, the student will be asked to actually see the tutor who marked it. So you'll have an opportunity to discuss with them. If they've done very badly, it may be case of referring them to the student support systems we have here in the University, or, if not, just identifying them within our course team as a student who is going to need support. But [in extreme cases] it also is a way of finding out whether that student is dyslexic and hasn't actually got appropriate things in place.'

The tutorial adviser added: 'In Performing Arts, I expect all staff to let me know of any problems with particular students and then I'll ask to see those students. We generally, all of us, are involved in marking the first assignment students do in the Guidance Unit. And we share those out among all the staff. And they'll pick up on any particular students who seem to have a problem there, and either I'll get their course leaders to see them or I'll see them.' He said that, initially: 'Some identify themselves and some-times you pick it up through the paperwork, but you don't always.' Students may not always admit their dyslexia on their admissions forms for a number of reasons, the two main ones being that either they fear they might be rejected because of their dyslexia or they do not want to be considered to be different from others. The tutorial adviser said: 'We generally find all sorts of problems about people who think they're dyslexic or they've lost the forms that say they are . . . it's a nightmare usually.' This he explained was due to the organizational difficulties of the students – endemic in their dyslexia. Difficulty in organizing their paperwork was part of the whole picture and of course added to the students' problems in gaining admission to a university course and in finding support. This tutor was, however, very active in seeking support for those who were identified as potentially dyslexic and wished for help. He would immediately refer them to the central support services for assessment. He said: 'The student services are very good I find. They can even lend them [the students] the money that they need. They lend them the money out of the Hardship Fund or somewhere like that to actually get the tests done if they need them done because they do cost over £150 . . . And then when they get their money they can pay that back.' Not all tutors interviewed were apparently aware of this (see the comments from the Engineering and the Health Studies tutors).

Writing

These tutors were very aware of the difficulties some of their students had with writing. Assessment is largely practice-based, but writing is involved in this too. Students were expected to keep a journal as a reflective practitioner in many of the units on this course. The course leader said: 'Last year students were required to hand in a full journal which could be a big file if they're documenting what they've done in each session and the work that's set in directed learning time and independent learning time . . . Now we've altered our practice to try to accommodate the needs of those students [those with writing problems]. So what we've done now is to ask students to just hand in a 2000 word synopsis, because the journal has a weighting in the assessment of some units. Which means they can keep their own notes in whatever way they see fit, be it on tape or whatever form it suits them which means that it doesn't have to be a written . . . I mean not that it ever had to be typed . . . but it doesn't have to be written in the same way.'

Reading

The course leader pointed out that in a drama course students will have to do a lot of reading. She explained some of the accommodations they made in order to lessen the burden of this for students with difficulties: 'The students have to do a lot of reading. . . . For example, in the first year I teach textual analysis. In that unit we use about six play scripts . . . It became apparent last year with a student on that course who was dyslexic, that actually asking them to read a play over the space of a week and to keep the journal and to work towards their assignment work was just far too much . . . So now, all the students are given the information about that unit way in advance so that they can get hold of the play copies . . . and for that particular student what I did was actually indicate which scenes we would be working on . . . so that if he actually physically could not read the play in the time that was available to him then he could [read the scenes in question].' The tutorial adviser also explained in addition that: 'What we would do is . . . working in drama we work in circles, obviously you know, so where you start can be significant. So we'll tend to avoid the student having to do that if we can. But the other thing is, if it's a small group we might give that particular student the piece the day before and say have a look at this before it comes round to the session.' These tutors also supported students in their writing by suggesting they hand in a draft of their ideas or a draft version for comment before the final submission (see quotes below under *Encouraging self-advocacy*).

Encouraging self-advocacy

Like many other tutors, the course leader also pointed out the importance of the student being willing to take responsibility for their difficulties and to look for help, if necessary. In order to encourage this from the beginning of the course she said: 'Again we have a culture that is very much about students being encouraged to seek support. So for example we may identify a student in the guidance unit who is struggling academically . . . The next assignment would be due in just before Christmas, which is their theoretical assignment for Semester 1 in the theory unit . . . we encourage students to hand in drafts or to hand in structures and staff will always make themselves available to read students' work. We spend a lot of time on supporting students in actually writing assignments . . . because again, because they're artists, the writing's sometimes something that can be . . . not even just for dyslexic students but for every student it's something that can be quite a traumatic undertaking.'

Note-taking

This course leader recognized the difficulty that dyslexic students may have with note-taking and said that: 'In the lecture-based aspect of the course . . . those sessions tend to be pretty interactive and we don't tend to just spout . . . I will prepare handouts with the key points and give them out, so students don't have to make notes in the same way . . . so they can just annotate and add, rather than sitting trying to scribble down notes . . . Also at the beginning of each session I always get two or three tape recorders, which again is absolutely fine. It's not a problem. It's just trying to think how to best support them.'

Assessment.

In relation to assessment, the course leader explained: 'We are a practice-based course so students don't suffer the pressure of exams. We use continuous assessment a lot, but we obviously have sound theoretical underpinnings that follow the practice through . . . These tend to be assessed by a combination of assignments and seminars . . . The vast majority of the assessment in the practice-based units is purely on process, contribution to the sessions, taking part in, devising, the research for the role and then actually the performance itself. And that's the same across drama and performance. They're very heavily practice-based.' Therefore, with students with dyslexia, the outcomes looked for are assessed far less by written output than on many other University courses.

Course approach to teaching, learning and student support

This course leader discussed the ethos of the courses which, she suggested, tried to engender a cooperative, inclusive, group work approach, appropriate to work in drama and supportive to all students. She said: 'Particularly in the drama courses there's such a huge emphasis on group work and supporting each other in the group. Actually, in both courses, because the nature of our work involves a certain amount of self-exposure, within a sort of safe . . . through the safety of fiction if you like, we have to encourage an openness and an ability to support one another and allow each other permission to take risks in performance. And those foundations are laid very early on in the course. So again, I think that's probably something hopefully everyone experiences.'

Organization.

In relation to self-organization problems, she also said that the particular demands of the course may be in some ways helpful to dyslexic students: 'I think the point about the drama course in particular is that it . . . the organization of self is always in relation to other. So [a particular dyslexic student] has had to organize himself throughout the year in order to be able to work with these other groups of people. And that shifts the emphasis outside yourself and I think it sharpens up the need to organize, and I think that people organize better because they're organizing for other people in a sense . . . you know he would tend to be late for ordinary classes, but when he was running the sessions he would always be there on time.'

Emotional adjustment and mental health.

When considering the problems of anxiety and low self-esteem, which can be very intrusive for students with dyslexia, this course leader was also quite positive about the particularly supportive role a drama course might play. She said: 'I guess the thing about drama is that it allows you the opportunity to fail, in the sense that the role that that you take is not you . . . and therefore, if it doesn't work out, it doesn't really matter because it's not you it's somebody else.' But, on the other hand, when the interviewer made the assumption that all students entering in to drama courses must be extraverts who loved an audience, she also added: 'I think there might be a tendency to underestimate the difficulty for some students [of drama] of speaking out in front of others, particularly if their self-esteem has been damaged over the years.' She cited the case of one particular student who had eventually been very successful, saying: 'He would be very quiet generally in class . . . not in practical work . . . but certainly otherwise he would tend to be quiet. But he'd be taking it all in. And always on a one-to-one he was very good.'

Supporting all students.

This tutor, along with several others, also said: 'I think some of the things that you put in place to support dyslexic students are actually good for all students. They're not massive steps to just provide that level of support. And I see students like the one I was telling you about – what a fantastic achievement.'

Staff attitudes

The course leader and the tutorial adviser both considered that, within their department, staff were supportive of students with dyslexia. The tutorial adviser was very interested in helping and supporting students with dyslexia and played a major role in facilitating their access to disability awards. He had established a good relationship with the student support services in relation to students with disabilities and their applications for financial support. He said: 'Staff are aware that it is a genuine problem and do what they can to support students but, obviously, increasingly given the numbers of students we have to deal with and the time constraints we face, you have to be certain that the student is helping themselves as well. That's why I make this particular effort to see that they have the computer equipment and software from the very beginning. If need be I write to the local authority and support the application.'

Staff support and information

The tutorial adviser also explained: 'Each year I check up on what the current state of things is with regard to awards there are available to students and I circulate either all new staff or if it's changed in any major way I circulate everybody in the school and let them know. So I circulate this basic information at least once a year.'

Health Studies

Identification

As noted in the previous chapter, this tutor emphasized the advantages in supporting learning given by the size of the course. She said: 'Our advantage is that we're a small course . . . and I know every single student . . . over the whole three years we have about 86. I can tell you all their names. I can tell you roughly all their profiles, simply because we're small . . . So in some ways for a student with a problem coming onto our course I think we're well placed (a) to pick it up and (b) to put something in place to help the student . . . Through our feedback and discussions with colleagues we are able to pick it up but I think where students are on huge courses doing units from all sorts of different divisions, where one tutor will mark that student's work and never see the student again . . . I wonder what kind of picture is picked up.'

A direct approach to the identification of students with difficulties and students with dyslexia was taken on this course. The tutor said: 'We have a study skills chunk at the beginning of year one which we're extending now that we do progress files in a more formal way and we're actually taking it right through the first semester, one hour a week.' In the course of this unit, the tutor would expect to identify any student who was struggling.

An additional problem, also noted by other tutors was the cost of the initial assessment for dyslexia. She remarked that some students on entry came to her and said they were 'mildly dyslexic'. When asked if she then recommended these students to go for a full assessment she said: 'Certainly but those that come with a mild problem don't usually take that up because, of course there's a big problem, they have to pay . . . I mean I think that's appalling how the government is looking for widening education and lifelong learning . . . but if this particular disability is to be identified you have to pay . . . I think the university should pay . . . with a careful filtering.'

Self-advocacy

This tutor noted that some students are reluctant to come forward and try to hide their difficulties. She felt it was important for them to realize that within their course there was a very supportive environment and it was the aim of the staff to support students through the course, rather than to try to identify those with a problem and to get rid of them. If the student has actually managed to pass all the hurdles and achieved admission to the University then the course tutors view their learning needs sympathetically, as long as the students themselves are prepared to put in the work to help themselves. This tutor said: 'Shy bairns get nowt . . . they do struggle and we say come and talk to us, go to your unit tutor or your guidance tutor or me as course leader . . . and it's almost like some of these students need assertiveness training . . . unless you come forward . . . but if they've spent their whole formal education at the margins you know . . . to suddenly walk in and say I've got this essay to write, and I think I'm going to do it this way can you help me please . . . it's hard for them . . . but it does happen eventually . . . I hope.' But she added that quite often it is the students with problems that don't come forward, that do not attend personal tutorials intended to help them. As she said: 'Some of the students get to year two and they still haven't had a personal tutorial. They haven't been to see anyone. You can follow them up . . . but they don't come . . .' She added: 'I think it's a problem within our whole educational structures. We're picking up some casualties which have made it, but I wonder how many others people out there just are lost.'

Writing

The assessment for a number of the units on this course depends on the writing of essays of a social science type. This tutor agreed with the interviewer's interjection that learning to write good prose is hard. However, she explained that because they recognized the difficulties of a number of students, support for writing was built into the course. She said: 'Writing well is very hard . . . but most of our students who do struggle get a lot of support from me and the study skills centre. They do use it. And we bring in the staff as well every now and then to do support sessions. We book them and they do a session with our students. Even for our third years who by this time one would like to think would have cracked it, to get at least a flow in writing . . . they come in at level three and what they do is very focused in terms of the students managing the whole of their dissertation report-writing . . . It's more to do with organized writing at that level and time management . . . which you know can add to the pressure which makes their writing wobbly.'

Course approach to teaching, learning and student support

This tutor also described how the course was structured towards the gradual development of the necessary skills to produce the third year research dissertation which was considered the culmination of the students' work. This approach is very different from that inherent in some degrees where students may accumulate modules of different types according to their preferences and what is available, but progression in the acquisition of particular skills cannot be achieved in the same way. She described the build up of research skills through a number of units: 'In Year 2, in a collaborative supported way, they actually do research and write it up, so they've had a kind of rehearsal if you like, for when they come to do their own. And I have a whole unit in the first semester of Year 3 where we look at proposal development . . . And, you know, the proof of the pudding – it's in their final dissertation . . . where they bring in the health analysis, they bring in the research, they bring in the writing and of course the big thing is communication.'

Individual case example

This tutor described in detail the type of support they were able to give to a young student who had been identified as having difficulties after starting the course: 'There was one particular young student . . . we picked up in Year 1 that she was struggling. Her writing was peculiar, that's the only way I can describe it, and she seemed to have more trouble with anything to do with numbers. We set things in motion and she was fully assessed . . . it came back that she had dyscalculia. I'd never heard of it. Well of course there are no tutors in the way there are for dyslexia . . . but she was supported by the dyslexia tutor who helped her through the whole three years. She dropped honours because that was too much pressure, so she could do ten units rather than twelve . . . Her spelling was fine. It wasn't a spelling problem. But no capital letters . . . no punctuation . . . She got a computer from the disability allowance . . . she's from a family without a previous history of university education and they were so proud that she'd got here and she was so, so committed . . . never missed a session, very reliable, did her group presentation, did her stand up stuff when she had to. Very shy, but always did it . . . She wasn't learning a language. She started one . . . But it was very difficult for her to combine all the different types of learning . . . Her research was local. She didn't go away. It was her choice. And you know she wrote a report, and the writing was so good, I mean it was just . . . and I thought "Look at that . . . it's been worth it." And for her own personal standing . . . she got there . . . and she wrote coherently around nutrition and young people and culture . . . you know it was very good.'

When questioned about the effect of dyscalculia on the student's ability to cope with the statistical aspects of research the tutor responded: 'You know we tried to steer her more towards qualitative work . . . but she did produce graphs. There was no statistical analysis other than frequency charts . . . but she could handle that . . . she'd worked through enough preparation to be able to do that . . . So that was fascinating because, as I say I'd never heard of it before, and I really feel we were right to support her and keep her.'

To sum up her own feelings, the tutor said: 'I think she'll be fine, she'll be fine. She knew she had a problem at school, but because she's so determined . . . we're not looking at first class honours, but you know the value-added bit of her being here . . . She matured, she accepted that she has a difficulty but she worked with computers to produce a dissertation, I mean . . . you know tremendous. And we did our bit, but a lot of work went on behind the scenes with the dyslexia tutor . . . without that support I don't know how the student would have coped, so we thanked her for that . . . And you know there's so much of a kind of human thing in it . . . it's more than what's going on in here . . . I think you've got to look at what's going on, not the person or the subject. I like to think we're tuned in to give people a chance.'

History

The experience of tutors from different courses of students with dyslexia was very varied. Some had several students with varying degrees of severity of dyslexia every year and some had only come across one instance of the problem. It seems clear that individuals with these difficulties tend to be fairly selective in their approach to university courses and, in all likelihood, tend to have developed skills in particular areas less dependent on literacy, which compensate for their other weaknesses. They therefore will look for openings in areas which call for the particular skills with which they feel competent. Thus Drama might have two or three students with dyslexia a year, but the tutor from the History Department who was interviewed had experience of teaching only one student with dyslexia during his eight years of teaching at the University.

This tutor, teaching on a course where words, language and argument are the essence, said, in relation to supporting the learning of students, that 'We tend to look at the written output at the end and perhaps we should pay a bit more attention to how the dyslexic students deal with the earlier stages of this process starting with the lectures.'

Individual case example

This tutor had had no previous experience of dyslexia until he had become involved recently with the case of one student, identified as dyslexic prior to reaching the University. He described the important roles of the student support services and the student's own acknowledgement of his problems and willingness to work on them. He described the difficulties that he observed in the student's writing and how his skills in this area evolved and developed with the aid of the student support services. He said: 'One of the things he mentioned was . . . the problem of not simply formulating correct sentences but also, in a way more significantly from the point of view of historical work, of formulating an argument. And I'd noticed that in some of his essays. Some of the essays I marked at around 57 or 58 where there was quite a bit of material there but the argument hadn't been developed as well as it might be. And that's something I know he's had counselling with or advice . . . from the student services in terms of trying to set out at the beginning what the essay question's about and so on. He's certainly made a serious attempt to overcome his difficulties. When he talks about it explicitly then it makes it much easier for a tutor to respond constructively.'

Marking

This tutor considered the suggestion that, since dyslexia affects skills and activities which are completely integral to one's development as a student of history, it might be appropriate to make some allowance for this at the point when marking is carried out, in the marking process. He said: 'I did have a discussion with a former external [examiner] about this particular student actually, in terms of whether we should make allowances in our actual marking, and basically his line was that really we should just mark it as it is, like the others . . . obviously you don't penalize for poor spelling and stuff like that, but you mark as is and then leave it to the procedures relating to mitigating factors. Which I think is probably the fairest way to do it. To make allowances or some marks . . . that would be too difficult.' However, he was advocating the position that dyslexia could be seen as a chronic problem which could be considered as an 'extenuating circumstance' or mitigating factor when it came to the discussion of marks, the passing and failing of units and the allocation of degree categories.

Note-taking

A comprehensive unit guide is provided by the tutor. He saw no problem in students tape-recording lectures if that was necessary to them.

Staff attitudes

He felt that there was a positive attitude within his department towards this student's disability and said: 'We've not really discussed it as a group, but, talking to individual members of staff about this student, there was a positive attitude to his disability.'

Identification

Since dyslexia had rarely been encountered in the students taking History courses to date, no particular procedures were in place to identify their difficulties. In relation to more general skills difficulties which students might have, this tutor said that there was a unit which aimed to address the development of basic skills necessary for the course, but he said, 'Some of the students don't seem to see the relevance of it.' The unit was under review by a working party.

Psychology

Course approach to teaching, learning and student support

In psychology, on quite a large course with an intake of around 90–100 students a year, the experience was that perhaps one student a year might be identified as being dyslexic, usually before they entered the University. Little direct acknowledgement of this was made at the point of learning. However, the production of substantial handouts was the norm for all lecturers. No lecturer would object to a student tape-recording his/her lectures or seminars, and advice was given on appropriate software for use on the course if the student was seeking advice on the use of their Disability Allowance. The importance of good writing in essay-type examinations and in reports of empirical projects was stressed, as these form the bulk of assessments. Students could go to the central services for support but there was no direct involvement with these on the part of the department. Extra time was given to students in examinations.

Staff awareness

The tutor explained that, although all staff would have knowledge of dyslexia as defined in the research literature, most would have little practical experience of the range of functional difficulties involved: 'I think, if there's a lack of knowledge then there really has to be some sort of dissemination of knowledge about (1) the various sorts of difficulties that individual students might have, (2) under what sorts of learning context they're likely to arise and be emphasized, and (3) strategies in a sense for intervention and then you can know in advance well if there's going to be difficulties here how can you cope with that. My feeling is that we don't think along those lines at all. We concentrate on teaching delivery and structuring that most efficiently. You might consider, OK, how do I deliver this in relation to individuals who struggle with a topic or individuals who are very competent with a topic so there'll be that sort of mixed ability consideration, but you can have that, I think, without thinking explicitly about individuals who are going to have particular difficulties. So, in that sense, for me the best way to approach it is to formalize the process so that we have an idea of where the difficulties are.'

Fashion Marketing

Course approach to teaching, learning and student support

In most departments in the University, teaching and learning takes part in groups of varying sizes apart from occasional one-to-one tuition in personal tutorials. However within the School of Art and Design within which this course was situated, one-to-one teaching is the everyday norm. The tutor explained that: 'They're lectured in a large group and we see them in a studio as large groups, but they're set tasks and you see them once or twice in that day for 10 minutes. So your day is divided into 10–minute slots. So they will see somebody once or twice in that day and then they have to get on with the next bit and the next bit. But then you might see them twice in a week, you know on two separate days in that week, that group'. *Interviewer:* '*So they're very much in here working every day?*' Tutor: 'They're in here 5 days a week.' *Interviewer: 'Having very regular short slots of input?'* Tutor: 'Right, and that's how you get to know them personally and you can help them. And then they get obviously personal tutorials as well which are a longer stretch, 20 minutes. But you're there, going through their course with them if you like. And there are times when you have to see more of them and there are times you can see less. But they're generally on the premises and around somewhere. So I feel like you live through their difficulties with them. It's quite a guiding role that we play with them through the projects that they have to do . . . it's not that distant lecturing role at all. So, in terms of support, because we teach the students on a one-to-one basis and there are 40 students in a year, it is quite hard work. But we give them personal support in that we treat every one as an individual.

General support

This tutor reported that, after a student had been identified as dyslexic, use was made of the central student support services, as well as concessions being made within the department. 'And what we would do is to give someone with dyslexia an extension so that we would say look we know you've got difficulties here. And we would try and find them the extra help in terms of referring them through to the central learning support services or if it caused other difficulties we would refer them to student counselling.'

Identification

The arrangements for identification were not as clear-cut as in the drama course but the tutor was fairly confident that a student's problems would be soon recognized. She said: 'But the minute you get the first assignment back you would realize there were problems . . . and you can tell also in the organization of the work, how they approach the work. I mean I would say that I think that most people would come to us those that stand out . . . And some will come with a certificate.'

Admissions

This tutor pointed out that for a course like hers and for others in the Art and Design Department, the most important criterion for admission was not the students' A Level grades but their ability to produce interesting and creative design work. In relation to admissions, she said: 'It's more to do with . . . in terms of A Levels grades we ask for C and above . . . but we look at their portfolios . . . and we look at any grades, and you get some students with fantastically talented portfolios and we just wouldn't bother to think about a grade particularly. We take them on . . . it's them, what they can offer and what we can offer them, in terms of their potential . . . and you know what gives you the greatest satisfaction is that you can take somebody on and see a huge improvement. It's a four year course. They do a year in industry and we see a massive improvement in some students . . . well, it's not a massive improvement, it's really them achieving their potential. There must be many out there that never get a chance . . . it's such a shame, you could almost open a dyslexic art college.'

Emotional adjustment and mental health

This tutor was very aware of the extra stress and anxiety suffered by many students with dyslexia due to problems with organization, multitasking and literacy demands. She said: 'What I've seen in dyslexic students is just a complete breakdown almost . . . "I can't go on, I'm leaving, that's it. I can't handle this any more. I never want to see another garment as long as I live. I've burnt out." I've had that on a number of occasions. And it's just that they're tired out. Absolutely tired out. And what I've done on those situations . . . I don't know whether it's the right thing, I've sent them home for a week, just said "Don't even think about it, don't think about it. Just go home." And I mean I've done that three times so far. And when they've come back they've felt fine again . . . Because I thought they have to work so hard to keep up, that they've just exhausted themselves. If you take the pressure off them and I say "Look we'll give you an extension . . . Just stop there. Go home, even if it's just for a weekend or whatever, take a long weekend . . . just go and watch television, turn off." It seems to help. They've just reached the end of the line. They're completely stressed out. But I mean that happens to other students as well, not just to dyslexics. I think there's a lot of pressure on students to succeed. They come with the expectation – a lot of students – that they're going to get a good degree, almost like you can order one.'

This tutor was very aware of the ways in which emotion may affect cognition. She said: 'And the self-belief, I think, there's a problem as well . . . you know they need a lot of emotional support . . . They tend to . . . I'm thinking of individuals here. They can be on a real high and then they just hit real lows. Completely lose confidence. It's a confidence thing definitely . . . If you look at someone finding out when they're 18, 19 20, when we get them they've obviously been through quite a traumatic time coming through school . . . Thought of as lazy, idle day-dreamers . . . there's no credit given for day-dreaming which is a shame. You look at how narrow the curriculum is now. It doesn't allow for the odd and unusual. It doesn't allow for the slightly off-beat person.' She had known a student who had severe dyslexia, identified at the age of 10 and sent to a special school for children with dyslexia. She said: 'He was very lucky in that that gave him the confidence to go on . . . but he would just have been written off. But I wonder what society thinks is going to happen to those people that can't read and write when they come out?'

Staff attitudes and awareness.

This tutor, who had a dyslexic individual in her family, was very tuned in to the problems of dyslexia. She said: 'I think we could help them more than we do . . . I'm obviously very aware of all these things but I think other people probably aren't as sympathetic. May be, you know, I think that you can't help it if you've got a personal interest in these areas, being more sympathetic. And I think that what we need to do is to make it more obvious to the team members how to pick up on the students' difficulties and what strategies we can put on place for those students. I went to a conference that was held here in Visual and Performing Arts. Someone came in here and talked about dyslexia and it was so interesting . . . That's where I've gleaned most of my information . . . And she was explaining about things that you can put in place to help. I've implemented some of them myself, but getting other members of a department or team to implement those and seeing it as serious is more difficult.'

Positive side of dyslexia

This tutor also wished to stress the positive benefits of dyslexia in terms of the development of visual understanding and visual thinking. She said: 'The other side of the story is that there are things that dyslexics have got, that dyslexics have, that other people don't. And there are people lacking in the general population, who are ever so smart with the written word but who have completely no visual understanding . . . but nobody pulls them up, they don't have a hard time. But they are responsible for a lot of ugliness in the world. You think, "How can that have happened?". You know you see the monstrosities in terms of planning, town planning that go on and you just think! . . . I'm sure it's because of that and I think that causes a lot of problems in the world. And you know what someone who has that wonderful visual thinking and reasoning can come up with kind of outweighs the difficulties – well it would outweigh the difficulties in an ideal world.'

Writing and marking

This tutor discussed the case of one student with severe dyslexia and his problems with writing. She said: 'And he did everything on the computer. But a computer doesn't solve all the dyslexic skills problems . . . because you need to know quite a bit about spelling for it to help you. And I mean all his 'I's were little 'i's – never had a capital I. And there were no para-graphs, no beginnings, no ends, it was just a stream. And I marked his work and I just had to let that go really. You can't hold it against him, considering where he'd got to and how he'd got there . . . you just have to let that be. You just have to look at the content rather than the grammar. It was the content that I was looking at. And that was very good, very interesting. But, I mean it was like travel writing – it was sparky and dynamic and it started at the beginning and it ended at the end and it was like speech.'

Conclusions re support provided by academic staff

1. University staff can be extremely creative and sympathetic in their approaches to helping these students with aspects of their work. These approaches can include:

- support for writing by staged presentation of work
- assistance from the student support services in-built to the course
- aspects of the course designed to be gradually developmental to the necessary skills for all students
- lessening of the work load by the provision of additional prior information about tasks; provision of study support materials on the Web
- provision of full lecture-notes prior to lectures
- provision of materials which are organized in ways that make them easily accessible to students with dyslexia (e.g. by colour-coding).

2. Self-advocacy is of great importance. If a student has dyslexia then they can best serve their own interests by explaining and discussing their needs and difficulties with members of staff.

3. Some courses within the University have an inclusive ethos and have developed teaching and learning approaches which are designed to be supportive to all students, not only those with dyslexia.

4. Some courses within the University have specific mechanisms in place to facilitate the identification of students with literacy difficulties.

5. Some course tutors are also active in supporting students in their application for certification as dyslexic and their application for the disability allowance.

6. Some courses or disciplines will play more to the dyslexic student's strengths and will therefore be supportive to them in a major way, while others by the nature of the discipline studied will face the students with their difficulties at every turn.

7. It is important to recognize that the student with dyslexia will require not only support with learning, but also emotional support to promote self-confidence and lessen the effects of stress.

Support for academic staff

The questionnaire survey of staff (conducted in summer 2000) showed that only 4/38 (10.5 per cent) had had training in relation to dyslexia and the needs and difficulties of students with dyslexia at the university. The source of training for one respondent was not the university in which she was currently employed but the Open University, for whom she was a tutor. This respondent was very enthusiastic about the training and support given by the Open University (see comments on support above). Twenty-nine out of 38 staff (76 per cent) said that they would avail themselves of training in dealing with dyslexic students if this was available. One staff member was unsure, and eight (21 per cent) said that they would not take up such an opportunity. Some of the latter commented that they were already very pressurized with 'extra' demands and activities over and above their normal duties and that they did not feel that they would have sufficient time to take up the opportunity. Several staff made comments about the need for the raising of the awareness of university teachers about the problems and needs of dyslexic students. One respondent wrote: 'Due to many of these students being poorly organized we need patience when working with them – some staff do not understand this. Some still have the view that claiming to be dyslexic is "trying to find excuses".'

Staff were also asked what further information they would like to receive about individual students with dyslexia. Between 50 and 60 per cent of the respondents said that they would like information on reading, writing and organizational difficulties. Staff also suggested that the following types of information about aspects of student's coping would be helpful:

- how to help learning
- spotting dyslexia, and distinguishing between dyslexic students and other students with difficulties in expression
- how to understand more clearly the nature of their difficulties
- how to make effective allowance for their problems
- how to support them to ensure satisfactory presentation of written work routinely
- reports explaining actual problems
- details of the nature of their problems with numeracy.

The following comments and suggestions were made:

- that it would be helpful to find a way of making clear to staff that what seemed like disorganization and excuses for slow, poor quality, late work might be attributable to the nature of the dyslexic student's difficulty and not just to idleness and lack of effort/interest

- that if we want to encourage students to become autonomous learners we should beware diminishing student autonomy by being over-helpful and directive
- the problems of dyslexia may be less than the problems of those who are tired from the necessity of having paid work in order to cope financially or the cultural problems of overseas students – of course, some dyslexic students will have paid work, which will add to their burden and some overseas students may also be dyslexic
- it is important for students to be given support to enable them to use appropriate techniques as well as for lecturers to be given training.

In the interviews carried out with staff (described above in Chapter 7), staff were asked what support and help they would like to receive in supporting students with dyslexia. The suggestions from the tutors from the different departments are given below.

Computing and Maths

This tutor suggested that the information needed was 'Something like the Open University gives us. For instance: you've got a student with schizophrenia. Here's a little handbook that we've produced on schizophrenia and the signs and symptoms, and here's some specific advice on how to handle this student . . . This student has a specific problem and you need to deal with him differently to the others, in the same way as if you had a visually impaired student.' She also suggested that it would be useful to receive a list of contacts from whom it would be possible to obtain advice. She said: 'With the OU it just comes automatically and there's a name and telephone number on the top of the sheet and it just tells you who to contact about this person if you need to know more, if you want any further help. If you telephone them they are very helpful.'

This tutor also suggested, as did one or two others, that there was a need for a designated person who understood dyslexia, and possibly other disabilities or differences, to be responsible for liasing between the central support services and the courses where the students were studying. This person could then be responsible for making sure that all staff within the department were aware of the students' difficulties and the type of support they might need and could also act, if necessary, as a channel for information from the student to the staff, although this should not be done to the detraction of the importance of students themselves liasing with individual tutors over their needs and taking responsibility for finding solutions to their difficulties.

Education

The tutor in the education department said that their particular concerns were over the admissions process and the need for the University management to understand that, although they were willing to receive dyslexic students, there was a problem in relation to the assessment and evaluation of the course and in relation to the students' possible failure of the current literacy and/or numeracy assessments at the end of the course. Discrimination on the grounds of disability is not permissible, therefore she said: 'I think we need specific support for our course with the whole of the interview process. The admissions process is going to be important and an up-front institutional decision about it is needed, rather than leaving the department to cope with external stick. I think there has to be much more an up-front policy and an awareness of the difficulties of some professions, with professional training.'

Engineering

This tutor said that currently he did not receive information about students with dyslexia and that he would appreciate a formal mechanism by which that information was received within the department and disseminated. He was aware that students might not always want their difficulties to be widely known but he said: 'Those of us who got the infor-mation and are sympathetic to dyslexic and dyspraxic students I'm sure would keep it confidential.' He also said that he would prefer the oppor-tunity to discuss the students' difficulties face-to-face but knew that there was not always time for such an in-depth exploration.

Initial information

He said: '. . . in a less than an ideal world if you do have to have the services interposed initially so that the ice can be broken . . . I would just think as much information as they were able to put down . . . because the student may be able to speak to someone who was uninvolved with the course a lot easier than talking to someone who is involved with the course.' He was also very aware that the students might not be very self-aware in relation to their strengths and weaknesses as a university student. He said: 'If we catch these kids at the beginning of the first year, I would think that they are not in a position to know which of their difficulties is going to be a problem as far as the course is concerned, so from that point of view I think that members of staff should be made aware of all of their particular problems.'

Staff awareness

'I think that we've just got to be aware that it's a very traumatizing condition for people and all the time they're with us we've got to try to support them and say "Look we're aware of what the problems are and you're the only one who's going to overcome it." And if they do come here on terms with it I think the worst thing we can do is to sort of beat them and say "You've not coming up to standard." So we do need to be aware of it. I think if we're getting more of them coming through the schools because of better screening et cetera we've got to face up to it.'

Drama

Initial information

The tutor from this department was impressed with the dissemination of information more recently. She said: 'I think certainly the way that the University disseminates information about students with disabilities has improved a lot over the last few years. And now, particularly with dyslexic students whose special need is registered with the central departments and we actually do get information about that student . . . also we've had very helpful and positive suggestions about how best to support that student. Some of it we had taken on board and were doing already but certainly we've had information about that student – if you could give them handouts, if you could give them more time, if they need to be given time to plan things perhaps further in advance of the other students in the group . . . and it's been very helpful I think. That's something I've noticed coming through recently with our current students. There are two students in Year 1 Performance who are quite severely dyslexic. I've had letters from the Students' Services from the Study Skills Unit which have been quite specific about the sort of things the students need . . . That's great. That's very helpful. It also means that you can make sure that everyone who teaches that student has that information, because to be honest that's a bit of a problem. Again not so much with us because we've only got six staff, but in a department of 20 or more, I can imagine that if you were trying to make sure that each of those that teaches that student . . .'

Staff attitudes and awareness

'I think people in general simply don't have the information, they don't . . . I've come across in discussions with other colleagues, not with my colleagues, not even necessarily from the School of Art . . . they can be very sceptical about whether dyslexia exists or whether . . . they think it's a made-up phenomenon. And I think there's certainly a lack of awareness of the different aspects of difficulty which a dyslexic student can face. People assume that it's all to do with reading and spelling . . . So I think information and I think specific training are needed.'

Health Studies

Identification

'I think it would be nice if we did identify by the end of semester 1 those students who have an ability but are going to need a lot of help. We can set up a support group and it could run for the whole of the next semester and they could be helped with their skills – but that's a resource issue.'

Resourcing

This tutor, as above, suggested that a support group for those students with dyslexic-type difficulties would be helpful, but this was a resource issue. She also commented on the difficulty some students have in coping with the library layout and cataloguing and the fact that there were no members of staff nowadays to help students on the floors where the books were held. 'And now that there's hardly a member of staff, other than on the ground floor. You're very much on your own. I think we could probably do more to help students.'

She also pointed out that the creation of dyslexia-friendly materials for units could be extremely time-consuming and was therefore another resource issue. She said: 'I know one of my colleagues teaching Year 1 Research had a second semester assessment which involved reviewing an article. She went through a huge amount of hassle to identify articles, check it out with the copyright . . . And I mean she spent hours and hours and hours and hours across the whole health and social type analytical or political literature . . . and came up with about five articles that were she felt were accessible to Year 1 and not too unreasonable in terms of diffi-culty . . . and then had to go through "Can I get these photocopied to give to the students so that they can practice with them?" and she put together a very good workbook for them . . . but you know it was about 100 hours she spent doing that, a huge amount of time . . . and you know in principle, in terms of support, you can think of all sorts of creative ways to do it . . . but I have to say time is at a premium . . . in an ideal world you know yes, yes. We already do a lot but that is a problem. But I think again if the University believes in helping people who wouldn't otherwise have made it then it needs resourcing.' This tutor felt that this resourcing should be provided not just in terms of equipment but in the end really what was needed was human support.

History

Initial and general information

This tutor backed the need for more specific information about dyslexia in general and the needs and profile of any specific student in question. He said: 'I don't think there's ever been any specific checklist of points or symptoms that I've actually seen which would have this all set out so that when you get a dyslexic student you can look at it and say right, be prepared for XYZ . . . So it was very much a case of picking this thing up. Obviously I knew the problems of formulating words and sentences and that was apparent in some of the essays, particularly early on, but other things like the short-term memory loss I had no idea about it . . . In the case of another student who suffers from multiple sclerosis, we were given or sent an email by the disabilities officer outlining some of the problems this creates in terms of studying, which you know is quite useful to have.'

Psychology

Initial and general information

A similar response to that from the History tutor was obtained from the Psychology tutor. He said: 'No psychologist in our division would deny any sort of knowledge of dyslexia, but on the other hand most people would say that they have a general concept of what dyslexia is, but actually 99 per cent of the staff probably do not have any real notion of the range and the constellation of difficulties so, if that's the case, how can we as tutors start to understand where difficulties might lie . . . So, in that sense, I think the best way forward is to make sure staff are informed, make sure that they know the learning context where difficulties are likely to arise and also have some notion of where intervention and the nature of intervention can be effective. I don't know how much information we have on that at the moment as members of staff.'

He considered that it was important that the general information should be public and available to both staff and students. He said: 'I think what I would also like to see . . . I would like to see it go into a general handbook. Then at least, if we can have identified to us as staff where difficulties are going to arise, then there's no reason why students can't be given that and, of course, if we're going to formalize that and somebody were to take responsibility . . . Then again I would like to think that students would know who to approach because, at the moment, I think it would go through a personal tutor, if it goes through anybody at all. It occasionally comes to me, but only as a second order, not first order so I think there are a lot of things on the staff side where things could be formalized, but I think there are things on the students' side in terms of information briefing.'

He felt that, if students were to be comfortable with their dyslexia and to feel confident in coming forward to discuss their problems then 'the more explicit the framework is the better, because if literally it can act as a scaffolding then, because if they know that it's there and they know that it's there for them, then there might be more encouragement for them to make use of it.'

Fashion marketing

Initial and general information

When asked what information she received at the moment the tutor replied: 'Generally you just get the student saying "I am dyslexic" and you take that on at face value. Or you get students with very poor spelling or they come with a certificate that says "I am dyslexic" and that's it.' She was very aware that dyslexia is a catch-all term which can involve a wide range of problems and that individuals with dyslexia are very variable in the number and extent of the difficulties with which they present. She said: 'There's a whole host of problems . . . It's one of those words which is just a coverall. It covers a multitude of problems. I wouldn't know where to begin to try and address all of them. But if you had a profile that came with the students, say from school, or from the Dyslexia Institute that said the student has problems with . . . a, b, c, d . . . Then it would be great. Then you could take those into consideration. Then you could even try remedial improvement work on those . . . Some have problems with numeracy . . . some are really good at numeracy. Some are fantastic lateral thinkers it's very difficult – as I say some sort of profile would be great.'

Conclusions re support required by staff

Overall, there are a number of general conclusions which can be drawn from this fascinating survey:

1. There is a lack of knowledge and understanding of dyslexia amongst the majority of University staff.
2. Training and general information for all staff are needed to change this state of affairs.
3. University staff who are aware of the trials and traumas faced by individuals with dyslexia are very willing to provide as much support as can reasonably be expected, given the other demands upon them.
4. There are resource implications if the need for support is to be fully met.
5. Staff would welcome the provision of a copy of the dyslexic student's profile of strengths and weaknesses, and support and advice on supporting their learning.
6. Staff would also welcome the identification of an individual member of staff within each course who would be responsible for receiving and disseminating information about dyslexia in general and about the needs of individual students in particular.
7. Many staff consider that students other than those identified as dyslexic have similar difficulties, particularly with writing. The supports which can be created to help dyslexic students would be helpful to students in general.
8. There is an unresolved issue around the marking of the work of students with dyslexia. Should dyslexia be regarded as a chronic extenuating circumstance and allowances be made for this in the marking procedure itself, or in the presentation of cases at Examination Boards?

CHAPTER 9

The perspectives of student support staff

Southside University has developed its support for students with dyslexia over the last 10 years, and is acknowledged to be among the leading universities in terms of the support it offers. The university has come top of the national league table for widening participation in higher education. Key members of the student assessment and support team at Southside University were interviewed, including:

Sally – disability services manager
Maggie – disability support adviser
Pam – disability support tutor
Jim – chartered occupational psychologist

What was striking was that all four of them came from a background of working with adults and were very committed to the idea of equality and justice for the students they supported. They all stressed the importance of teamwork in providing effective support.

Sally – disability services manager

Sally came from a background in staff training and development and had used these skills to develop a well organized and dynamic support service. Her role is to draft policy on disability issues and develop new projects to improve the overall service. She has set up a number of working parties to develop and improve disability support within the University. A current example is a specific learning difficulties working party which has been developing guidelines for the admission of students with dyslexia to initial teacher training courses at the university (Cain and Riddick 2001).

Q: How have you developed the service for dyslexic students?

A: Right . . . well I'll try and give you a sort of pocket history, I arrived here in November 92 and there were already students at the university who declared dyslexia . . . out of about . . . just over a hundred . . . students that had declared a disability or a specific learning difficulty to the university, the great majority of those were dyslexic learners, so I prioritized my work and my efforts towards the greatest number of students I possibly could, so that meant one of the first things I wanted to get my teeth into was this issue of dyslexia and raising awareness across the institution and providing support in an organized and measured way for the students. So, that's the direction I headed in, not to the exclusion of others, but that was a priority at that time One of the first things I did was to look at setting up an infrastructure and developing contacts and finding out by talking to students what they needed as individuals, which also gave me a good range of ideas of what we should develop as a basic provision.

I joined in November so a lot was concentrated on providing for individuals but one of the first things I did was . . . we needed students assessing because there was a lot of people coming to me, saying 'I think I'm dyslexic' or I am dyslexic and this is the report I've got . . . and it was a side long and it was somebody who had been given extra time for an examination when they did O Levels . . . which is all fine, but wasn't what we needed here . . . so I wanted to get to a stage where students who presented to us could, whatever their level of awareness or diagnosis was, could just jump onto the system and continue along it. So we have people coming who just are struggling and don't know why . . . so we needed to be able to respond to those and we had people, who say I've just been diagnosed and I need x, y, z support . . . so it was the whole lot at once . . . so I established contact with somebody who could conduct assessments for students here and the University paid, of course, because the cost of it is very prohibitive to students . . . very prohibitive . . . to lots of families.

Q: Was that an issue, getting the assessment paid for or was that fairly straightforward to arrange?

A: No it wasn't (an issue) actually at the time because the University was quite forward looking then and said, this is an area we need to do something about and it had just been the widening participation paper, the original one . . . so there was money . . . there was money for me to get equipment . . .

Q: So it was part of that widening participation?

A: It was really the start of it here so there was cash available at that stage . . . since then of course, budgets have diminished . . . but what we've always managed to do is use the access fund as allocated by government for students, to purchase assessments for students . . . One of the first things I also wanted to do and thought about . . . the feeling that I was getting was that a lot of students felt isolated and like they were the only one and I knew from my own work in the first few months that this isn't so, so what I thought was, we need some sort of contact for these people . . . for students who feel like this and who need guidance, so as well as establishing the assessment mechanism . . . we set up a support group and really all the University does is pay for tutors . . . two very experienced and qualified tutors, to come in and work with whichever students turn up to the support group and there's usually a good regular core of anywhere between eight to a dozen . . . and others drift in and out as they will . . . and the remit I gave is that we have students with dyslexia here . . . all different levels of experience . . . abilities . . . different degrees, different years of study, they all need some guidance and assistance . . . so the support group established itself very quickly and it's run since 93 I think, every year, and it now is in the shape and form where it continues as it originally did, whereby the first thing in the new academic year the group of students who meet, will decide what subjects they want to cover . . . under the guidance of the tutors.

Added to that, what we've also done now, because we've got two tutors and we can wangle it like that, is we've got half hour slots, for one-to-one . . . it's not ongoing and it's not everlasting for an individual student, but it's helpful, because if they're struggling with something in particular, like say in pharmacology where spellings are so important . . . and the change of one letter can really change a prescription . . . those students have got to get spellings right, so they might come in and say, well let's work out a multi-sensory approach for these five spellings . . . and use the half hour like that. Somebody might have an essay question that they need to be sure they've interpreted correctly. I mean you will know yourself the array of things that students need . . . in short sharp bursts . . . and that's what the one-to-one sessions will do.

Then we were lucky enough in 94 . . . I applied for and got money from HEFCE . . . under the provision for disabled students and special needs . . . to develop . . . 'Get Sussed' . . . so I set up a dyslexia working party, we had probably about five or six students with dyslexia who came in and contributed to that, as much as they could and wanted to . . . and that was invaluable . . . then at a later stage we got learning development services people in . . . then the module went up for validation and has been running now . . . this will be the fourth year it's run I think . . . and we always have a decent cohort of students and the feedback is 99.9 per cent positive . . . the one thing that always strikes me about it is that when students come back . . . the next year after they've done 'Get Sussed' . . . they said, you know I didn't realize that that bit would be so helpful . . . and so it's applied knowledge, but not immediately . . . and the whole idea of 'Get Sussed' came because we had a group of students who were already marginalized and pressurized in terms of time, and at that given time any additional support they wanted had to come on top of all of the other degree and work, which was just compounding the issue . . . it was making life tougher, you know by pressurizing students who were already on the edge of pressure . . . so what we decided to do then, is get something validated so these students could do the same support work we'd developed but do it as part of the degree, so the module obviously had a theoretical element to it as well, there are a few sessions in it looking at what dyslexia is, and what a specific learning difficulty is . . . what assessment processes there are . . . how to interpret your own ed. psych.'s (educational psychologists) report, here we have the finished article sent to us from the ed. psych. and then we contact the students saying, 'We've got your report back, make an appointment and we'll sit there . . . talk you through it and explain it . . .' and those sessions usually last for about an hour and a half . . . because if we were just to send it to the student, I think they wouldn't get as much from that, or there's more room for misinterpretation if we didn't do it this way . . . Plus of course, we always say to the students, receiving your diagnostic assessment report from the psychologist is the first step . . . is the beginning of our work with you really, because it diagnoses the issue and highlights your strengths and weaknesses and from those strengths and weaknesses we can start to develop a strategy for you as a person.

And you know, I've had students come back . . . who say, 'My grade points have gone up two or three since I've done that you know, because I'm more organized and I'm clearer about what I'm doing,' and of course if students can't get to do 'Get Sussed', there's the support group available to them, and thankfully a lot of students do get the disabled students allowance within which, if there's a need, we ask for funding for multi-sensory tuition and we've got lots of students who get it from year one and they get multi-sensory tuition right throughout their degree . . . an hour a week, an hour and a half a week . . . so a student could be in a position where they can get one-to-one tuition, they can attend a support group and do 'Get Sussed', but they're the lucky few, er . . . but at least there are three options there or a combination of options, so somebody somewhere will always get something hopefully . . . often it's depending on funding . . . sometimes it's dependent on timetabling . . . but we always do what we can, we always try and . . . we always try and be excessively flexible and if it needs applying pressure on a programme leader to release some-body a little bit, then we do it, you know, but sometimes the timetabling doesn't allow.

Q: So do you sometimes feel you're having to be an advocate for the student?

A: Sometimes yes. When a student presents to us, you never say, oh this is a typical student because everyone is coming at it from a different angle, they've got all of their experiences as a young child and then an adolescent in education and they're often awful experiences, terrible experiences, so they've got that . . . depending on whether or not they were formally diag-nosed and when and what support they got or didn't get after that, whether it was explained to them or not . . . whether or not the student understands themself what it's all about, so the first thing we do is find out where the student's at, taking into account all of these sort of background things . . . before we even get to supporting them here, you've got to go through all like that stuff . . . the main thing is we work with the student at a pace which they're comfortable with . . . we always say that you'll get three things from us . . . that's honesty, confidentiality and the feeling that you are in control . . . now with some students, they naturally take that mantle on very quickly, because they're organized, they're together . . . they may be very aware of their dyslexia and understand it thoroughly . . . and at the other end of the spectrum are those students who don't have any of those three features, if you like . . . and it's a question of enabling them or giving them the oppor-tunity to develop their self esteem . . . their confidence . . . their understand-ing and then their skills and knowledge . . . so with some students you can get them to see . . . us regularly . . . all of the time to begin with and eventu-ally as they become more confident, so their contact with us . . . with their own knowledge . . . within their own control . . . diminishes . . . or becomes less frequent . . . I mean we're always here . . . with other students it takes a long time and they never ever get fully to where you want them to be in the three years but you can only go as fast as the student can really . . . when I say it's fast, it doesn't mean we're pushing people along . . . we're encouraging them a great deal and supporting them, because we're as quick to say, don't be such a lazy so and so . . . or that was your fault . . . in our view, why didn't you do that, or you can't expect people to be telepathic . . . unless you're willing to contribute towards the development of your skills . . . and to put your time, you can't expect everyone else to do it, while you're not bothering . . . so sometimes that message takes a little bit to click but that's few and far between, because I find that a lot of the students who get here with the level and the severity of the difficulties they've got . . . often undiagnosed . . . don't need to be motivated.

Q: Yes, yes . . . they have to be motivated to come right through the years of school

A: Yes, they're more motivated than most people I know to get this far with the difficulties they've got . . . and the no support that they've had . . . so motivating students is often not an issue . . . sometimes allowing students room to express themselves and to have an outlet for frustrations in development . . . because they've got through, you know, statutory education suppressing feelings or having their feelings suppressed by others . . . at the end of the day, you know much better than I if they've got through education . . . being educated about how uneducable they are really . . . it's a crude way of putting it but if people tell you enough times that you're silly and you're thick, you'll eventually believe them even if you know in your heart to begin with . . . and if it starts from a very young age and the older a . . . I find the older the students are, the more entrenched these views are.

Q: Yes, yes . . . and they probably went to a school at a time when, there were much more negative attitudes.

A: I'm not saying it's great for younger pupils today, it's not . . . but then there was also the physical . . . it was almost a physical sort of, er . . . degradation of people as well as the sort of intellectual degradation of someone . . .

Q: Yes . . . that's very true.

A: So anyway students come with all these different backgrounds and experiences, and our first job is to get their confidence and explain to them what we can and can't do . . . what their part will be and how, if they're going to benefit to the maximum that they're going to have to do their bit, and then just take it from there . . . how we approach things varies enormously depending on the student. So we help them to get diagnosed and then from that we use their profile of strengths and weaknesses to develop a strategy which might include disabled students allowance and all sorts of stuff.

Q: You've obviously done a lot . . . how important do you feel it is to get the teaching staff involved and more aware?

A: Oh it's crucial. We could be as informed and as expert advisers as anyone could have wished for, but unless the people who do the teaching, who mark the work, who set the exams, who go with students on field trips, who communicate with students and teach . . . unless they . . . have a level of understanding and a number of approaches . . . then our work is not futile, because there's always that one-to-one stuff for the student, but it could never achieve its maximum for the students . . . so the academic and other staff . . . resource centres and labs . . . their awareness is of crucial importance . . . which is why one of the first things I did when I arrived here was go and see the university staff training manager and got him to fund . . . which he has done since then . . . a series of staff training courses and we have one which is three half days on dyslexia . . . it's an understanding and awareness of it and then it's very much how educators . . . academics . . . can support students in the class.

Q: Yes . . . so what sort of response do you feel you get?

A: Generally very good . . . and I like nothing better than when you sit and talk to somebody and you can almost see a light bulb going off in somebody's head . . . because some of it . . . disability awareness generally . . . some of the basic concepts of it . . . is so basic and simple that, I don't know whether people imagine it's too difficult to grasp . . . and you've got to be a big theorist to hang onto the basic principles of it, but you don't. So when you've got training courses where people have signed up for it themselves, you're what I call preaching to the converted, almost . . . in which case you've got a very open welcome audience who are keen to find out . . . when you go into something say, like a Cert Ed where staff have to go . . . because it's part of their agreement to become qualified and so on . . . then you may get . . . more scepticism and that stuff . . . but again you've just got to beat them to the challenge. I don't present things in an academic way . . . I'm very much person-centred . . . student-centred thing . . . I mean the University's got a policy here . . . the reason I had the policy was I was getting tired of wasting my time speaking to staff who said, I don't think dyslexia exists . . .

Q: Yes.

A: . . . and I thought, I'm not here to have an intellectual argument with you about its existence, this University says it exists so it does . . . so I thought, right we'll have a blooming policy for it and that way I'll just say . . . I respect your personal views, but keep them to yourself, because this University has a policy for dyslexia, this University believes it exists and it says, these students are entitled to x, y, z . . . you're an employee of this University therefore you must follow this procedure and practice and support the students . . . it's not to say . . . we all have our prejudices . . . but the key to that is to own them and to keep them in our own heads and our own hearts . . . and to deal with them ourselves and work through them . . . easier said than done, but that was the reason I had a policy.

Q: In the time you've been here, has the scepticism lessened?

A: Yes, well put it this way, I think awareness has risen, there are still people who are very sceptical . . . and they could no doubt provide very cogent arguments . . . but the fact is that I think awareness and under-standing has increased . . . I think difficulties come when teaching staff are pressed for time, and sometimes then they feel as if, oh lord, I've got to do an extra set of overhead prints and things like that . . . now it's essential for the student and . . . I might sit here and say, well it'll only take you 15 minutes, but that 15 minutes might have been earmarked for a hundred other things and it might have been at a bad time . . . I don't accept it as an excuse . . .

Q: . . . You have got a lot of different students who are all, wanting differ-ent things.

A: . . . that's right yes . . . and if you teach large groups and you've got ten different groups and you've got, you know, three students in each of those groups, that's a lot of extra effort, but my point is, once it's organized, once you've done it once, if you're at the photocopier, print off 20 sets of your notes . . . instead of one for that one student, then next time you have somebody and you do that lecture, next semester, you've got them there already. I think a lot of it is good organization as well . . .

Q: Yes . . . I think sometimes . . . although it sounds very basic it's about not doing certain things . . . not turning round and making disparaging comments.

A: Yes . . . attitude is a great thing . . . and one of the staff development courses that I wanted is called, disability equality, because it's just highlighting . . . again planting a seed, hoping such a little light will go on about how powerful language is . . . and how what we say sometimes, we don't mean it, but it can have an impact on a student so yes, attitude and the way staff approach students and discuss the issue is very important . . . for example, if you go into a lecture and somebody shouts . . . all the dyslexic students come here please . . . and I'll give you your handouts . . . oh . . . wonderful . . . we may have worked with those students and they don't mind the lecturers knowing, but they don't necessarily want their peers to know and that's their prerogative . . . and then suddenly it's announced to all and sundry . . . and they're made to feel second class . . . . that doesn't happen a great deal, but when it does, the impact is massive on someone . . .

Q: Yes . . . I found with interviewing children that one of the things they hated was this . . . the way extra time was handled for exams, it made them feel very shown up . . .

A: Which is why here when I have accommodations for exams, we find out what that student wants . . . . it's their exam.

Q: Presumably the number of students has increased . . . because of better, identification . . . is it beginning to level off, or is it still increasing?

A: The increase has slowed down, but it's still increasing . . . I mean the ratio of students with disabilities and specific learning difficulties to those who don't have them . . . has increased every year . . . last year I think it was one in 15 students.

Q: Yes.

A: Fortunately we're still . . . at one stage I mean it was . . . each year we were jumping up 200 per cent or something . . . well I don't have to say, the sort of implications in terms of resource. We don't have enough resources, full stop . . . absolutely . . . I've got staff who are magnificent . . . they'll do wonders . . . wonders . . . work themselves to a frazzle sometimes . . .

Q: Particularly things like the one-to-one support, do you have to limit that in some way?

A: We try not to . . . we really don't have any rules about students accessing our support except that at the moment we're only accessible for student appointments three out of five days a week, that's to enable us to time to do all the follow-up stuff and, er, the paperwork and the admin and but we never say, ten sessions and you're out, sort of thing, or six appointments and that's your whack . . . or you can only have one a month . . . because it would be wrong to do that . . . some students need an awful lot of very regular contact . . . and that might diminish over time and often it does . . . our aim, is to get the students to develop their skills and to become confident independent learners . . . they'll feel happy about approaching other parts of the university on their own to trigger what they need, and to discuss issues pertinent to the dyslexia.

Q: What about the whole issue of . . . when they're finishing and moving on, do they want advice about whether they should declare.

A: Oh yes all the time . . . should I put that I'm dyslexic on my application form? Well I have an answer which is so well rehearsed now because it's the only one I can really give . . . which is . . . it is a choice that you must make and the only advice that I can give you is, if it's an application to a particular company, find out that company's view and practices . . . do they have a policy and a practice for supporting people . . . employees with dyslexia, see if they have got the two ticks, positive about disability . . . you can never tell a student what they should and shouldn't do.

A: I keep saying to my team, I can't wait till five, ten years time when we've got a lot of our graduates who've had dyslexia, who are actually out there in jobs . . . who are heads of year at schools, who are teaching or who are personnel officers . . . who are head of a . . . some organization . . . and they're in a position to apply their experiences, their accrued knowledge . . . but more importantly their attitudes . . . and I think that's when we'll start to see a change . . . er . . . but it'll be slow, but I cannot wait for that . . . because then we have a great network of people out there in employment that . . . students then coming through with similar diffi-culties, they won't be facing the same amount of difficulties . . . or, they'll have more havens ready standing . . .

Q: Yes that would be great.

A: I do think that . . . you must have support at the very highest level in any organization to get anything done . . .

Q: Yes, I was going to ask if you felt you'd been well supported by the University?

A: To begin with, oh yes . . . an awful lot . . . but universities are like any other organization, you know, they feel the bite of hard times financially, and when that happens, budgets and resources are cut a little bit and other priorities come along and part of my job, I suppose, is to keep disability issues high profile, but that's very hard . . . sometimes when you've got a lot of work to do and when other managers are all . . . very senior staff.

Q: What sort of things do you do to try and keep it high profile?

A: Well, last summer I did a review of disability right across the Univer-sity . . . now I've been wanting to do that for ages . . . but you always really need an external lever or a stick or carrot and . . . I used HEFCE's base level report on providing support for disabled students and I used the QAA Code of Practice for supporting disabled students . . . now if you can do something and say to senior managers, it's not just my idea . . . but look, HEFCE is in it, QAA and of course but now there's the Disability in Education Bill . . . but those sort of things are good . . . because you say, so it makes sense to start integrating and planning now. Because we were so successful here, which is illustrated by the increased number of students and the good reputation Southside's got in this field, there's a danger of people thinking that they've achieved, that they've done it . . . we've ticked that off our list . . . well it couldn't be further from the truth, because there's always room for improvement, and there's always better things to do and more things to do . . . and oh yes, we're probably in the top five in the country, but look, we don't do that . . . or we need to do more of this . . . so it was useful to be able to point out to people, yes we are very good, but we're far from perfect . . . far from it . . .

Q: Yes . . . to maintain that performance . . . you've got to keep moving forward, haven't you?

A: Well yes and you can't do that without resources . . . and of course our priorities are the students so maximum time must be devoted to them, and when that happens, obviously you do fall behind with development . . .

Q: Yes . . . so you're having to balance those elements.

A: That's hard . . . that's the hardest thing for me really.

Q: Yes. How do you evaluate what you're doing?

A: Personally, I evaluate it through my own team, and just listening to . . . what their work entails . . . they're the people who deliver stuff . . . if you've got a team of good staff who you trust implicitly to do the work well, which I have . . . and who you know are good professionals . . . then you know if they say something's not right, that something's not right . . . if they say something is going well, it's going well and it's successful so I never ever undervalue the feedback I get from the staff . . . the same thing applies, to feedback that we get from students . . . because we've got a lot of one-to-one contact and because we've got a great deal of contact with some students, we get a lot of anecdotal feedback and some of it's in compliments and we take that on board and obviously talking to staff like yourself, and other academics throughout the institution. But officially there's a Disability Working Party, which is a University-wide thing and it's got student representatives . . . the president of the Students Union is involved, so there's that feedback and that forum.

Maggie – disability support adviser

Maggie had a background in working on projects supporting adults with learning disabilities. When she started her role as support adviser there was little formal training available. She feels she has largely trained on the job by attending a number of specialist courses and obtaining specialist qualifications. Her role is to see students through the initial assessment process and identification of their support needs. She carries out the initial dyslexia screening, briefs students on the psychological assessment and, after it has been carried out, talks through the subsequent report with them. In conjunction with the recommendations of the psychological report, she evaluates the learning needs of the individual student and identifies the support needed to meet these needs. Where appropriate, she helps students to apply for the DSA (Disabled students allowance).

Q: Do you see students with a whole range of disabilities?

A: Every disability except mental health, we're not geared up for that, you name it we do it. All of it, I wouldn't be happy just specializing in one area.

Q: No, I think it gives you more of a context in which to understand particular problems if you have that overall view.

A: And I think you can have a dozen people with the same disability or impairment and each one would be different, it could be down to the level of the disability and the severity of the disability and it could be down to people's own opinions.

Q: Yes.

A: Their own self-esteem and personality drive and previous experience of support.

Q: When do you tend to first see students, do some of them come along before they've been assessed and say 'Well I think I might have a problem'?

A: Yes, we offer a screening test, which is the DAST (Dyslexia Adult Screening Test).

Q: Oh yes.

A: The dyslexia adult screening test which I helped in the piloting of, so I've done it for a few years now and when it first came out it was a marvellous thing because it meant that you weren't relying on subjective impressions. Prior to that we were having to look mainly at people's own perceptions and how difficult they thought it was whereas this gives a measured ability scale.

Q: Have you any idea of what percentage don't go on then to have a full assessment?

A: A third roughly.

Q: What sort of feedback do you give to those that don't go need to go on to full assessment?

A: Well that that depends on where the areas of difficulty are. It's usually what we're getting through now which is quite common is mature students who haven't studied for a long time so they're not used to all the different techniques of the study skills that we use. So we usually refer students to one of two places, either learning development or basic adult education departments. I think a lot of the stigma's gone from attending basic adult education, it's not like the past.

Q: So are people fairly happy with that or do they find it threatening or inappropriate?

A: Yes, they've gone there [basic adult education or learning development] if they've got no problems in processing speed and they've got a problem with spelling. Then I refer them on to there, sometimes they go sometimes they don't. Sometimes they get back to me and say by the way this is brilliant. But a lot of the time I think it's down to practice, they're just not used to studying, they're not organized they don't know how to organize themselves so we'll give them advice on how to get organized. But you still have to refer them on because we can't deal with every student with a slight difficulty.

Q: But in a sense you are directing them?

A: Oh yes.

Q: Yes, so they're not just being abandoned?

A: No, even students from franchised colleges as well, they come in and they have access to facilities.

Q: Yes, I noticed quite a few from Denman College when we got the questionnaires back. What I noticed was that they did seem more likely to say the assessment was fine but then they didn't feel they had the follow-up support because they're there and not here.

A: That's true but what we've tried to do since then is work with the disability support advisers within the college.

Q: Yes, so when you've seen students and you've done that initial screening and you decide they do need to go on for a full assessment do you talk to them about what that will entail or what happens then?

A: Briefly, I tell them what the timetable's going to be, hopefully we can give them a date there and then. I briefly describe what's involved. I went through the assessment myself so I now know exactly what the students are going to go through.

Q: Do they want to know what will be involved? What the content will be?

A: Yes, but obviously I can't tell them exactly what it's going to be but I'll say you'll be doing things like tests similar to what we've done today.

Q: Yes, so they've got something to go by.

A: I also tell them that there's a lot of dialogue and going into the history of previous education and family background and things.

Q: What sort of range of responses do you get at that point?

A: At that point, it's usually they're relieved but at the same time then the stress starts to come in because then the threat of the ability comes, that's one of the main things the students worry about is their actual ability.

Q: Yes, I've had a few students who've said they put off being assessed for dyslexia because they're worried that they might just be thick and not dyslexic.

A: Yes, that's the main concern I think with most people although you get some students who will say 'I know I'm not thick.' I think it's mainly that they start to doubt their ability because whatever it is going to be it's going to be official. They also worry about the cost even though I've already told them that it's free.

You can try and reassure them and say 'Look it's going to be fine.' From experience, questions about previous education, how you found life at school, of course that in itself opens up a whole can of worms, it can be very emotional sometimes and the emotion usually comes at the assessment.

Q: Yes.

A: For mature students it's a fact the oldest person we actually assessed I think it was 67.

Q: That must be quite amazing to have lived your life till then and then had this different view of yourself, that must take some getting used to I'd expect.

A: Very emotional but it gave me a wonderful insight because it was shortly after I'd started and it gave me a wonderful insight into all the generations back in the history of education and how it's changed now in schools to how people's attitudes have changed because at 67 when he was at school, totally different ball game, and he would be caned every day because he couldn't do certain things. But it was a very good experience for me, I learn a lot from people's own experiences.

Q: When they've had the assessment you seem to liaise quite a bit with Jim in that he's giving you some indication afterwards of how somebody has fared.

A: As soon as he's finished the assessment, if you haven't got them back to back, he'll come down and he'll say 'Right, this is the rough results, this is where the problem areas are' and he also gives me information if there's going to be any other help they need, counselling things like that, he goes right through the whole thing. I always get the reports sent to me, it never goes straight to the student because it can be misread, it can be misunderstood.

Q: And are they okay about that, you don't get any who question that?

A: No I just say that's what will happen once the assessment's over and Jim [assessing psychologist] will give them the feedback.

Q: So he gives them a bit of feedback.

A: Yes, he gives them a little bit of feedback and then gives me it, I'll get the report sent to me and then we literally talk them through it.

Q: So this is when he's had time to do like a proper report do you mean?

A: Yes, it's usually about three weeks after the assessment. But if for example the student needed instant support and needed tuition putting in place straightaway or they needed equipment Jim would just say 'We'll do it' and what I would have to do then is I would just contact the student and give them a little bit of feedback and say 'We can't go into it in detail but you know you've got difficulties, this is what we need to do in the interim until we can get you the correct information' and they're fine with that. But you can't, you can't hit the students with too much all at once, you know after the assessment we say there's only a little bit of feedback because they're brain-dead by the end of it.

Q: Yes.

A: And even if it's a small thing I'll say 'Ring me' and they quite often do. And I quite often get students once I've gone through the report with them and they'll ring me and I'll say 'Take it away and read it at your leisure' or usually they get families to look at it and the family come and query 'What does this word mean?' or 'What does this score mean?' and I'll get them to ring me.

Q: It seems to me it's quite a difficult balancing act producing a report that's readable and understandable but at the same time is technically comprehensive enough and stands up to official scrutiny.

A: I think we've cracked that. What I usually do is I'll read through it, I'll highlight the main areas, I don't read through the whole thing and if there's a complicated sentence I'll translate it into a comprehensible form and I'll say 'Well basically that means you're not processing the information properly it's not going in there correctly' and things like auditory and visual memory.

Q: Yes, it's words we get to take for granted.

A: That's right and I try to be very well expressive when I talk to people I'll make it quite visual.

Q: Yes, one of the things we were interested was whether knowing they were dyslexic raised or lowered their self-esteem, we found more said it did raise the self-esteem but there were some that said it lowered the self-esteem.

A: Yes, it varies, I would agree that it raises it more often than it does decrease it but again I think it depends on people's previous experiences.

Q: Yes.

A: One of the main things that we have to get over is not the actual diagnosis because by the time they've been through the assessment they know it's going to be some type of disability. It's once they get to know the severity of it and once I tell them how we can improve their skills, improve their technique and their ability to do their course, then they jump right back to school or college and a lot of the time the students will get hung up on what they could have been and that's very difficult.

Q: Yes, there's a few of them that came through angry about their wasted time at school.

A: Yes, and 'I'm going to go back to that school, I'm going to do this' and I'll really concentrate on this first, we need to get students counselling for it which we quite often do and we'll refer them onto the counsellors.

Q: Oh right so they have separate counselling in addition to the kind of support your service gives?

A: Yes, I don't do counselling.

Q: What percentage would you say go on to counselling?

A: It's a few.

Q: Presumably sometimes it's all wrapped up with lots of other issues?

A: It is but sometimes students can go and only have two counselling sessions and it does the trick, it's what they needed to do and others I've got some students who have counselling every week all the way through into their final year.

Q: The students that you see who've been assessed before, how do you find they react to being assessed again? Do they see it as a bit of a pain or a chore having to be reassessed or what's their attitude to it?

A: If they don't see the necessity of having another I'll explain why. Usually if you explain about the need to have it for the disabled students allowance then they're OK.

Q: Yes, they can see the purpose of it.

A: They know they're going to get it but if I say to them 'Well we need the information so that we know how to support you' they look as if to say 'Yes but I can do this and I can do that and I can do the other', but quite often when we have reassessments the students don't know the level of their capability, they don't understand dyslexia.

Q: Yes, I noticed that with some of them although they've been assessed before until they had it done here they weren't that clear.

A: No, they don't even know what underlies their difficulty. I have this little drawing that I did of the brain. I'm really not very good at drawing and its a great ice breaker and I'll say 'Do you know how it works?', I never yet had a yes. I'll demonstrate to them and you can see them thinking 'I wonder now if that's why I just doze off in lectures' and I'll say 'Precisely'.

Q: With having a son who's dyslexic one of the things I've come to realize is that you learn as you go along and its a developmental thing and what it means to you at eight is different to twelve and 16 and 18 so I suppose it's a process that goes on into adult life . . .

A: Yes, that's right and they're all different. We have some students who don't want support or anything said to their tutors and it's so frustrating because they're often the ones who really need it.

Q: Is that because they see it as a stigma or what?

A: Yes.

Q: They're worried about how they'll be responded to?

A: There's a lot in education [the education department].

Q: I've been interviewing trainee teachers and they're often made to feel not legitimate, I don't blame them I can see why they're very wary of declaring. Presumably that's perhaps decreasing, students who don't declare.

A: It is I think once people get here and they see the support available and they see it actually working because you don't necessarily need to notify the lecturers to get people in the support group or to get them one-to-one tuition.

Q: Yes, so they can feel safe here even if they don't feel safe in their department.

A: That's right it's a confidential service and you usually find that once people access the support system then I'll say to them, 'What do you want your lecturers to know?' They'll say 'Well what exactly will you be telling them?', and then I'll show them the memo and we'll talk through it. What I usually do is I'll say 'Look I'll do a memo and you take it away and have a look and if there's anything you want to take out' because you never send anything out without the student's approval.

Q: One of the things we also asked students about was once they'd been assessed whether that changed their coping strategies and more said yes but there were still some that said no. I wondered what your impression was of what they do once they've had the assessment and are having ongoing support?

A: A lot of the time it's positive and I think a lot as to how a student is going to react is in the initial feedback session because if you don't finish the session on a very positive note and if you're not able to give them examples of definitely something to be improved and you don't believe in what you say then they'll pick it up and they'll doubt you.

Q: Yes, so it's kind of giving them the confidence to think that they can succeed that changes can be made?

A: And that they could be changed in a certain way and sometimes I'll even do if I think there's still a doubt I'll get them to choose a word that they're having difficulty with and I'll do the multi-sensory and I'll break it down and I'll say to them 'Right, at the end of the session I'll ask you that' and 99 per cent of the time they'll remember how to spell that word and that just makes them believe change is possible.

A: I tell them it's going to be hard work and I don't tell them it's going to be an easy ride.

Q: That is an issue isn't it? I think it's one that sometimes perhaps gets a bit overlooked but it is it does mean extra work. Do you find different students respond to different sorts of ideas or suggestions? I mean do you have to tailor what you're doing to different students?

A: Yes, constantly and you usually find that a lot of students already have a lot of strategies in place – my job is to make them aware of those. Bring them out, in that strategy you're doing multi sensory learning here and they'll look and I'll say 'You don't even know that that's what you're actually doing' and so that that's encouraging. But some students will get very upset about the assessment and some will turn it around and they'll get very political about it.

Q: Yes.

A: I'm dyslexic and the world needs to know it and I don't care what anybody else thinks and you just get extremes.

Q: Yes, it's interesting isn't it, it's that social model of disability perspective coming in which is fair enough, it's the world that needs to change and not you.

A: That's right, but saying that there's a lot of students who think that it should be them that improves their skills because they know that they can improve their skills. That they can present themselves in written form much better then they think, it's their responsibility and that people shouldn't just ignore spelling errors.

You've got to be diplomatic about the previous support when sometimes you just want to explode and say 'What on earth have you been doing?' We've had people coming in where the whole support package has been based on DAST.

Q: I think there needs to be a gold standard for reports because they're so hugely different and the assessments people come in with, the information that's in them is so different.

A: We've had students whose assessments can differ between psychologists. We've had students in where somebody's said the difficulties are minor and I've doubted it, I've worked with a student and I've really really doubted it, and we'll have them reassessed again and it's a lot more severe than what was originally reported.

Q: So if they've been assessed before do they still have to a full assessment or do they just have a more literacy-based assessment?

A: No they have a full assessment.

Q: Right.

A: We can work with an assessment that's about three years old.

Q: So if they had one for A Levels or something?

A: Yes, then you know we can work with that but usually we have students reassessed or we tell them where to go to get reassessed before they start. I think you should be assessed regularly.

Q: Yes, the only reservation I've got is having experience of a child who was first assessed when he was seven or eight he's now just starting his A Levels and he's just going to have another assessment so this is his fourth already and he gets quite stressed every time.

A: Oh that's a lot.

Q: This is what's going to happen in the future if people are picked up when they're young they get their initial assessment, you might need one when you do your SATs or something, you need one for GCSEs, you need one for A Levels that's already up to four. One of the students on the questionnaire said she'd been assessed four times.

I noticed most of the students, we asked them whether they got the DSA and most of them said yes so presumably does that fairly automatically follow from the assessment?

A: Yes, when I do the assessment feedback I run through the report, I give them the scale for percentiles to show where their abilities are so they can actually physically see any gaps. Then what we do is I look through the list of recommendations and I tell them how we're going to implement these recommendations which means the application for DSA. Then I explain what's going to happen about DSA, I write it down, then I give them information on the DSA and I tell them to go away and then to get back to me. I'll say to them 'Every time you've got a query or you're not sure about something' that they just ring us.

Q: That system seemed to work very well, they all seemed to be saying yes they got the DSA, there hasn't been any problem.

A: With applications to DSA it's a bit easier now because we have the access data here and I'm one of the assessors at the access centre.

A: The education authority would refer students to an access centre, some would allow students to apply themselves. We try to take away a lot of the responsibility for that because students are already trying to cope with their course, you can't present them with all this other work to do. It's quite a complicated procedure so what we usually do is if the student doesn't want to have an access centre assessment I have to explain to them it's not going to be a test it's a totally different thing. It would be about technology and such. We have these guidelines if a student is confident enough to do their own application then they can do it themselves and I'll proofread it but they usually bring it back to me to check.

Q: I wanted to ask you about what's your relationship to the teaching departments?

A: We never get to meet in person I have to say, but that's probably because I don't have the time to actually get out. Sally does a lot of or does most of the policy work or review work and I get to do the face-to-face.

Q: More of a hands-on.

A: Yes, and I much prefer it that way I have to say. But as for lecturers I get to talk to people over the phone when there's a problem, obviously through email which is very impersonal, I get lecturers ringing me up on some advice on certain situations with students and the disability support tutors.

Q: So what what's the difference, Maggie, between you and the disability support tutors?

A: The disability support tutors are more there for the day-to-day contact, they're actually in a better position than me in some cases because they know all the staff and students to talk about.

Q: So what's your official title?

A: Disability support adviser.

Q: So what's the difference in your role and the tutor's role?

A: The tutor's role is more for if there's any day-to-day diagnosis needed. I'm always here from start to finish, I make my own technology and support assessment, the disability support tutors are there to try and implement once the support's been organized.

Q: Yes, so it's the day to the day support.

A: Once the support's been organized then the disability support tutor is there to ensure that the support is where it should be.

Q: Just coming back to this relationship with departments, presumably you must find it frustrating at times when you're doing a lot to try and support and help the students.

A: Very frustrating, very frustrating, you get some members of staff who are good at supporting students but you usually find that those members of staff will support every student.

Q: Yes, it's a kind of attitude of mind almost, isn't it?

A: But you get some lecturers and I've got one example that I have to deal with where the understanding of the disability is rubbish, absolutely rubbish and you still get some lecturers who say they just can't spell. I get a lot of students coming to me who from the confidentiality thing about different lecturer's reactions and I so wish that they would make it a complaint, there's no way they're going to and I must have about three a week.

Q: Yes.

A: I have to say it's written policy that they're allowed this. I get a lot of feedback from students about members of staff but a lot of the time your hands are totally tied.

Q: It's a shame that there isn't more statutory training for staff.

A: Oh tell us about it. I've said general disability training should be compulsory.

Q: Yes, I agree.

A: For every member of staff.

Q: Because the problem is otherwise the people who are sort of anti it never do the training.

A: I think it's in every department, you get the odd one or two or you get a lot of staff who are very supportive but their hands are tied.

Q: Yes, it seems to me it's a long-term problem, you're here providing a really good support service and it's how to make the best of that by involving the whole university.

A: I think because they're such a good team here we tend to take a lot of the responsibility away from the lecturers, lecturers know that if there is a problem the students will come to us.

Q: It's a bit the same issue that they used to have in schools when they had remedial departments and in a sense a lot of ordinary teachers didn't take responsibilities so it's a structural issue about whether having really good central support services is good or not?

A: What we try to do now is get the departments doing more. Say for instance the exams, we've always organized all the exams and a lot of the time if a student needs speciality equipment or a reader or a scribe then we would do it here and it just got where there was just too many students for us, so what we've done now is we've given it back to the schools.

Q: Yes, so they're having to organize it.

A: The school has to organize it.

Q: And then they do have to think about the issues for it don't they?

A: That's right so it's raising awareness there but it's a little bit by little bit, it would be wonderful to have an adviser for each school.

Q: Do you get any impression about the different literacy demands of different courses or modules?

Q: One of the things we were wondering about, is if courses or modules could have some kind of literacy rating so at least when students were choosing they'd be aware of what the literacy loading of different courses are likely to be.

A: Yes, that would really help . . .

Pam – disability support tutor

Pam is one of several disability support tutors employed on a sessional basis by the university to do both one-to-one and group work with students. Three of Pam's adult children have dyslexia (two and a half as she likes to jest). She was involved when they were young in setting up local dyslexia support and for several years was head of a local branch of the Dyslexia Institute. She trained to work specifically with dyslexic adults and has done so for a considerable period of time. She also does sessional dyslexia support work for other local universities so she is well placed to take an overview of some of the critical issues involved in providing support.

Q: You were saying you do some group work, what tends to happen in the groups?

A: In the groups well we advertise a group session in both places and whoever is interested comes and generally the first semester we do a variety of study skills. I've got a list of topics that we normally cover and in the first meeting I ask them which ones and what order they'd like them in. Then in the second semester I always do spelling because by then they know each other. I don't think you can do spelling in the first semester because they're too embarrassed, but you can do it in the second one because they're at home with each other by then . . .

Q: Right, so even though they're all dyslexic they're still quite embarrassed about their spelling?

A: Oh yes.

Q: Interesting.
    When they first come along at the beginning Pam what do you think are their priorities, what's kind of worrying them most or they most want help with?

A: Oh that's very variable there's not one thing it's a whole range of things.

Q: So it could be?

A: A raft of things that you do in study skills, so some people are absolutely terrified of presentations but that applies to nondyslexic people as well of course. A lot of them it's note-taking, quite a few of them it's reading for comprehension from the volume of reading that they have to do, and it will be essays for all of them. Mostly they don't complain about spelling but they're generally quite pleased when you do it but that's you know to start with, especially the first years think that their spellcheckers are going to fix it, it's only after you've tried a spellchecker they know it doesn't.

Q: Yes, do they give you any comments about the attitude of the course they're on or is that something they don't really talk about in group sessions.

A: Oh they do. They compare the compassion of their courses.

Q: Or lack?

A: Or lack of, and if you've got a particularly uncompassionate course you're generally kind of lined up for some sympathy from the rest of the group.

Q: I was going to ask you about that, how far you felt the groups as well as providing specific study skills are about providing general support from each other and knowing they've got somebody like you to believe in them.

A: I think it's a bit of each, and what else is good the very first group I ever had at Northside so that's 1996 they all are still in touch. Not only with me but with each other. And at Southside where they wait in a sort of central waiting area some people quite deliberately come quite early mostly and then they have their chat and then they often go off afterwards to the pub from both places and at the end of term sometimes we all go out have a meal or something like that.

Q: In the one to one sessions do you tend to start with study skills or do you just see what it is the students want?

A: See what they want.

Q: Yes

A: And if it becomes obvious while we're doing things that there's something that they really need to know when we've got over the immediate and urgent like the already overdue work. The work that's already past its final extension then I would say 'Look it is becoming obvious to me that you do need this, but you also need this' but if they don't want to do it then I wouldn't do it but I might suggest it.

Q: So you start with the student's priorities?

A: Yes.

Q: But then you would be proactive in sort of saying what would help.

A: If I thought there was a serious lack, otherwise what I do is I just introduce it as we come to it, so if it's something like apostrophes or something like that I would just sort of do it when I came upon it in an essay.

Q: When you first meet a student, Pam, do you have a copy of their report or do you have any kind of background information?

A: Yes, we have copies of their reports usually, odd times we don't, but mostly we do. When we don't it's because they've been assessed and somebody's said they need urgent help and so they've come before the assessment's actually been written and completed or it's you know not available or something but mostly you can have a look at the assessment first.

Q: Right, so are you ever in the position of having to explain an assessment to a student that's just been done.

A: Well, quite frequently not just those who've just been seen but also those who've been seen years before.

Q: Right

A: Because they'll say 'I can't do so and so' and I may say 'Well, no, you won't be able to because you've got a problem with so and so' and they'll say 'How do you know that?' So then if you start going to the scores and saying 'Well because of that, that and that', then they'll say 'And what does this mean and what does that mean?' Mostly when students come they're quite relaxed and well fairly relaxed anyway but if they seem tense I do often ask them if there's anything about their report that they want to know. Because sometimes they just feel like they have been told about it but it hasn't sunk in or they say they went through it and somebody spent an hour with me and I couldn't remember or I've forgotten since or I can't believe this can be solved because they said I can't do this but I can do that.

Q: Yes, do you find it helpful to have their report or it does it not make much difference in a sense to what you do or how you relate to them?

A: I don't mind not having their report but it's better if you do it's better practice to have it. Sometimes it doesn't make any difference to what you do because sometimes you've just got to get on with getting their essays done and whatever and so you've got to go through the question analysis and the brainstorming and everything so that they can do their essay. But if it's study skills it's extremely useful to have the report because then you can look for ways and when you're looking for learning styles and things like that it's really useful to have the report. Sometimes you find horrendously that people who have absolutely no auditory short-term memory at all, perhaps not none but very low score, are relying on an auditory channel to remember things because it never occurred to them that there were other ways of writing it down apart from in words so like little caricatures or flow-charts or something like that rather than pages and pages of writing.

Q: So because you work at both Southside and Northside what from your experience do you think are the basics of a good support service for students?

A: I think they need to have somebody they can go and talk to. I think the staff that they deal with, their subject staff, they need to know and preferably be fairly supportive. And as well the staff need to understand exactly what it means to be dyslexic because some of them just think it means you can't spell, some of them think it means you can't read at all and they don't realize all the other things like copying. Somebody said to me once 'Well I'm not asking her to spell I'm asking her to copy' and you think if only they knew! And you say 'Well, copying is reading and spelling and well what do you do when you copy when you look up you read it you remember it and write it down' and I had a lecturer say once 'He can't read it back but he must be able to because he copied it.'

Q: Yes.

A: So you think mmm.

Q: So are you ever involved in any sort of staff training or staff awareness raising?

A: I have done some staff awareness, yes, and the staff who come to things like that are generally very keen to learn, it's the ones that don't come that you have to worry about.

Q: Yes.

A: And sometimes individual members of staff will just ring up and ask about things in general not individual students in particular, although occasionally they do that too.

Q: Obviously every student's different, I just wondered if you got any sort of feel of what factors make that difference. Is it largely down to personality or does the severity of their problems make a big difference – what are the things that you think are the key differences?

A: I think the key differences are what has happened to them in the past.

Q: Yes, that's a good point.

A: I really do.

Q: Yes.

A: I just feel that so strongly I could cheerfully slaughter some people.

Q: Yes.

A: People will say to me and I remember this you know various little horrors and you think oh no wonder. You can't have wrote it, it's so awful!

Q: Yes, in a way that's one of the things presumably as a student you have to learn to do, to be your own advocate in a way if that's not a role you've ever learned to develop in the past.

A: And they have a lot of trouble with the self-directed learning because they just don't do it. They haven't got the ability to catch it up at the end when they haven't done it.

Q: So do you get students presumably who range a lot in age from young to quite mature?

A: They range from about 18 to 50-something.

Q: Do you find the more mature students have better study skills or does it not work like that?

A: You find that the more mature students mostly are really really pleased when you tell them something and they see the sense in it and they're thrilled to bits and they adopt it and they take it away and they're thrilled.

Q: Yes.

A: But some of the mature students are still kind of bogged down in why did nobody find out sooner. They're stuck on the horrendous time at school but really what they need to be doing isn't thinking about that now, they've got to get on with what they're doing now and move on and you know I keep saying to them that Nelson Mandela thing because I reckoned if he could everybody could.

Q: Yes.

A: And you know he said they asked him if he will go after the people who'd put him in prison, and he said 'We haven't got time to bother about the past, we have to think about the future.' I think that's fantastic and a lot of people see elements of their dyslexia as something which isn't part of the dyslexia and they're looking for a cure for that bit and that is a bit time-wasting as well, because really you've got to accept that it is going to take you longer, you are going to have to spend longer and that's it really. You will have other things that might help you but there's no way round it you can't take a tablet tonight and wake up in the morning spelling and even if you could there'd be a lot to do.

Q: Yes.

A: So that's a bit of an element as well. Some of the younger ones I think there's a problem because some of them have had help at school which they didn't find particularly rewarding and therefore they don't want to access help now.

Q: Yes, do you think the fact that you've got personal experience of dyslexia helps you in having more insight or empathy with the students you see or not really?

A: Well I think it might have done at the beginning but I think by now I've probably seen so many . . . well no it probably does because you remember better, you hear the stories but if you've actually lived with the stories it's probably, yes you're probably right, it probably does.

Q: Do you ever disclose at all or say well you know my son is.

A: Oh yes, all the time.

Q: Yes.

A: All of them, I mean all three of them, I just say 'Oh yes one of mine da da does so and so and the other one oh yes she did that' and I do, yes all the time. I just don't think it matters, people say to me 'Are you dyslexic?' and I say 'No I'm not but a lot of my family are.'

Q: Yes.

A: But they don't mind, they tell people so?

Q: Oh no, I was seeing it as an asset in a way and again that it might make them feel more relaxed with you if they know that you know what it's like and so on.

A: I think as well the home-sickness for some of the dyslexic people in their first year might be worse because I think they will have had, they're also being deprived of that layer of support that they would have had at home.

Q: Yes, that's a good point, yes. One or two of the female students have said their fathers have always proofread their work. Again there's this whole issue of who you can trust or ask to proofread for you and for some people that's not an easy thing to do.

A: No, it's actually quite scary as well because I saw some work the other day and said to a student 'Did you proofread this?' and he said 'Oh no, my flat mate did, he's really good at English' and I thought 'Oh it's terrible.'

Q: I think the whole thing of asking for help is something some people find easier to do than others.

A: Oh yes, it's really hard to ask for help isn't it. I always give out my phone number and say if you really get panicky or upset just ring and people have said to me well they'll ring you all the time but they don't.

Q: Yes, I find that I do that, and I think it's people having that kind of psychological safety net is the important thing.

A: Yes, definitely

Q: Do you talk with the other support tutors about what you're doing or your roles? Are you all very different in what you do or is there a certain level of similarity in what you do?

A: Some of us do the same, there's a group of us that do the same and there's some people who see their role as sort of dealing with the spelling and the study skills as almost a subject.

Q: A technical kind of approach?

A: Yes, and that's just the difference in people I suppose. Well I do that too, it's just what the student wants but basically there are a number of us who ask the students what they want. But sometimes the students don't realize what sorts of things they could have you know so you can influence them then.

Q: Yes, and you don't always articulate or know what you want to start with.

A: Yes, so sometimes you have to probe a little bit and say do you have any work outstanding that we maybe we could look at or something like that. Because obviously if somebody's got several things late for deadlines the last thing you want to be doing is spelling rules you know, because what's important is that they get their work in and so we need to be looking at analysing questions and planning and that sort of thing.

Q: Yes, and I suppose more kind of personal life skills about how you identify the time to do the work and how you fit paid work in.

A: Definitely yes. Of course that's a big thing the paid work now, a lot more of them are having to do a lot more paid work around Northside, it's scary how much work some of them are doing.

Q: Yes, I know.

A: And it must be even worse for the dyslexic ones.

Q: Well I was thinking that Pam, it's a good point, you may need longer to read and to do work and as you say the bottom line seems to be they have to be prepared to spend the extra time. You think, well, the ones who really need the money they're in a very difficult position.

A: It's quite upsetting sometimes when I look at the time they're working.

Q: So it sounds as if what you're saying is that some people focus more exclusively on study skills as a kind of subject, whereas others of you are doing that but within more of a life context of coping with ongoing work . . .

A: I think it's better if it's more like the 'Get Sussed' module if you focus the work, sort of connect the study skills to the work rather than spend an hour dealing with a particular skill. Unless they come and say 'Look I really need exam techniques' in which case you can spend an hour doing exam techniques.

Q: From the evaluations we did, all the ones who had one-to-ones rated it very positively and there's a lot of them rated it as the number one thing out of the various supports that they got. I was going to ask you about a bit more about the 'Get Sussed' module Pam. I know it's been running for some time now.

A: Yes, I've only been doing it for the last two years and it covers the study skills things so it covers spelling, reading, presentations, time management, just certain rules of spelling, obviously you can't do a lot of spelling because it's only a 13 week module. There's two weeks of theory, the first week is on the sort of theories of dyslexia and the second week is the assessment and how to understand it or interpret it. Then you've got the range of exam techniques, memory skills, things like that, things they would like to learn and then we revisit a couple of things later on and the aim of that is that they shouldn't necessarily have to do extra work so they bring for example a plan of an essay. And you have to show with your portfolio that you're doing the things that we've covered in the session so maybe you'd want to plan perhaps a linear plan and a line map and a diagrammatic plan or something like that you know and then you'd like a first draft of an essay and then a corrective draft of an essay so that would go in as one section. Then for reading you would get maybe them to photocopy something that they'd read and show how they'd picked out the bones of what they'd read which might be either a running record or highlighting or whatever. So it's quite good because not only does it give them the opportunity to find out about the different things but it gives

them the opportunity to actually try them and that's something sometimes that you have to do in the one-to-ones as well. Because if somebody
comes and says they're having difficulty with reading and you suggest a
new way for them to do it it's quite important that you say 'Well when you
come next week perhaps you could bring something that you've done so I
can see how you got on.'

Q: So in an informal way you're setting them homework in a sense?

A: Well, targets I think.

Q: The evaluation was very positive for those students who came to 'Get
Sussed' but I got the impression it's only a fairly small proportion of
students because of the timetable?

A: Well sometimes it's the timetable because I had a girl yesterday who
was desperate to come but the first hour clashes with one of her core
modules so she has to go to that and that's really unfortunate.

Q: So is it just run once, is it run in the first and the second semester?

A: No, just the second semester because that's to give new people the
chance to be assessed because some people haven't been assessed when
they come, you see, and you have to have been assessed to get onto the
module.

Q: Yes, but overall do you feel it's a useful way of offering support, something like this 'Get Sussed' module, or do you think there are problems
about it as a support mechanism?

A: I think it's a good way of offering support but it's more suited to people
who haven't had support in the past.

Q: Right.

A: I think that the difficulty with the course is because of the spectrum of
dyslexia, the continuum of dyslexia, if you get somebody who's severely
dyslexic on one side and somebody who is only mildly dyslexic. Well,
'only', that's not really an 'only' is it but mildly compared with the person
who is severely, it's a big, a big difference and therefore what is set up to

deal with one is really going to be wrong for the other whichever way you do it, and obviously you can differentiate within the session but if all you look at is the book then you can't.

Q: One of the issues that I find quite difficult is the occasional student who doesn't perhaps distinguish between what are problems to do with their dyslexia and what are more general conceptual problems that are not particularly related to the dyslexia.

A: Yes, definitely or motivation problems. They often say 'Well I can't do that because I'm dyslexic' and you have to say 'Well you know you need to be able to do this and we'll have to find some strategies.' I sometimes do thinking skills with those ones.

Q: Yes, so there are ways around it. It's difficult to say because everybody's so different but how long do you tend to see a student for if you're doing individual sessions with them?

A: Well, some students you see for the whole three years, other students you might just see for ten or 15 weeks and maybe they might come back at the end and some you see in the first year and then they feel quite confident and I'll just say 'Well just ask for some more if you need it.'

Q: Do you get students asking for advice on whether they should declare when they apply for jobs?

A: Yes, it's very difficult to know what to advise. Basically I opt out of that one, send them to see the disabilities advisers or careers and say ask them which is really a cop-out but it's because I don't know.

Q: I think, well, you're right though because it's a sort of fifty-fifty thing, isn't it, that in some cases it is going to be a disadvantage and in other cases it is better to say so.

A: Well, my son, when he applies for jobs he always says he waits till he gets to the interview and then he says 'I am dyslexic and that means that I do have problems with this and this and the way I deal with that is I use a laptop all the time, never use anything else. So that's all right and I use something or other else for something else but because of that I'm really better than some people at all the other bits' and then he tells them about that.

Q: Excellent.

A: So I do say to them if you are going to tell them explain to them how you're going to get round it and say what you're good at, you know present it as positively as you can but I do hang fire on telling them whether or not to disclose it because I don't know.

Q: I think that's exactly right, that's what we're saying with dyslexic trainee teachers that you've got to say what your coping strategies are and what kind of strengths it gives you.

Q: The other thing is the different support tutors have perhaps come in from different training routes. Because you had already done work with adults, hadn't you, at the Dyslexia Institute?

A: I'd worked with adults and I'd worked with adults at other places as well at Leap and places like that. I think perhaps people who have only worked with children, it might be harder for them, maybe it's easier for those of us who have dealt a lot with adults.

Q: Yes, you're probably used to having a more kind of equal relationship perhaps?.

A: I think so because obviously if you're used to teaching children particularly children in classes it must be quite hard to go in and say 'Okay what do you want to do today?' Mind you, some of the students really don't like that approach either, some of them just look at me and say 'Well you're the teacher.' I say 'No I'm not.'

Q: Yes, do you find your relationship does change over time if you see somebody for a while?

A: Yes, it does really, sometimes not so much because sometimes you have a sort of a affinity with people and others, it takes a little while or even, I think, sometimes you don't necessarily have to work at it per se I think it's a time thing. I think they just sort of get used to you and what you do and they begin to feel more comfortable

Q: Do you have any talks with the people who actually carry out the assessments for students or not?

A: I talk to the psychologists that do it, yes.

Q: Yes, so would that be in a general sense or about specific students?

A: Sometimes they talk to me about specific students and sometimes we just chat in general when we meet just or sometimes if I'm doing screenings I might ask, if I'm puzzled, I might say 'Why would I get this and this?' and he might say 'Ask that and that.'

Q: Is there anybody else who you liaise with?

A: I see the disabilities advisers, I see them lots. That's quite useful because sometimes you can go and say 'Can so and so have so and so?' or something like that.

Q: Just going back to the support you give students are there any things that you find are harder to teach people or help people with?

A: Sometimes it's when their sentence structure is absolutely fine for speaking and absolutely terrible for writing and because it's just like a second skin it's really hard to stop them doing it. I think it's because it's part of their speech and so it's automatic, isn't it, we've got automaticity there and that's going to be really hard to change.

Q: How far do you feel that self-esteem or confidence plays a role in how they cope with their dyslexia?

A: I think it's huge.

Q: Yes.

A: I think it's absolutely huge and I think as well particularly those, if they've had a lot of support somewhere before, and then they come here and they don't get it and they're already a little bit weak in the self-esteem, it absolutely crashes, you know, it's like a nose-dive thing.

Q: Yes, so that's an important element?
A: I think it's a huge element in some people and they just don't believe in themselves anymore and so until you've shown them that they can do it there's very little progress can be made because they're just so hesitant

and diffident and you know that the more hesitant and diffident you are the worse everything gets and the more stressed you get and harder it is to take notes and write essays and so on . . .

Q: So how do you tend to tackle that?

A: I don't know, I must do something, mustn't I? I think just showing them the sorts of things that they can do or pointing out to them when they've got something right.

Q: Success, yes.

A: And getting a bit of success and saying 'Look you, can do this now and soon you'll be able to do that' and sometimes I just tell them that they're going to be able to do that and I know they are because I'm determined to help them. I supported somebody for a little while and the psychologist actually come and said that he didn't recognize him.

Q: Oh really?

A: He said he thought he was a completely different young man, he said 'That isn't so and so out there is it?' and I said 'Yes' and he said 'Well what have you done to him?' and I said 'Nothing' but obviously I had! It's a matter of giving them some self-belief and I don't really know to be honest how I do it.

Q: Do you find that having done so much work that you've refined your own skills in how to help people?

A: Yes, actually it's funny you should ask that today because just last week I looked at something and then I thought right so you need to do that that and that and they just looked at me as if I was manna from heaven! And I did think to myself a few years ago I wouldn't have been so sure that that was all you had to do. Because even though when you start working with students everybody tells you that you don't need to know the subject because we're not there for content but you somehow feel deep down that maybe you really do need to know something about the subject before you can answer the question. Then you realize that actually you don't, you just have to know what questions to ask and they know the answers to that and what you really have to do I think is to give them like a coat hanger and they can put the coat on it but you have to make the coat hangers. You do spend time thinking about them when you're at home and sometimes you just get this flash of inspiration and you can ring them up the next day and say 'I've been thinking next time you're doing so and so, try this and see if that works.'

Q: Oh great

A: But I think it is a big advantage if you've done a lot.

Q: Yes.

A: I think the only way to do a lot is do a bit isn't it?

Jim – chartered occupational psychologist

Jim became involved in assessing adults with dyslexia through working as an occupational psychologist for employment services. He is employed on a sessional basis by both Southside and Northside Universities to carry out psychological assessments. He does this on a virtually full-time basis and has built up considerable experience and expertise in this area. Many but not all the students who filled in the questionnaires (and had their latest assessment at university) would have been assessed by Jim.

Before the face-to-face assessment he sends students a detailed questionnaire which asks a number of yes/no questions about their reading, spelling, writing, number, memory skills, and general organization particularly in learning situations.

Jim was asked in the interview if he has a 'standard package' he uses for the assessment or whether he varies it.

A: Generally I've a standard package, although sometimes I'll do extras.

Q: Do you always carry out a full assessment?
A: Nearly always because their prior assessments vary so much.

With the majority of students Jim includes the following:
- preliminary questionnaire
- discussion of student's educational background and present coping strategies
- Wechsler Adult Intelligence Scale-III UK (WAIS)
- Wide Range Achievement Test (WRAT) Word, Spelling, Arithmetic

- free writing task – to assess writing speed, spelling, grammar, punctuation, and handwriting.

Like many assessing psychologists, he breaks his written report down into sections with the more technical details of the standardized tests used and the scores obtained in the appendix.

Report format:
Background and objectives
Summary of profile of abilities and attainments
Conclusions and recommendations
Appendices: 1 – Description of tests; 2 – Test scores.

As part of the background section Jim explains the purpose of different components of the overall assessment.

Jim works closely with the disability support team at Southside. Maggie, the disability adviser, briefs students in advance about the nature of the psychological assessment. She informs Jim of any students who are particularly anxious or worried about the assessment. At the end of the assessment, if time permits, after feedback to the student Jim also feeds back to the disability adviser. When asked how his views have developed on what constitutes a good assessment he replied:

A: It's about teamwork.

Jim stresses the importance of giving some initial feedback at the end of the assessment:

A: In 90 per cent of cases I know what the outcome is. It's important to tell them something, because they've gone through all that ordeal.

Q: What sort of responses do you get?

A: Immense relief – 'I'm not thick, I'm not thick' – that comes out over and over again.

Chapter 10

Conclusion

Recent thinking acknowledges that dyslexia cannot be viewed in isolation and needs to be located within wider issues of social justice and equality (Diniz and Reid 2001; Johnson 2001). In the context of higher education, dyslexia can be seen as part of the debate over increasing access and widening participation. Ozcan (2000), in a review of recent policy, notes that even though the numbers of students with disabilities have increased at universities, they are still under-represented in comparison to the wider population. Because of the key role of literacy difficulties in descriptions of dyslexia it has presented a particular challenge to traditional models of higher education which see high literacy standards as central to academic learning (Pollack 2001; Riddick 2001b). The new Special Educational Needs and Disabilities Act, which amends the Disability Discrimination Act of 1995, comes into force in September 2002. This makes discrimination against disabled students unlawful in both the pre- and post-16 sectors. Corlett (2001) points out that part of being 'non-discriminatory' involves making 'adjustments', including changes to policy and practice. She comments:

> . . . the concept of adjustments will also require educators to look at some fundamental issues regarding their academic and subject disciplines and the methods used to teach and access these.

The Dyslexia in Higher Education Report (Singleton 1999) gave a list of recommendations on supporting students with dyslexia:

Immediate priorities:

- establishing a policy for dyslexia for the whole institution

- developing a programme of staff awareness on dyslexia, especially for key staff such as admissions tutors, examination officers, counsellors and careers advisers.
- instigating special examination and assessment arrangements for students with dyslexia
- providing assistance to students with dyslexia when making DSA applications.

Second stage priorities are:

- covering the cost of diagnostic assessment for students with dyslexia
- providing technological support and training
- developing a regular programme of study skills tuition
- creating a screening programme for students who are suspected of having dyslexia
- considering how library facilities can be adapted or augmented in order to assist students with dyslexia
- creating guidelines for the marking of work of students with dyslexia.

Our intention has been to look at some of the issues involved in meeting these recommendations from the perspective of students, support staff and academic staff. As Singleton's follow-up report (Singleton and Aisbitt 2001) indicates, some institutions are moving towards these targets more rapidly than others. At the time of the study, the University of Southside had met most of these targets and the University of Northside was moving towards them. What was encouraging was that where most of this support was in place and was of high quality, students were largely positive about the assessment and specialist support services and reported that they were using a range of effective coping strategies. Singleton (1999) notes that the provision of study skills support has often been contested on the DSA application. In our research, students cited specific study skills and organization strategies as their two most important coping strategies, thus underlining the importance of provision that enables them to develop these.

Of concern were the mixed experiences that students encountered in their academic departments. Perhaps because dyslexia is a 'hidden' or 'not evident' disability, some staff have not accepted its legitimacy and have made comments to students that it is hard to imagine they would make to a student with an evident disability. In some departments there still seems to be a lingering notion that how staff respond to dyslexia is a matter of choice and individual academic freedom. Increased awareness and training have been recommended for staff and the wider student body (Singleton 1999), but at an institutional and departmental level it needs to be made clear that discrimination is not acceptable. The feedback from students indicates that many of them feel that they do encounter some unsympathetic, indifferent or uninformed departmental staff. From a student's point of view, it is difficult to tell in advance which tutors/lecturers are sympathetic, and this makes some of them reluctant to disclose or self-advocate. In our interviews several tutors/lecturers commented on the need for students to identify themselves so that they could be offered help, but this approach is undermined if students are uncertain of the response they will receive. Many academic staff (as witnessed by our interviewees) are supportive but, ironically, with widening participation, are teaching greatly increased numbers of students and are frustrated at the limited amount of time they have to support individual students. Some institutions do have departmental or subject area specialist support, often in the form of a disability tutor or equal opportunities coordinator. As with the situation in schools, there is the need for a SENCO-type role (special educational needs coordinator) in departments, who oversees and develops support at this level and provides training, resources and help to individual members of staff. In looking at the issue of student retention, Moxley et al. (2001) emphasize the importance of 'at risk' students having a working relationship with somebody who values their learning in higher education. At present, most of the resources are concentrated within specialist central support services; without wishing to dilute this, it is important that more resources are available at departmental level and that stronger links between specialist and departmental support are formed so that students receive an integrated support service. Decisions need to be made at a departmental level on issues such as marking, providing notes, and, as part of the widening participation culture, creating a dyslexia-friendly environment.

This is not suggesting that dyslexic students should be a privileged group and, indeed, many of the features of a dyslexia-friendly environment would be of benefit to a large number of students. Posting lecture notes on the web, for instance, is of benefit to all students. Study skills modules or courses are commonplace in further and higher education institutions, and many of these contain key elements of the support that students with dyslexia value, including how to get organized, specific study skills and awareness of own learning styles. Cottrell (1999), for example, has produced a study skills handbook for all students, which was piloted in part by students with dyslexia and dyslexia support tutors. There are many instances of good practice and innovative projects across higher education institutions but support is still patchy and attitudes variable. As shown in our interviews with academic staff support is sometimes dependent on good will and personal interest rather than systematic organizational structures and collective positive departmental attitudes.

The Higher Education Report on Dyslexia in its summing up outlined what it saw as the future major research and development needs, which included among others:

- improved identification procedures that are appropriate for adults with compensated dyslexia
- development and validation of new psychometric tests and other assessment techniques that are appropriate for use at higher education level
- promotion of a better general understanding of dyslexia amongst staff and students in higher education, and among the population generally.

A key element of this book has been to review the overall assessment of dyslexia and to look in detail at aspects of the assessment of reading, spelling, writing, and numeracy.

Careful thought needs to be given as to how such 'psychological' approaches can be used to enable and empower individuals rather than underline a deficit model of dyslexia. We would argue that further research and negotiation is needed with individuals with dyslexia to find out in what context and framework such information can be helpful. As Kirk et al. (2001) point out, the purpose of formal identification is not to simply to denote people as being dyslexic but to explain their difficulties.

Although there has been considerable documentation of people's experiences of dyslexia at the biographical level, there has been relatively little research which has systematically investigated how individuals come to terms with living with a cognitive difficulty or difference within a particular cultural and educational context. We concluded that, where students agree, a collaborative and non-intrusive approach could be taken to assessing their level of self-understanding and personal well-being.

Of concern are those students who do not fit the criteria for dyslexia but do have a cognitive profile which suggests some form of specific learning difficulty, and who are clearly in need of help. As with autism, where an autistic spectrum is now clearly recognized, some of these cases might be resolved by moving in the future to a dyslexia spectrum. This would have 'classic' or severe cases of dyslexia at the core, widening out to milder or more selective dyslexia-type difficulties which are encountered by an increased range of students. A dyslexia-friendly institution would be well placed to support this wider range of students. An alternative or complementary approach is to heighten awareness of the overall concept of specific learning difficulties (or cognitive differences) and to focus on negotiating with individual students a clear understanding of what their particular specific learning difficulty (or cognitive difference) means. In reality, everybody has a unique cognitive profile, and, with the advent of computer screening programmes like StudyScan (Zdzienski 1997), all students can have increased awareness of their cognitive profile and learning styles. It may help to normalize the experiences of individual students if they are seen within this more inclusive conceptual framework. What is clear is that many students need help in translating or negotiating the 'label' or written feedback they are given, both in terms of personal understanding and the development of coping strategies. In listing the difficulties and negative experiences that students with dyslexia have encountered there is a danger of presenting what disability theorists term a 'personal tragedy' model of disability. There is a need, especially with adults, to move from a support to an empowerment model where dyslexic students can articulate their own needs, coping strategies and strengths.

The inclusion of students with dyslexia in higher education can be considered at three levels:

- personal
- organizational
- political.

In looking closely at assessment and individual support we have concentrated on the personal. But in understanding how this assessment and support is delivered we have also considered some of the organizational issues. Although we have said relatively little about the political level it is there as a backdrop to our research, particularly in the policies and funding designed to widen participation and increase inclusion in higher education.

We thought it important also to adopt an 'inclusive' approach to our research, which ranges from experimental cognitive research, through rating scales, questionnaires and semi-structured interviews, to in-depth interviews. We would argue that research from differing methodologies and perspectives is needed to try and develop a multi-faceted view of dyslexia in higher education. We would hope that dialogue between these perspectives would extend and enrich this understanding and inform directions for future research and practice.

References

Aaron PG, Phillips S (1986) A decade of research with dyslexic college students: a summary of findings. Annals of Dyslexia 36: 44–65.

Ackerman PT, Dykman RA (1996) The speed factor and learning disabilities: the toll of slowness in adolescents. Dyslexia 2(1): 1–21.

Adams JW, Hitch GJ (1997) Working memory and children's mental addition. Journal of Experimental Child Psychology 67(1): 21–38.

Alarcon M, DeFries JC, Light JG, Pennington BF (1997) A twin study of mathematics disability. Journal of Learning Disabilities 30: 617–23.

Anderson K (1997) Gender bias and special education referrals. Annals of Dyslexia 47: 151–62.

Badian N (1999) Persistent arithmetic, reading, or arithmetic and reading disability. Annals of Dyslexia 49: 45–70.

Bandura A (1997) Self Efficacy: The Exercise of Control. New York: Freeman.

Bandura A, Jourden FJ (1991) Self-regulatory mechanisms governing the impact of social comparison on complex decision making. Journal of Personality and Social Psychology 60: 941–51.

Battle J (1992) The Culture-Free Self-Esteem Inventory. Austin, TX: Pro-ed.

Bereiter C, Scardamalia M (1983) Does learning to write have to be so difficult? In Freedman A, Pringle I, Yalden J (eds), Learning to Write: First Language/Second Language. London: Longman.

Boder E (1973) Developmental dyslexia: a diagnostic approach based on three atypical reading-spelling patterns. Developmental Medicine and Child Neurology 15: 663–87.

Boetsch EA, Green PA, Pennington BF (1996) Psychosocial correlates of dyslexia across the life span. Development and Psychopathology 8: 539–62.

Bradley L, Bryant PE (1983) Categorising sounds and learning to read: a causal connection. Nature 301: 419–21.

Brandys CF, Rourke BF (1991) Differential memory abilities in reading and arithmetic disabled children. In Rourke BF (ed.) Neuropsychological Validation of Learning Disability Subtypes. New York: Guilford.

Bruck M (1990) Word recognition skills of adults with childhood diagnoses of dyslexia. Developmental Psychology 26: 439–54.

Bruck M (1992) The persistence of dyslexics' phonological awareness skills. Developmental Psychology 28: 874–86.

Bruck M (1993) Component spelling skills of college students with childhood diagnoses of dyslexia. Learning Disability Quarterly 16: 171–84.

Brunsden V, Davies M, Shevlin M, Bracken M (2000) Why do HE students drop out? A test of Tinto's model. Journal of Further and Higher Education 24: 301–10.

230

Butterfield EC, Hacker DJ, Albertson LR (1996) Environmental, cognitive and metacognitive influences on text revision: assessing the evidence. Educational Psychology Review 8(3): 239–97.

Campbell R, Butterworth B (1985) Phonological dyslexia and dysgraphia in a highly literate subject: a developmental case with associated deficits of phonemic processing and awareness. Quarterly Journal of Experimental Psychology 37A: 435–75.

Cain S, Riddick B (2001) Developing policies and practice to support student teachers with dyslexia. Conference paper, 5th International BDA Conference, York.

Carron G (2001) Professional development in student support and guidance. University of Sunderland 8th Annual Teaching and Learning Conference.

Cassidy T (1999) Stress, Cognition and Health. London: Routledge.

Castles A, Coltheart M (1993) Varieties of developmental dyslexia. Cognition 47: 149–80.

Chemers MM, Hu L, Garcia BF (2001) Academic self-efficacy and first-year college students' performance and adjustment. Journal of Educational Psychology 93(1): 55–64.

Chinn S (2001) Learning styles and mathematics. In Peer L, Reid G (eds), Dyslexia – Successful Inclusion in the Secondary School. London: David Fulton.

Chinn S, Ashcroft J (1998) Mathematics for Dyslexia, 2nd ed. London: Whurr.

Clayton P (1994) Using computers for numeracy and mathematics with dyslexic students. In Singleton C (ed.), Dyslexia and Computers. Hull: Dyslexia Computer Resource Centre.

Coltheart M, Masterson J, Byng S, Prior M, Riddoch J (1983) Surface dyslexia. Quarterly Journal of Experimental Psychology 35A: 469–95.

CRE (1996) Special Educational Needs Assessment in Strathclyde: Report of a Formal Investigation. London: Commission for Racial Equality (CRE).

Conners F, Olson RK (1990) Reading comprehension in dyslexic and normal readers: a component skills analysis. In Balota DA, Flores D'Arcais GB, Rayner K (eds), Comprehension Processes in Reading. Hillsdale, NJ: Lawrence Erlbaum Associates. pp 557–79.

Cornet S (2001) Special Educational Needs and Disability Act. Skill – National Bureau for Students with Disabilities. www.skill.org.uk.

Cottrell S (1999) The Study Skills Handbook. London: Macmillan Press.

Coventry D, Pringle M, Rifkind H, Weedon C (2001) Supporting students with dyslexia in the maths classroom. In Peer L, Reid G (eds), Dyslexia – Successful Inclusion in the Secondary School. London: David Fulton.

Cowen SE (1988) Coping strategies of university students with learning disabilities. Journal of Learning Disabilities 21: 161–64.

Crème P, Lea MR (1997) Writing at University: A Guide for Students. Buckingham: Open University Press .

Dalton B, Winbury N, Morocco C (1990) 'If you could just push a button': two fourth grade learning disabled students learn to use a computer spelling checker. Journal of Special Education 10(4): 177–91.

Denckla MB, Rudel RG (1976) Rapid automatized naming (RAN): dyslexia differentiated from other learning difficulties. Neuropsychologia 14: 471–79.

Deponio P, Landon J, Mullin K, Reid G (2000) An audit of the processes involved in identifying and assessing bilingual learners suspected of being dyslexic. Dyslexia 6(1): 29–41.

Diniz A, Reed S (2001) Inclusion – the issues. In Peer L, Reid G (eds), Dyslexia – Successful Inclusion in the Secondary School. London: David Fulton.

Dutke S, Stoebber J (2001) Test anxiety, working memory, and cognitive performance: supportive effects of sequential demands. Cognition and Emotion 15(3): 381–89.

Edwards J (1994) The Scars of Dyslexia. London: Cassell.

Everatt J, Smythe I, Adams E, Ocampo D (2000) Dyslexia screening measures and bilingualism. Dyslexia 6(1): 42–56.

Eysenck MW (1988) Trait anxiety and stress. In Fisher S, Reason J (eds), Handbook of Lifestress, Cognition and Health. Chichester: Wiley.

Farmer M, Riddick B, Sterling C, Simpson B (2001) Assessment of the functional needs of dyslexic students in higher education. Paper presented at the 5th British Dyslexia Association International Conference, University of York, UK.

Farmer M, Riddick B, Sterling C, Simpson B (in prep.) The assessment of the writing of HE students with dyslexia.

Fawcett, AJ (2001) Dyslexia: Theory and Good Practice. London: Whurr.

Fawcett AJ, Nicolson R (1996) The Dyslexia Screening Test. London: The Psychological Corporation.

Felton RH, Naylor CE, Wood FB (1990) Neuropsychological profile of adult dyslexics. Brain and Language 39: 485–97.

Fitzgerald J, Markham L (1987) Teaching children about revision in writing. Cognition and Instruction 4: 3–24.

Fletcher JM, Shaywitz SE, Shankweiler DP, Katz L, Liberman IY, Stuebing KK, Francis DJ, Fowler AE, Shaywitz BA (1994) Cognitive profiles of reading disability: comparisons of discrepancy and low achievement definitions. Journal of Educational Psychology 86: 6–23.

Fonseca M (2001) Differences between reading regular and irregular words in Portuguese and English. Undergraduate dissertation, South Bank University.

Gamaroff R (2000) Rater reliability in language assessment: the bug of all bears. System 28: 31–53.

Gaudry E, Spielberger CD (1971) Anxiety and Educational Achievement. New York: Wiley.

Gerber PJ, Reiff HB, Ginsberg R (1996) Reframing the learning disabilities experience. Journal of Learning Disabilities 29(1): 98–101.

Gilger JW, Pennington BF, DeFries JC (1991) Risk for reading disability as a function of parental history in three family studies. Reading and Writing 3(3–4): 205–17.

Gillis JJ, Light J, DeFries JC (1995) Comorbidity of reading and mathematical difficulties: genetic and environmental aetiologies. Journal of Learning Disabilities 28(2): 96–106.

Gillis JJ, DeFries JC (1989) Validity of school history as a diagnostic criterion for reading disability. Reading and Writing 1(2): 93–101.

Gilroy D, Miles TR (1986) Dyslexia at College. London: Methuen.

Gilroy D, Miles TR (1996) Dyslexia at College, 2nd edn. London: Routledge.

Gilroy D (1995) Stress factors in the college student. In Miles TR, Varma VP (eds), Dyslexia and Stress. London: Whurr.

Goswami U (1999) The relationship between phonological awareness and orthographic representation in different orthographies. In Harris M, Hatano G (eds), Learning to Read and Write: A Psycholinguistic Perspective. Cambridge: Cambridge University Press. pp 134–56.

Gottardo A, Siegel LS, Stanovich KE (1997) The assessment of adults with reading disabilities: what can we learn from experimental tasks? Journal of Research in Reading 20(1): 42–54.

Gough PB, Tunmer WE (1985) Decoding, reading and reading disability. Remedial and Special Education 7: 6–10.

Gregg N (1983) College learning disabled writers: error patterns and instructional alternatives. Journal of Learning Disabilities 16: 334–38.

Gross-Glenn K, Jallad B, Novoa L, Helgren-Lempesis V, Lubs HA (1990) Nonsense passage reading as a diagnostic aid in the study of adult familial dyslexia. Reading and Writing 2: 161–73.

Hacker DJ, Plumb C, Butterfield EC, Quathamer D, Heineken E (1994) Text revision: detection and correction of errors. Journal of Educational Psychology 86(1): 65–78.

Hanley JR (1997) Reading and spelling impairments in undergraduate students with developmental dyslexia. Journal of Research in Reading 20(10): 22–30.

Hatcher J (2001) An evaluation of the types of provision appropriate for dyslexic students. Paper presented at the 5th British Dyslexia Association International Conference, University of York, UK.

Hatcher J, Snowling M, Griffiths Y (in press) Cognitive assessment of dyslexic students in higher education. British Journal of Educational Psychology.

Henderson A (1998) Maths for the Dyslexic. London: David Fulton.

Hitch GJ (1978) The role of short term working memory in mental arithmetic. Cognitive Psychology 10: 302–23.

Hughes CA, Suritsky SK (1994) Note-taking skills of university students with and without learning disabilities. Journal of Learning Disabilities 27(1): 20–24.

Jansons KM (1988) A personal view of dyslexia and thought without language. In Weiskrantz L (ed.), Thought Without Language. Oxford: Oxford University Press.

Joffe LS (1983) School mathematics and dyslexia: a matter of verbal labelling, generalisations, horses and carts. Cambridge Journal of Education 13(3): 22–27.

Johnson M (2001) Inclusion: the challenges. In Peer L, Reid G (eds), Dyslexia – Successful Inclusion in the Secondary School. London: David Fulton.

Joshi RM, Williams KA, Wood JR (1998) Predicting reading comprehension from listening comprehension: is this the answer to the IQ debate? In Hulme C, Joshi RM (eds), Reading and Spelling: Development and Disorder. London: Lawrence Erlbaum Associates. pp 319–27.

Kinsbourne M, Rufo DT, Gamzu E, Palmer RL, Berliner AK (1991) Neuropsychological deficits in adults with dyslexia. Developmental Medicine and Child Neurology 33: 763–75.

Kirk J, MacLoughlin D, Reed G (2001) Identification and intervention in adults. In Fawcett AJ (ed.), Dyslexia: Theory and Good Practice. London: Whurr.

Landon J (2001) Inclusion and dyslexia – the exclusion of bilingual learners. In Peer L, Reid G (eds), Dyslexia – Successful Inclusion in the Secondary School. London: David Fulton.

Lea MR, Street BV (1998) Student writing in higher education: an academic literacies approach. Studies in Higher Education 23(2): 157–72.

Lefly DL, Pennington BF (1991) Spelling errors and reading fluency in compensated adult dyslexics. Annals of Dyslexia 41: 143–62.

Lejk EV (2000) Creating a mathematical CAL application for use by students with specific learning difficulties. MSc (CBIS) Dissertation, University of Sunderland.

Lerner JW (1989) Educational interventions in learning disabilities. Journal of the American Academy of Child and Adolescent Psychiatry 28: 326-31.

Low J (1996) Negotiating identities, negotiating environments: an interpretation of the experiences of students with disabilities. Disability and Society 11: 235–48.

Lubs HA, Rabin M, Feldman E, Jallad BJ, Kushch A, Gross-Glenn K (1993) Familial dyslexia: genetic and medical findings in eleven three-generational families. Annals of Dyslexia 43: 44–60.

MacArthur CA, Graham S (1987) Learning disabled students composing under three methods of text production: handwriting, word processing and dictation. Journal of Special Education 21(3): 22–42.

MacArthur CA, Graham S, Haynes JB, DeLaPaz S (1996) Spelling checkers and students with learning disabilities: performance comparisons and impact on spelling. Journal of Special Education 30: 35–57.

Maccoby EE (1988) Gender as a social category. Developmental Psychology 24: 755–65.

Maccoby EE (1990) Gender and relationships: a developmental account. American Psychologist 45: 513–20 .

McKissock C (2001) Counselling and supporting adults with dyslexia. In Hunter-Carsch M (ed.), Dyslexia: A Psychosocial Perspective. London: Whurr.

McLoughlin D, Fitzgibbon G, Young V (1994) Adult Dyslexia: Assessment, Counselling and Training. London, Whurr.

McNaughton D, Hughes C, Clark K (1997) The effects of five proofreading conditions on the spelling performance of college students with learning disabilities. Journal of Learning Disabilities 30(6): 643–51.

McNaughton D, Hughes C, Ofiesh N (1997) Proofreading for students with learning disabilities: integrating computers and strategy use. Learning Disabilities Research and Practice 12: 16–28.

Malmer G (2000) Mathematics and dyslexia. Dyslexia 6(4): 223–30.

Manis FR, Custodio R, Szeszulski PA (1993) Development of phonological and orthographic skill: a two year longitudinal study of dyslexic children. Journal of Experimental Child Psychology 56: 64–86.

Manis FR, Seidenberg MS, Doi LM, McBride-Chang C, Petersen A (1996) On the bases of two subtypes of dyslexia. Cognition 58: 157–95.

Manis FR, Seidenberg MS, Stallings L, Joanisse M, Bailey C, Freedman L, Curtain S, Keating P (1999) Development of dyslexic subgroups: a one-year follow up. Annals of Dyslexia 49: 105–34.

Marolda MR, Davidson PS (2000) Mathematical learning profiles and differentiated teaching and strategies. Perspectives 26(3): 10–15.

Matthews G, Davies DR, Westerman SJ, Stammers RB (2000) Human Perfomance: Cognition, Stress and Individual Differences. Hove, UK: Psychology Press/Taylor and Francis.

Miles TR, Miles E (1992) Dyslexia – A Hundred Years On. Buckingham: Open University Press.

Miles TR, Miles E (1999) Dyslexia – A Hundred Years On, 2nd edn. Buckingham: Open University Press.

Miles TR, Haslum MN, Wheeler TJ (1998) Gender ratio in dyslexia. Annals of Dyslexia 48: 27–55.

Miles TR, Varma VP (1995) Dyslexia and Stress. London: Whurr.

Morais J, Cary L, Alegria J, Bertelson P (1979) Does awareness of speech as a sequence of phones arise spontaneously? Cognition 7: 323–31.

Moxley D, Durack A, Dumbrigue C (2001) Keeping Students in Higher Education. London: Kogan Page.

Nicolson RI, Fawcett AJ (1997) Development of objective procedures for screening and assessment of dyslexic students in higher education. Journal of Research in Reading 20(1): 77–83.

Ozcan K (2000) Creating enforceable civil rights for disabled students in higher education: an institutional theory perspective. Disability and Society 15(7): 1041–63.

Pennington BF, Van Orden GC, Smith SD, Green PA, Haith MM (1990) Phonological processing skills and deficits in adult dyslexics. Child Development 61: 1753–78.

Pollak D (2001) Access to higher education for the mature dyslexic student: a question of identity. Paper presented at the 5th British Dyslexia Association International Conference, University of York, UK.

Pritchard RA, Miles TR, Chinn SJ, Taggart AT (1989) Dyslexia and knowledge of number facts. Links 14: 17–20.

Quicke J, Winter C (1994) Labelling and learning: an interactionist perspective. Support for Learning 9: 16–21.

Rack JP (1994) Dyslexia: the phonological deficit hypothesis. In Fawcett AJ, Nicolson RI (eds), Dyslexia in Children: Multidisciplinary Perspectives. Hemel Hempstead: Harvester Wheatsheaf.

Rack JP (1997) Issues in the assessment of developmental dyslexia in adults: theoretical and applied perspectives. Journal of Research in Reading 20(1): 66–76.

Rack JP, Snowling MJ, Olson RK (1992) The nonword reading deficit in developmental dyslexia: a review. Reading Research Quarterly 27(1): 29–53.

Rapp LC (1988) Proofreading skills and writing proficiency: error detection, editing accuracy and linguistic competence. ERIC Document Reproduction Service No. ED 307 82.

Raskind MH, Higgins E (1995) Effects of speech synthesis on the proofreading efficiency of post-secondary students with learning disabilities. Learning Disability Quarterly 18(2): 141–58.

Rickard Liow R (1999) Reading development in bilingual Singaporean children. In Harris M, Hatano G (eds), Learning to Read and Write: A Cross-linguistic Perspective. Cambridge, UK: Cambridge University Press. pp 196–213.

Rickard Liow S, Poon, K-L K (1998) Phonological awareness in multilingual Chinese-speaking children. Applied Psycholinguistics 19: 339–62.

Riddick B (1996) Living with Dyslexia: The Social and Emotional Consequences of Specific Learning Difficulties. London: Routledge.

Riddick B (2000) An examination of the relationship between labelling and stigmatisation with special reference to dyslexia. Disability and Society 15(4): 653–67.

Riddick B (2001a) Dyslexia and inclusion: time for a social model of disability perspective? International Journal of Sociology of Education: in press.

Riddick B (2001b) The experiences of teachers and trainee teachers who have dyslexia. Paper presented at the British Dyslexia Association International Conference, York.

Riddick B, Farmer M, Sterling C (1997) Students and Dyslexia: Growing up with a Specific Learning Difficulty. London: Whurr.

Riddick B, Sterling C, Farmer M, Morgan S (1999) Self-esteem and anxiety in the educational histories of adult dyslexic students. Dyslexia 5: 227–48.

Riding RJ, Rayner SG (1998) Cognitive Styles and Learning Strategies. London: Fulton.

Rourke BP, Conway JA (1997) Disabilities of arithmetic and mathematical reasoning: perspectives from neurology and neuropsychology. Journal of Learning Disabilities 30: 34–36.

Rudel RG (1981) Residual effects of childhood reading disabilities. Bulletin of the Orton Society 31: 89–102.

Rutter M, Yule W (1975) The concept of specific reading retardation. Journal of Child Psychology and Psychiatry 16: 181–97.

Sattler JM (1982) Assessment of Children's Intelligence and Speed Abilities, 2nd edn. Boston: Allyn and Bacon.

Sawyer C, Francis ME, Knight E (1992) Handwriting speed, specific learning difficulties and the GCSE. Educational Psychology in Practice 8(2): 77–81.

Sawyer C, Gray F, Champness M (1996) Measuring speed of handwriting for the GCSE candidates. Educational Psychology in Practice 12(1): 19–23.

Shaywitz SE, Shaywitz BA, Fletcher J, Escobar M (1990) Prevalence of reading disability in boys and girls. Journal of the American Medical Association 264(3): 998–1002.

Siegel LS (1989) Why we do not need intelligence test scores in the definition and analyses of learning disabilities. Journal of Learning Disabilities 22(8): 514–18.

Siegel LS (1992) An evaluation of the discrepancy definition of dyslexia. Journal of Learning Disabilities 25(10): 618–29.

Singleton CH (Chair) (1999) Dyslexia In Higher Education: Policy, Provision and Practice. Report of the National Working Party on Dyslexia in Higher Education. Hull: University of Hull.

Singleton CH, Aisbitt J (2001) A follow-up of the National Working Party survey of dyslexia provision in UK universities. Paper presented at the 5th British Dyslexia Association International Conference, University of York.

Snowling MJ, Goulandris N, Defty N (1996) A longitudinal study of reading development in dyslexic children. Journal of Educational Psychology 88(4): 653–69.

Spielberger CD, Gorsuch RL, Lushene R, Vagg PR, Jacobs GA (1983) State-Trait Anxiety Inventory. Palo Alto, CA: Consulting Psychologists Press, Inc.

Stanley N, Manthorpe J (2001) Responding to students' mental health needs: impermeable systems and diverse users. Journal of Mental Health UK 10(1): 41–52 .

Stanovich KE (1986) Matthew effects in reading: some consequences of individual differences in the acquisition of reading. Reading Research Quarterly 21: 360–407.

Stanovich KE (1988) Explaining the differences between the dyslexic and the garden-variety poor reader: the phonological-core variable-difference model. Journal of Learning Disabilities 21(10): 590–612.

Stanovich KE, Nathan RG, Zolman JE (1988) The developmental lag hypothesis in reading: longitudinal and matched reading level comparisons. Child Development 59: 71–86.

Steeves KJ (1983) Memory as a factor in the computational efficiency of dyslexic children with high abstract reasoning efficiency. Annals of Dyslexia 33: 141–52.

Sterling C, Farmer M, Riddick B, Morgan S, Matthews C (1998) Adult dyslexic writing. Dyslexia 4: 1–15.

Thomas E (2000) Opening address. Dyslexia in Higher Education Art and Design Conference. Report available from The Surrey Institute of Art and Design, University College, Farnham, Surrey.

Tinto V (1987) Leaving College. Chicago: University of Chicago Press.

Torgesen J (1989) Why IQ is relevant to the definition of learning disabilities. Journal of Learning Disabilities 22(8): 484–86.

Turner M (1997) Psychological Assessment of Dyslexia. London: Whurr.

Turner Ellis SA, Miles TR, Wheeler TJ (1996) Speed of multiplication in dyslexic and non-dyslexics. Dyslexia 2(2): 121–39.

Vogler GP, DeFries JC, Decker SN (1985) Family history as an indicator of risk for reading disability. Journal of Learning Disabilities 18: 419–421.

Wagner RK, Torgesen JK (1987) The nature of phonological processing and its causal role in the acquisition of reading skills. Psychological Bulletin 101(2): 192–212.

Wechsler D (1981) Wechsler Adult Intelligence Scale – Revised (WAIS-R). New York: Psychological Corporation.

West T (1991) In the Mind's Eye. New York: Prometheus Books.

Wilkinson GS (1993) Wide Range Achievement Test, 3rd edn, revd. Delaware: Jastak Associates.

Winch C, Wells P (1995) The quality of student writing in higher education: a cause for concern. British Journal of Educational Studies 43(1): 75–87.

World Federation of Neurology (1968) Report of Research Group on Dyslexia and World Illiteracy. Dallas: World Federation of Neurology.

Zdzienski D (1997) StudyScan. London: PICO Educational Systems Ltd.

Zimmerman BJ (1989) A social-cognitive view of self-regulated academic learning. Journal of Educational Psychology 81: 329–39.

Index

Aaron PG, 28
academic staff
   support of, x
   see also staff attitudes, staff awareness, staff
     support
ACID tests, 18
Ackerman PT, 54
admissions
   on Fashion Marketing courses, 170
advocacy
   for students, 186
   see also self-advocacy
Aisbitt J, viii, 225
Alarcon M, 54
Anderson K, 75
anxiety, 43, 63–66 *passim*, 120
   on Drama courses, 161–62
   and mathematics, 55, 56
   State-Trait Anxiety Questionnaire, 66
   and verbal IQ, 64
argument quality (writing)
   assessment and, 41–42
arithmetic
   and maths compared, 52
   mental vs written, 53
   see also mathematics
Ashcroft J, 58
assessment, 11–23, 210
   background indicators, 21–22
   on Computing and Maths courses, 123,
     153
   coping strategies in, 101–12
   core indicators, 15–18 *passim*
   on Drama courses, 128–29, 160–61

and emotional adjustment, 60–67
of grammatical errors, 50
on History courses, 133
importance of fedback, 223
initial, viii, 193
of lexical choice errors, 50–51
in maths, 56–57
of numeracy, ix, 52–59
phoneme counting, 15
post-assessment, 197–98
practical issues, 80–81
principles of, ix
prior information on, 81–82
of spelling errors, 50
'standard package' for, 222
stress of, 196
students' perceptions of, ix
of writing (skills), ix, 31–51
see also assessment of students' writing,
   experiences of assessment
assessment of students' writing, 31–51
   demands of different courses, 48–50
   grammatical errors, 39
   handwriting speed and output, 35–38
   ideas organization/argument quality,
     41–42
   proof-reading and revision, 45–48
   recommendations, 50–51
   text output method, 42–45
   vocabulary and semantics, 40–41
auditory short-term memory
   lack of, 211
automaticity
   dyslexics vs non-dyslexics, 54

background indicators, 21–22
    educational history, 22
    genetic loading, 22
Badian N, 52, 54
bilingual children
    underidentification and, 74–75
Boetsch EA, 62
Bruck M, 16, 17, 21
Brunsden V, 108, 111
Butterfield EC, 46
Butterworth B, 7

Campbell R, 7
Carron G, 114, 115
chartered occupational psychologist
    interview with, 222–23
Chemers MM, 64
Chinn S, 58
Code of Practice for supporting disabled
        students (QAA), 192
cognitive performance
    and emotional state, 64
compensated dyslexia, 14, 19–21 passim
computers
    as a coping strategy, 109
    and mathematics, 59
Computing and Maths courses, 121–23
    support for academic staff, 175–76
    supporting students, 151–54
confidence
    see self-confidence
Conway JA, 54
coping strategies in/after assessment,
        101–12, 201
core indicators, 15–18 passim
    IQ, 19
    nonword reading, 17–18
    phonemic awareness, 15–17
    short-term memory, 18
Corlett S, 224
Cottrell S, 226
counselling, 199
    after assessment, 90
    need for, 116
    for stress, 66–67
course requirements, ix–x
    different literacy demands, 207
    matching students to courses, 139
course size/structure

course 'compassion', 208–9
    differences, 208–9
    on Health Studies courses, 129–30
    on History courses, 134–35
course-specific difficulties, 117–47
    Computing and Maths, 121–23
    Drama, 127–29
    Education, 123–25
    Engineering, 125–27
    Fashion Marketing, 136–39
    Health Studies, 129–32
    History, 132–35
    Psychology, 135–36
    relevant questions to raise, 140–42
    Singleton Report on, 117–18
Coventry D, 54
Cowen SE, 107
criticism
    sensitivity to, 114
Culture-free Self-esteem Inventory, 65–66

Davi(??)son PS, 58
deficit
    see functional deficit
delayed dyslexia (Manis), 9
diagnosis, 1–10 passim
    ambiguity in, 13–14
    anti-IQ argument in, 5–6
    mis-, 23
differential diagnosis, 1–10 passim
digit span
    impaired, 18
Disability Discrimination Act (1995), 224
Disability in Education Bill, 192
disability ratio, 190
disability services manager
    interview with, 182–93
disability support advisor
    compared with tutors, 205
    interview with, 193–207
Disability Support Allowance (DSA), viii
disability support tutor
    compared with advisors, 205
    interview with, 207–22
Disabled Students Allowance (DSA), 194,
        204, 225
disciplines
    demands of different, 48–50
    see also courses

discrepancy criterion, 2
Drama courses, 127–29
   support for academic staff, 177–78
   supporting students, 157–63
Dykman RA, 54
dyscalculia, 53
dyslexia
   ACID tests of, 18
   approach of companies to, 191
   dearth of adult research, 12
   defined, vii, 1
   delayed, 9
   different causes of, 8–9
   gender prevalence of, 74
   identifying students with, 1–10, 156
   lecturers' reactions to, 205–6
   motor problems and, 12
   phonological, 8–9
   positive side of, 172
   and psychosocial functioning, 62
   'recovered'/compensated, 14, 19–21
      passim
   scepticism about, 189
   staff attitudes to, 49
   and stress, 61–62
   supporting students with, 151–73
   surface, 9
   in trainee teachers, 219
   see also emotional adjustment
Dyslexia Adult Screening Test, 194
Dyslexia in Higher Education (Singleton)
   Report (1999), vii, viii, 27, 61, 66, 68,
   70, 74, 80, 90, 116, 148, 192, 224–25,
   227
   on evaluation of needs, 117–18

Education courses, 123–25
   support for academic staff, 176
   supporting students, 154–56
educational history, 22
Edwards J, 62
emotional adjustment, ix, 60–67
   on Drama courses, 161–62
   on Fashion Marketing courses, 171
   see also anxiety, self-esteem
Engineering courses, 125–27
   support for academic staff, 176–77
   supporting students, 156–57
essay writing, 41

see also writing
evaluation of assessment experiences,
   68–117
examinations, 206–7
   extra time in, 109, 148–49, 190
   special arrangements in, 42
   technique in, 216
experiences of assessment, 68–117
   assessment itself, 82–88
   coping strategies, 101–112
   evaluating assessment, 88–90
   evaluations of support, 112–116
   feedback to students, 90–93
   prior experience, 75–80
   self-esteem, 98–101
   self-perception, 93–98
Eysenck MW, 64

Farmer M, 24, 32–34 passim, 40, 43, 49, 120
Fashion Marketing courses, 136–39
   support for academic staff, 180–81
   supporting students, 169–70
Fawcett AJ, 12
Felton RH, 19
free writing task, 223
functional deficit indicators, 19–21
   single word reading, 19–20
   single word spelling, 20–21

Gaudry E, 64
gender differences in dyslexia, 74
general backward poor reader (GBR), 2
general disability training, 206
genetic factors
   loading, 22
   in mathematics, 54
'Get Sussed' module, 106–7, 111, 185, 186,
   216
Gillis JJ, 53–54
Graham S, 38
grammatical errors (writing), 39
   assessment of, 50
group support
   on Education courses, 155
   group work, 207–8
   see also support

handwriting speed/output, 35–38
Hanley JR, 12, 16, 17

Hatcher J, 12, 16, 29, 35–40 *passim*, 47
Health Studies courses, 129–32
    case example, 165–66
    support for academic staff, 178
    supporting students, 163–66
'hidden disabilities'
    and labels, 97
History courses, 132–35
    case example, 167
    support for academic staff, 179
    supporting students, 166–68
Hughes CA, 37
hyperlexics, 4, 5

ideas organization (writing)
    assessment and, 41–42
identification (procedures), viii
    on Drama courses, 157–59
    on Education courses, 156
    on Engineering courses, 157
    on Fashion Marketing courses, 170
    on Health Studies courses, 163, 178
    on History courses, 168
inclusion,
    of dyslexic students, viii, x
indicators
    background, 21–22
    core, 15–18 *passim*
Initial Teacher Training courses, 125
intelligence
    anti-IQ argument, 6
    and reading ability, 5–6, 10
    see also IQ
interview protocol (academic staff), 146–47
interviews
    chartered occupational psychologist,
        222–23
    disability services manager, 182–93
    disability support advisor, 193–207
    disability support tutor, 207–22
IQ
    anxiety and verbal, 64
    as an indicator, 19
    see also intelligence
isolation (feelings of), 184

job applications, 218

Kirk J, 227

labels, 97
Lea MR, 26
Lefly DL, 20, 21
lexical choice errors
    assessment of, 50–51

MacArthur CA, 38
McLoughlin D, 28
McNaughton D, 47
Malmer G, 53
Manis FR, 9
marking
    on Fashion Marketing courses, 172–73
    on History courses, 167
Marolda MR, 58
matching students to courses, 139
Mathematica for Students, 59
mathematics
    anxiety/self-esteem and, 55, 56
    and arithmetic compared, 52
    assessment and, 56–57
    computers and, 59
    difficulties, and genetic factors, 54
    gaps in knowledge, 56
    input/output problems, 55
    Mathematica for Students, 59
    working memory problems, 55–56
    see also arithmetic
Mathwise (NAG), 59
Matthew Effect, 14
mature students, 212–13
    demands upon, 60
memory
    Computing and Maths courses and, 122
    on Education courses, 123
    see also auditory short-term memory
mental health
    see emotional adjustment
Miles E, 53
Miles TR, 53, 62
misdiagnosis, 23
Morais J, 13
motivation of students, 187, 218
motor problems, 12
Moxley D, 226

'new' universities, 40
Nicolson RI, 12
nonword reading, 17–18

note-taking
    on Drama courses, 160
    on Engineering courses, 125–26
    on History courses, 134, 168
    on Psychology courses, 136
numeracy
    assessment of, ix
    on Computing and Maths courses, 123
    on Fashion Marketing courses, 139
    on Health Studies courses, 131
    on Psychology courses, 136

one-to-one tuition, 109
oral communication skills
    on Health Studies courses, 132
    on History courses, 134
oral language
    on Education courses, 123
organizational skills
    on Computing and Maths courses,
        152–53
    on Drama courses, 161
    on Education courses, 123, 155–56
    on Fashion Marketing courses, 137
    on Health Studies courses, 131–32
    on Psychology courses, 136
orthographic memory, 9
Ozcan K, 224

Pennington BF, 20, 21
phonemic awareness
    and first language, 7, 15–17
    phoneme counting, 15
    phoneme deletion, 16
    pig latin task, 16
    spoonerism task, 16
phonological deficit
    dyslexia and, 3–5 *passim*
pig latin task, 16
Pollak D, 26
Poon K-L K, 7
proof-reading
    competence in, 51
    exercise, 33
    and revision (writing), 45–48
Psychology courses, 135–36
    support for academic staff, 179–80
    supporting students, 168–69
psychometric tests, 227

psychosocial functioning, 62

questionnaire
    design, 68
    for university teaching staff, 142–46

R & D needs, 227
rapid naming, 18
Rapp LC, 46
reading
    compensatory logographic, 7
    on Computing and Maths courses,
        121–22, 151–52
    on Drama courses, 128, 159–60
    on Education courses, 123
    on Engineering courses, 125, 156
    on Health Studies courses, 130
    on History courses, 132
    on Psychology courses, 135
    see also other 'reading' entries
reading ability
    intelligence and, 5–6, 10
reading aloud
    stressful nature of, 84
reading comprehension, 5
    diagnostic ambiguity of, 13
reading errors
    incidence of, 20
reassessment, 200, 203
regularization errors, 20
resource constraints, 191
resourcing
    on Health Studies courses, 178–79
Rickard Liow S, 7
Riddick B, 53, 61, 63, 84, 97
Rourke BP, 54
Rudel RG, 28
Rutter M, 4

self-advocacy, 65
    on Drama courses, 160
    on Engineering courses, 156–57
    on Health Studies courses, 163–64
    see also advocacy
self-belief, 221
self-confidence
    on Drama courses, 129
self-efficacy beliefs, 64–65
self-esteem, 63, 198–99, 220–21

and assessment, 98–101
and coping strategies, 98–101
self-perception
    and assessment, 93–98
    and coping strategies, 101–12
SEN coordinator
    need for, 226
sequencing
    on Computing and Maths courses,
        122–23
    on Engineering courses, 126
    on Psychology courses, 136
short-term memory, 18
Siegel LS, 4, 6
single word reading, 19–20
single word spelling, 20–21
Singleton CH, viii, 27, 36, 40, 42–43, 45,
    48–49, 56, 225
spatial organization problems
    on Engineering courses, 126
Special Educational Needs and Disabilities
    Act (2002), 224
'specific reading difficulty', 3
spellcheckers, 109
spelling
    on Computing and Maths courses, 122
spelling errors
    assessment of, 50
Spielberger CD, 64
spoonerism task, 16
staff attitudes, 49
    on Drama courses, 162, 178
    on Fashion Marketing courses, 172
    on History courses, 168
    to student dyslexia, 118, 121–39
staff awareness, 211
    on Engineering courses, 177
    on Psychology courses, 168–69
staff views
    on student support, 148–81 passim
Stanovich KE, 3, 5
State-Trait Anxiety Questionnaire, 66
Sterling C, 40
Street BV, 26
stress
    of assessment, 196
    dyslexia and, 61–62
    of reading aloud, 84
student debt, 60, 107
student loans, 107

student services, 115–16
student-centred approach, 189
study skills handbook, 226–27
StudyScan, 228
support
    for academic staff, 174–81
    and coping strategies, 101–12
    on Drama courses, 161, (staff) 162–63
    -groups for students, 67, 184
    with mathematics, 57–59
    staff views on student, 148–81 passim
    student, on Fashion Marketing courses,
        169–70
    student, on Health Studies courses, 165
    student, on Psychology courses, 168
    of student services, 115–16
    students' evaluation of, 112–16
    see also group support, support staff
support staff
    perspectives of, 182–223
    support tutors, 49–50
    see also other 'support' entries
support of academic staff, x
support of students
    Computing and Maths courses, 151–54
    Drama courses, 157–63
    Education courses, 154–56
    Engineering courses, 156–57
    Fashion Marketing courses, 169–73
    Health Studies courses, 163–66
    History courses, 166–68
    Psychology courses, 168–69
support tutors, 49–50
Suritsky SK, 37

test batteries, 11–15 passim
text output method (writing)
    assessment and, 42–45
text production
    speed of, 50
thoughts organization
    on Computing and Maths courses, 122
    on Fashion Marketing courses, 137–38
Torgeson J, 5–6
Turner Ellis SA, 53

universities
    'new', 40
    widened admissions, 1

Varma VP, 62
vocabulary and semantics (writing), 40–41

Wechsler Adult Intelligence Scale (WAIS),
    2, 4, 6, 14, 19, 24, 222
    arithmetic, 56
Wells P, 26
Wide Range Achievement Test (WRAT), 2,
    19–21 *passim*, 24, 222
    arithmetic, 56
Winch C, 26
writing
    assessment of students', 31–51 *passim*
    on Computing and Maths courses, 123
    on Drama courses, 128, 159

on Education courses, 123–24
on Engineering courses, 125
on Fashion Marketing courses, 138,
    172–73
free writing task, 223
on Health Studies courses, 130–31, 164
on History courses, 133
problems of students, 27–29
on Psychology courses, 135–36
quality of student, in HE, 26
students' perspectives on, 29–31
see also handwriting speed

Yule W, 4